SAFE JOURNEY

AN AFRICAN ADVENTURE

GLENN L. PACE

DESERET
BOOK

SALT LAKE CITY, UTAH

The author wishes to make it clear that the opinions and views expressed in this publication are those for which he and he alone is responsible. This is not a Church publication and has not been written under assignment of or at the request of the First Presidency or the Quorum of the Twelve Apostles.

Quotations from *Church News* are used by permission.

Library of Congress Cataloging-in-Publication Data

Pace, Glenn L.
　Safe journey : an African adventure / Glenn L. Pace.
　　　p.　　cm.
　Includes bibliographical references and index.
　ISBN 1-59038-231-5 (hardbound : alk. paper)
　1. Pace, Glenn L.　2. Mormon missionaries—Africa, West—Biography.　3. Mormon missionaries—United States—Biography.　I. Title.
　BV3542.P29 A3 2003
　266'.93'092—dc22　　　　　　　　　　　　　　　　　　　　　　2003019508

Printed in the United States of America　　　　　　　　　　70582-7162
Phoenix Color Corporation, Hagerstown, MD

10　9　8　7　6　5　4　3　2　1

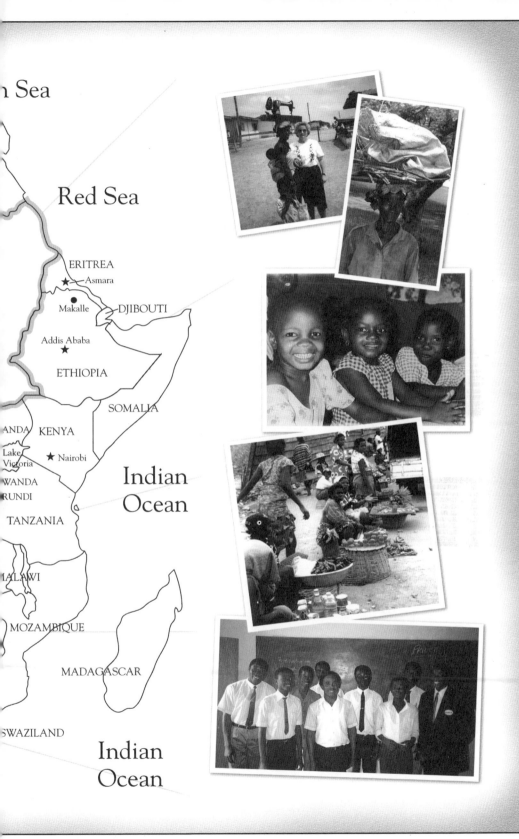

SAFE JOURNEY

*Dedicated to the Saints in Africa
and my wife, Jolene*

CONTENTS

List of Photographs ix

Preface xi

Timeline of the Gospel Work in West Africa xv

1   The Master's Plan 1

2   The Ethiopian Famine—An Initiation 21

3   An Apprenticeship 49

4   The Call 89

5   Making Adjustments 109

6   Dissolved in the Work 139

7   The Temple Approval Roller Coaster 185

8   Free Fall 213

9   Golden Calves 235

10 Euphoria 253

    Epilogue 277

    Books Cited 279

    Index 281

LIST OF PHOTOGRAPHS

Elder Pace and children at a refugee camp 36

Refugees at a camp 36

Elder Ballard at a refugee camp 37

A toddler and mother at a refugee camp 37

Three children at a refugee camp 37

A mother fixing her daughter's hair at a refugee camp 40

An old man and a baby at a refugee camp 41

West African members with machetes clearing the land 51

Three Ghanaian girls attending a school 53

Elder Pace and Elder Bob Linnell at a new water well 53

A gas station 54

Thatched hut in rural Africa 59

Elder and Sister Pace with Samuel in 1992 61

Sister missionaries in Ghana 70

Michael and his priests quorum 71

A busload of Saints traveling to the Koforidua District 86

Sister Pace teaching Ghanaian children how to count 87

One of the Paces' grandsons sitting on their luggage 107

ix

Market in downtown Accra, Ghana 111

Sister Pace at a rural market in Ghana 111

Hard-working African woman 113

A woman with a sewing machine on her head 113

Area presidency of the Africa West Area 115

Area Authority Seventies in the Africa West Area 116

Sister Pace after a conference at Abak District, Nigeria 121

Bombed-out apartment, Monrovia, Liberia 128

Elder and Sister Pace and President and Sister
    Banyan Dadson 130

Elder Pace and President Jerry Kirk at the temple
    site in Aba, Nigeria 154

Mission tour with President and Sister Kirk in Nigeria 155

Sisters at a leadership training meeting in Nigeria 162

Demolished motel 164

President and Sister Kola Tusey 172

Priesthood leaders 173

Da Tar and Ava Bessey 175

Members traveling to a baptism in Gabon 178

Boys swimming in a tributary just before a baptismal
    service in Gabon 179

Young girl in Sierra Leone 220

Africa West Area office after a fire 226

Elder Pace and Elder Ballard at the Ghanaian temple site 255

Africa West Area presidency and Area Authority Seventies . . . 264

Elder and Sister Pace in native clothes 271

The Angel Moroni atop the Ghana Temple 273

The Ghana Temple, still under construction 274

PREFACE

M y wife and I were blessed to serve in the Africa West Area
for three years. It has been more than a year since we
returned to our home, and we are still in culture shock.
We expected to experience this upon our arrival in Accra, Ghana,
but not upon our return to Bountiful, Utah. It will take the rest of
this book to explain what I mean by that.

When friends and strangers alike discover we lived in Africa for
three years, they are full of questions. Africa has a certain mystique,
and I have found most people are fascinated with our experiences
and anxious to know more. It has been difficult to adequately convey my deep feelings about the experience. Returned missionaries
will relate to the frustration. They will recall coming home and having someone ask, "How was your mission?" The usual answer is
something like "great" or, more common, "awesome." Our most
common, short response was "It was an adventure." How do you
answer a question like that in twenty-five words or less? You can't.
Therefore, for my own peace of mind and sanity I am writing this
book. (Thank you for the therapy!)

It has been difficult to settle on an approach to accomplish my
objective, which is to share some experiences and perspectives gained
in Africa in such a way that you will be inspired and motivated, in

addition to being entertained and educated. I am convinced there is no approach or words that can convey the impact this experience has had on me personally. Nevertheless, the experience was so unique and the period of time in African Church history so pivotal that I am compelled to share it to the best of my ability.

There are at least four areas where Africa helped increase my vision:

1. There is a master plan and it is the Master's plan.

2. The rolling out of the kingdom in accordance with the Master's plan cannot be stopped.

3. Each of us has a role to play in the Master's plan and each of us can make a difference.

4. The Savior's love for his children is universal and the doctrines of the kingdom have a universal appeal.

If you will read this book with those points in mind, hopefully the exercise will result in something you can liken unto yourself.

You may never be asked to serve in Africa. Nevertheless, as part of the Lord's plan, we have all received our own individual, unique assignments. We were all taught the Master's plan in our premortal existence and were told what our role would be. When our time came to leave the comfort of our heavenly cocoon I believe we must have had a fond send-off by our Heavenly Father and others we loved.

In Africa, when you leave on a trip those around you use a phrase that became very endearing to me. They would simply say "safe journey." This is the reason I chose to title this book *Safe Journey*. My choice of the title has little to do with surviving the sometimes dangerous travel in Africa. It arises from the eternal perspective of a loving Father in Heaven seeing each of his children off as they left the only home they had ever known and ventured forth to whatever geographic area on this earth they had been assigned. I'm certain he desired each of us to have a *safe journey*, even though he was perfectly aware of the challenges we would face. It is hoped that this book will assist you in pressing forward with confidence in the Lord's plan and in yourself.

Please join me on this journey. I know that words alone—not to mention my inadequacies in using them—cannot possibly convey the feelings of my heart for Africa and the things she taught me. Nevertheless, I also know the Spirit can fill in many verbal blanks. I hope at the conclusion of this book you will be able to say with me, "God bless Africa and all her sons and daughters."

TIMELINE OF THE GOSPEL WORK IN WEST AFRICA

I n 1998, the *Church News* published a short history of the work of the gospel in West Africa. This gives historical background to much of what follows in this book.

"Although the Church has been in Nigeria for only 20 years, it has progressed rapidly. The following time line of the Church in western Africa lists the significant dates of the development of the Church there.

"1950s—Church leaders became aware of West Africans interested in the Church. Many letters were sent to Church headquarters from the West African nations of Nigeria and Ghana, requesting literature and membership in the Church. The letters were written by devout Christians who had gained a testimony of the Book of Mormon.

"1960s—Numerous letters were received at Church headquarters. More letters were received from Nigeria and Ghana than the rest of the world combined. The Church responded by sending literature. Some Africans even established LDS bookstores. However, those seeking baptism were told they must wait. These Africans organized congregations. It was reported that there were more than 60 congregations in Nigeria and Ghana with more than 16,000 participants, none of whom were baptized.

"Glenn G. Fisher, president of the South Africa Mission, was assigned by President David O. McKay to visit these congregations. He was the first Church representative to visit these groups. In his visits, he found one group of congregations with more than 5,000 participants.

"1961—LaMar Williams, secretary to the Church Missionary Committee, went to Nigeria for a month long fact-finding visit. The first official meeting in West Africa was held Oct. 22, 1961, in the Opobo District, Nigeria. Some, including eight mothers with small children, had walked up to 25 miles to be at the meeting. The meeting included two hours of instruction and three hours of testimony bearing. Brother Williams was called as mission president, but was unable to get a visa to enter the country.

"1965—After working to get a visa for four years, Brother Williams, while in Nigeria, received an urgent telegram to return immediately to the United States. He was not told why but followed the directive. Upon his return to the United States in December 1965, the Biafran War began, with much destruction in the area where the unbaptized congregations of believers were located. Released from his call, Brother Williams gave to the Church Missionary Committee some 15,000 names of people in Nigeria who requested baptism.

"June 9, 1978—President Spencer W. Kimball announced revelation extending the priesthood to all worthy males.

"Nov. 9, 1978—Elder Rendell N. and Sister Rachel Mabey and Elder Edwin Q. and Sister Janath Cannon arrived in Lagos, Nigeria, as the first full-time missionaries.

"Nov. 21, 1978—Anthony Obinna, who had waited for baptism for 13 years, was the first of many converts baptized, and was set apart as the first branch president in West Africa. 'The seed of the gospel will grow into a giant tree. The Church in Nigeria will surprise all the world in its growth,' said Brother Obinna at the time. In one 24-hour period, the missionaries baptized 149 converts.

"1979—Within one year of the missionaries' arrival in West Africa, there were more than 1,700 members in 35 branches.

"July 1, 1980—The Africa West Mission was created.

"May 15, 1988—The Aba Nigeria Stake was created, with David William Eka as stake president.

"Feb. 14, 1998—President Gordon B. Hinckley arrived in Port Harcourt, Nigeria, the first Church president to visit West Africa.

"Feb. 16, 1998—The first temple in West Africa was announced for Accra, Ghana." ("Work in Nigeria Has Deep Roots, Flowers Quickly," *LDS Church News*, Feb. 21, 1998.)

1

THE MASTER'S PLAN

You cannot go to Africa without asking yourself some soul-searching questions, especially as they relate to human suffering. Why all this suffering? Why are so many Africans born into abject poverty, while so many of us, relatively speaking, are born into peaceful prosperity? Why did the Africans have to wait 148 years longer than my ancestors to receive the full blessings of the gospel?

Africa caused me to ask life-changing questions and provided me with life-changing experiences. I saw things I had never seen before and consequently confronted feelings I had never felt before. The experience created in me an intellectual and spiritual dichotomy where old questions were laid to rest while new questions were born.

The scenes that unfolded before my eyes during this mother-of-all-field-trips tested my perceptions of fairness, justice, and equity. My knowledge and understanding of the basic doctrines of the kingdom were relatively good. I'd been on a mission. I've been a General Authority for eighteen years. I am married and have six children and twenty-two grandchildren. I have lived more than sixty years and have experienced my share of the vicissitudes of life.

However, the African experiences induced an evolution of thoughts and feelings. To me, Africa more than any other continent forces one to come to grips with the "why" questions. It provides a wellspring for all the "If there is a God, how could he allow this to happen?" questions. It provides the ultimate experiences to raise the question of whether life is really fair. It provides a perfect breeding ground for cynicism.

In addition, rather than just being thankful for all I had, I experienced pangs of guilt for having too much. I felt guilty and ashamed for any part my forefathers played in slavery. I felt guilty and ashamed of my own country for the prejudice and racism that existed and still exists in many places.

We cannot begin to understand, let alone accept, these alleged inequities without the benefit of the eternal perspective the restored gospel provides us. For this reason I have written this chapter as a reminder of the big picture.

Another reason for placing this chapter at the beginning is to create a setting for an appreciation of the miraculous and historical unfolding of the Master's plan as it relates to the African people over the last twenty-five years. I hope it also explains the tremendous urgency I felt in trying to get a temple built for these great Saints so they could finally receive all the Lord has. This is the day of Africa, when their faithfulness and patience is being rewarded manyfold.

I knew the doctrine of the plan of salvation before I left for Africa. But it is one thing to have an intellectual knowledge and testimony of doctrine, and it is quite another to go through an experience that first tests your convictions and then solidifies them. Our testimonies of the gospel must eventually lead us to a literal conversion. We must internalize into our very souls the knowledge and testimony we have. For example, I had a testimony about life after death before my father, mother, and grandchild died; however, as a result of their deaths that testimony has been put to the test, and I have undergone a metamorphosis of my soul on that topic. In a similar manner, after various experiences on the continent of Africa, the plan of salvation has become more than just a comforting doctrine for my own life. It has become a critical key to obtaining the mettle to live with the seemingly unfair pain and suffering of others. Considering war, civil unrest, poverty, disease, famine, crime, and a host of other problems, every day is 9/11 for many in Africa.

Remembering the Big Picture

It is therapeutic to step back from the details of life and reacquaint ourselves with the big picture. A few years ago our family was vacationing at Colter Bay in the Grand Teton National Park. One night as we walked along a path in the darkness, I happened to look up to the sky and was overwhelmed at the clarity of the stars and the magnitude of the universe. I wondered how long it had been since I had lain on my back, stared at the sky, and let the concept of eternity and the glory of God's creations wash over me. It had been too long, and I therefore repented and soaked it in. Later that year I was reading some excerpts from John A. Widtsoe's *A Rational Theology*, which brought back some feelings of that night.

"Earth, stars and the vastness of space; yesterday, today and tomorrow; and the endlessly increasing knowledge of the relations of forces, present [a limitless] universe of numberless phenomena. Only in general outline can the universe be understood. In its infinite variety of expression, it wholly transcends the human mind.

"In the midst of this complexity, man finds himself. As he progresses from childhood to manhood, and as his slumbering faculties are awakened, he becomes more fully aware of the vastness of his universe and of the futility of hoping to understand it in detail.

"Nevertheless, conscious man can not endure confusion. Out of the universal mystery he must draw at least the general, controlling laws that proclaim order in the apparent chaos; and especially is he driven, by his inborn and unalterable nature, to know if possible his own place in the system of existing things" (*A Rational Theology*, 1).

Where do we fit in the vastness of existing things? Who are we?

We know each of us has always existed in some form. Scripturally we know that "man was also in the beginning with God. Intelligence, or the light of truth, was not created or made, neither indeed can be" (D&C 93:29).

Joseph Smith expanded on this scripture when he said, "I am dwelling on the immortality of the spirit of man. Is it logical to say that the intelligence of spirits is immortal, and yet that it had a beginning? The intelligence of spirits had no beginning, neither will it have an end. That is good logic. That which has a beginning may have an end. There never was a time when there were not spirits; for they are co-equal [co-eternal] with our Father in heaven" (*Teachings of the Prophet Joseph Smith*, 353).

Modern Church leaders have taught the same principle. Elder Spencer W. Kimball, then a member of the Quorum of the Twelve, wrote, "Our spirit matter was eternal and co-existent with God, but it was organized into spirit bodies by our Heavenly Father" (*The Miracle of Forgiveness*, 5).

President Marion G. Romney, speaking of people's divine origin as children of God, stated, "Through that birth process, self-existing intelligence was organized into individual spirit beings" ("The Worth of Souls," *Ensign*, Nov. 1978, 14).

There have been some lively debates about what an intelligence is. I like Joseph Fielding Smith's summary of the rhetoric: "Some of our writers have endeavored to explain what an intelligence is, but to do so is futile, for we have never been given any insight into this matter beyond what the Lord has fragmentarily revealed. We know, however, that there is something called intelligence which always existed. It is the real eternal part of man, which was not created nor made. This intelligence combined with the spirit constitutes a spiritual identity or individual" (*Answers to Gospel Questions*, 4:127).

We can say, then, that we became the spirit children of Heavenly

Parents and were nurtured by Deity. As George Q. Cannon so beautifully put it: "There was a period when we, with Jesus and others, basked in the light of the presence of God and enjoyed His smiles. We are the children of God, and as His children there is no attribute we ascribe to Him that we do not possess, though they may be dormant or in embryo. The mission of the Gospel is to develop these powers and make us like our Heavenly Parent" (*Gospel Truth*, 3).

The Family—A Proclamation to the World simply and clearly states, "All human beings—male and female—are created in the image of God. Each is a beloved spirit son or daughter of heavenly parents, and, as such, each has a divine nature and destiny."

Joseph F. Smith taught: "Every spirit that comes to this earth to take upon it a tabernacle is a son or a daughter of God, and possesses all the intelligence and all the attributes that any son or daughter can enjoy, either in the spirit world, or in this world, except that in the spirit, and separated from the body, they lacked just the tabernacle of being like God the Father" (*Gospel Doctrine*, 453).

And Brigham Young said: "I want to tell you, each and every one of you, that you are well acquainted with God our Heavenly Father, or the great Elohim. You are all well acquainted with him, for there is not a soul of you but what has lived in his house and dwelt with him year after year; and yet you are seeking to become acquainted with him, when the fact is, you have merely forgotten what you did know" (*Discourses of Brigham Young*, 50).

We have had a veil of forgetfulness drawn over our minds about these matters. As George Q. Cannon put it: "If we could understand the glory we once had with our Father in heaven, we would be discontented in dwelling in this condition of existence. We would pine for the home we left behind us. Its glory and its beauty, its heavenly graces and delights were of such a character that we would pine for it with that homesickness that men have some partial knowledge of here on the earth. . . . Wisely, in the providence of God, this knowledge is withdrawn from us. We can have a glimpse occasionally, through the revelations of the Spirit to us, of the glory there is awaiting us" (*Gospel Truth*, 8).

In the preface of this book I stated that *the Savior's love for his children is universal and the doctrines of the kingdom have a universal appeal.* While in Africa, I often marveled at how quickly the doctrines of the kingdom were understood and accepted by so many. Our American culture and the culture of our African friends are poles apart. However, the instant bonding and commonality we felt as we discussed the gospel was one of the many joys of serving there. It is my opinion that this hearkens back to the fact that we all knew these truths intimately prior to coming to this earth.

Most of us have had the experience of teaching someone the gospel and recognizing excitement in their eyes as the Spirit testifies to the truthfulness of the message. Their reaction consists of more than coming to accept a new truth. They are remembering something they already know. A common reaction is "Oh, I've always believed that!" My interpretation of that comment is "Oh, I remember that!"

Joseph F. Smith taught this truth: "All those salient truths which come home so forcibly to the head and heart seem but the awakening of the memories of the spirit" (*Gospel Doctrine*, 13).

Truman Madsen put it this way: "One has sacred moments in relation to persons, places, and situations which bear the subtle stamp of prior awareness, however elusive. . . . One hears truths expressed, 'hidden from before the foundation of the world,' and is pulled to them with overwhelming gratitude. Jesus Christ, who promised He would bring all things to our remembrance, defined all this and more when He said, 'My sheep know my voice'" (*Eternal Man*, 20–21).

"One begins mortality with the veil drawn, but slowly he is moved to penetrate the veil within himself. He is, in time, led to seek the 'holy of holies' within the temple of his own being. . . . There is inspired introspection. As we move through life, half-defined recollections and faint but sometimes vivid outlines combine to bring a familiar tone or ring to our experience" (*Eternal Man*, 20).

Elder Hugh B. Brown had similar observations: "Sometimes during solitude I hear truth spoken with clarity and freshness; uncolored and untranslated it speaks from within myself in a language original but inarticulate, heard only with the soul, and I realize I brought it with me, was never taught it nor can I efficiently teach it to another" (*Eternal Quest*, 435).

The Lord has said, "But the Comforter, which is the Holy Ghost, whom the Father will send in my name, he shall teach you all things, and bring all things to your remembrance, whatsoever I have said unto you" (John 14:26).

"I am the good shepherd, and know my [sheep], and am known of mine. . . . And when he putteth forth his own sheep, he goeth before them, and the sheep follow him: for they know his voice" (John 10:4, 14).

In summary, every person who has ever lived or will ever live on this earth is a spirit child of Heavenly Parents. We have lived with them and been taught by them. Their ultimate purpose has always been the same as that of their firstborn spirit child, Jesus Christ: "For behold, this is my work and my glory—to bring to pass the immortality and eternal life of man" (Moses 1:39).

The Law of Agency

While still in premortality, we were taught right and wrong and were promised that the way would be prepared for us to become like our Heavenly Parents. Laws existed in that premortal existence, and our priceless agency did not begin with earth life. Without law and agency there can be no individual progress. Elder Bruce R.

McConkie taught that there are certain principles that must exist before agency can have any meaning.

"Four great principles must be in force if there is to be agency: 1. Laws must exist, laws ordained by an Omnipotent power, laws which can be obeyed or disobeyed; 2. Opposites must exist—good and evil, virtue and vice, right and wrong—that is, there must be an opposition, one force pulling one way and another pulling the other; 3. A knowledge of good and evil must be had by those who are to enjoy the agency, that is, they must know the difference between the opposites; and 4. An unfettered power of choice must prevail" (*Mormon Doctrine*, 14).

Whenever numerous people are given a set of rules or laws, along with the freedom to obey, to disobey, and to work at their own speed, a diversity of outcomes will result. When we are dealing with a population as numerous as the "sands of the sea," one can hardly imagine the variety of children our Father in Heaven is dealing with. The wonderful thing is that he loves us in our diversity and has set up a plan that takes our various talents into consideration and allows everyone an equal chance to become like him.

Of this diversity in progress Joseph Fielding Smith said:

"God gave his children their free agency even in the spirit world, by which the individual spirits had the privilege, just as men have here, of choosing the good and rejecting the evil, or partaking of the evil to suffer the consequences of their sins. Because of this, some even there were more faithful than others in keeping the commandments of the Lord. Some were of greater intelligence than others, as we find it here, and were honored accordingly. . . .

"The spirits of men had their free agency, some were greater than others, and from among them the Father called and foreordained his prophets and rulers. Jeremiah and Abraham were two of them. . . . The spirits of men were not equal. They may have had an equal start, and we know they were all innocent in the beginning;

but the right of free agency which was given to them enabled some to outstrip others, and thus, through the eons of immortal existence, to become more intelligent, more faithful, for they were free to act for themselves, to think for themselves, to receive the truth or rebel against it" (*Doctrines of Salvation*, 59).

This observation is most dramatically illustrated by an event that occurred just prior to beginning our mortal probation here on the earth. It is hard to comprehend that one-third of our spirit brothers and sisters, all of whom had been nurtured by Heavenly Parents, would allow themselves to be deceived by one of their brothers and rebel against all they had been taught. Nevertheless, this is exactly what happened when the war in heaven began.

The account of a war in heaven provides irrefutable evidence that we had been taught the truth and had been given the agency to accept or reject what we had been taught. A brief summary of this event is provided by Elder Bruce R. McConkie:

"Following the pre-existent choosing of Christ and the rejecting of Lucifer to be the Redeemer in the great plan of salvation, Satan and one-third of the spirit hosts destined for life on this earth came out in *open rebellion* against the Father. The rebels 'sought to destroy the agency of man' and to modify the Father's plan so that salvation would come automatically to all who passed through mortality. Their rebellion against light and truth and their refusal to subscribe to the terms and condition laid down by the Father whereby salvation might be gained is called by John the *war in heaven*" (*Mormon Doctrine*, 828).

We can be assured that all who have lived upon the face of this earth kept their first estate and battled on the Lord's side in the war in heaven. We learn from Joseph Smith that "at the first organization in heaven we were all present, and saw the Savior chosen and appointed and the plan of salvation made, and we sanctioned it" (*Teachings of the Prophet Joseph Smith*, 181).

Whenever agency is combined with diversity in attributes, skills, talents, desire, and effort, diversity in progress is inevitable. Therefore, as it came time for the two-thirds of the hosts of heaven to begin their earthly experience, a variety of individuals emerged who would require a variety of earthly experiences.

The Role of Foreordination

With the Lord's complete understanding of each of us, he devised a plan for the time and bounds of our habitation. We know that the premortal lives members of the Church lived qualified them to be foreordained to be born during this favored (and challenging) time and to function in the assignments they receive. Joseph Smith said: "Every man who has a calling to minister to the inhabitants of the world was ordained to that very purpose in the Grand Council of heaven before this world was" (*Teachings of the Prophet Joseph Smith*, 365).

Such assignments as to the time, place, and circumstances under which we would be born fall under the category of foreordination. This principle is clearly taught in the Book of Abraham:

"Now the Lord had shown unto me, Abraham, the intelligences that were organized before the world was; and among all these there were many of the noble and great ones;

"And God saw these souls that they were good, and he stood in the midst of them, and he said: These I will make my rulers; for he stood among those that were spirits, and he saw that they were good; and he said unto me: Abraham, thou art one of them; thou wast chosen before thou wast born" (Abraham 3:22–23).

Elder Bruce R. McConkie explained foreordination as follows:

"To carry forward his own purposes among men and nations, the Lord foreordained chosen spirit children in pre-existence and assigned them to come to earth at particular times and places so that they might aid in furthering the divine will. These pre-existence appointments, made 'according to the foreknowledge of God the Father' (1 Pet. 1:2), simply designated certain individuals to perform missions which the Lord in his wisdom knew they had the talents and capacities to do" (*Mormon Doctrine*, 290).

Each of us has a role to play in the Master's plan and each of us can make a difference. I am impressed that one of President Gordon B. Hinckley's personal articles of faith is "I believe in myself. I do not mean this with egotism. But I believe in my capacity and in your capacity to do good, to make some contribution to the society of which we are a part, and to grow and develop. . . . I believe in the principle that I can make a difference in this world, be it ever so small" ("Pres. Hinckley Shares 10 Beliefs with Chamber," *LDS Church News*, Jan. 31, 1998, 3).

With the help of scriptures, words of the prophets, and our own personal revelation, we gradually come to an awareness of our true nature and destiny. Once we grasp this reality, we can obtain the faith to move forward and overcome any obstacle that stands in the way of our fulfilling our foreordained destiny.

Foreordination to perform responsibilities in the kingdom of God is the most obvious form of foreordination, but also very important is foreordination to the lineage through which we will be born and the nation where we will live. In Deuteronomy we read,

"When the most High divided to the nations their inheritance, when he separated the sons of Adam, he set the bounds of the people according to the number of the children of Israel.

"For the Lord's portion is his people; Jacob is the lot of his inheritance" (Deuteronomy 32:8–9).

President Harold B. Lee explained this scripture in the following way:

"It would seem very clear, then, that those born to the lineage of Jacob, who was later to be called Israel, and his posterity, who were known as the children of Israel, were born into the most illustrious lineage of any of those who came upon the earth as mortal beings.

"All these rewards were seemingly promised, or foreordained, before the world was. Surely these matters must have been determined by the kind of lives we had lived in that premortal spirit world. Some may question these assumptions, but at the same time they will accept without any question the belief that each one of us will be judged when we leave this earth according to his or her deeds during our lives here in mortality. Isn't it just as reasonable to believe that what we have received here in this earth life was given to each of us according to the merits of our conduct before we came here?" (*Stand Ye in Holy Places*, 16).

Elder McConkie carried the concept of foreordination even further:

"All men are the spirit children of the Eternal Father; all dwelt in his presence, awaiting the day of their mortal probation; all have come or will come to earth at an appointed time in a specified place, to live among a designated people. In all of this there is no chance. A divine providence rules over the nations and governs in the affairs of men. Birth and death and mortal kinship are the Lord's doings. He alone determines where and when and among what people his spirit children shall undergo their mortal probation.

"Is it inappropriate to ask: Why are there different races of men? Why is there a white, a yellow, and a black race? In the days of Israel's first bondage, why did the Lord send some spirits in the lineage of enslaved Jacob and others to their Egyptian overlords? Why were some spirits sent to earth among the Amalekites, the Assyrians, and the Babylonians, while others at the same moments found birth in the house of Israel? Why was Antipas sent as the son of a debauched and evil Herod, while John the Baptist came into the home of a priestly Zacharias and a saintly Elisabeth?

"All of these things operate by law; they are the outgrowth of long years of personal preparation in preexistence on the part of each individual; they come to pass according to the laws that the Lord has ordained. This second estate is a continuation of our first estate; we are born here with the talents and capacities acquired there. Abraham was one of the noble and great spirits in the premortal life. He was chosen for his mortal ministry and position before he was born, and as with the father of the faithful so with all of the spirits destined to be born as his seed" (*A New Witness for the Articles of Faith*, 512).

While it is very logical and even comforting to realize we have been born into a situation resulting from our preparation in the premortal realm, it is also dangerous to jump to many conclusions as to the exact whys and wherefores. If we are not careful we can begin to make judgments about people and their circumstances of birth. While we can be certain that many were called to certain positions because they were among the "noble and great ones," there are also many other factors the Lord would take into consideration prior to determining the circumstances under which we would be born. Other variables might include the circumstances that would give us the best chance to succeed or the group of people we may be able to influence the most.

Thanks to the restoration of the gospel we know many things, but there is much we don't know. The most important thing to consider in this discussion is that the bounds of our habitation have been determined by a God who is omniscient, omnipotent, and omnipresent.

Elder McConkie describes these attributes as follows:

"He is omniscient. He has all wisdom, all knowledge, and all understanding. . . . There is no truth he does not know, no wisdom hidden from his view, no laws or powers or facts for him to discover in some distant eternity. His wisdom and knowledge are absolute and have neither bounds nor limitations. He knows all things now; he is not progressing in knowledge; he is not discovering new truths; there are no higher spheres than the one in which he now walks. Were it otherwise he could not be the Creator of galaxies unnumbered; were it otherwise, he could not hold the universe in his hands and govern and control all things. Indeed, his glory and greatness and goodness exist and are because he knows all things and is the source of all truth. And if such were not the case, men could not exercise faith in him unto life and salvation, for they would know that he might someday discover some truth that would destroy immortality, or eternal life, or the whole scheme and system of things."

The second attribute Elder McConkie mentions is omnipotence. "He has all power, all might, and all dominion; He is the Almighty. He has power to do all that he wills to do. He is the Creator of worlds without number. If it were possible to number the particles of millions of earths like ours the sum obtained would not be a beginning to the number of his creations; and the whole sidereal heavens, all of which are the works of his hands, move through the midst of immensity at his word. Truly he is infinite and eternal without limits or bounds. His power is immeasurable, his might is without end, and his ways cannot be fathomed. There is no power yet to be gained that he does not now possess. If it were otherwise, our faith in him could not be other than limited and partial.

"God is Omnipresent. By the power of his Spirit, God is everywhere present at one and the same time. There is no place on earth or in heaven or through all the broad expanse of boundless space where his presence is not felt. Though he is a personage of tabernacle, . . . though he is an individual set apart from all others, a person separated from all other persons, yet his senses are infinite and there is no limit to the power of his mind. He can hear and see and know all things at one and the same time—all by the power of his Spirit. . . .

This Spirit that is everywhere present is also called the light of Christ" (*A New Witness for the Articles of Faith*, 52–53).

A firm testimony of these attributes immediately brings us to the realization that the Master's plan is sound and fair. We can be assured the Lord knows what he is doing. We may have questions because our finite mind cannot comprehend the infinite. There may be many questions that will necessitate our withholding judgment. We must accept some things on faith. However, we can be absolutely certain that the bounds of our habitation have been set by a God who knows this was the next step in the Master's plan to give us an equal opportunity to come back into his presence and receive all that he has. Each of us as a daughter or son of Heavenly Parents have received the genes of godhood. Irrespective of our place of birth, a plan is in effect to bring those genes into full maturity, even if this earth life never exposes us to the complete truths we learned in our premortal state.

The suffering many have had to endure in order to receive their bodies on this earth will be but a small moment. Unfortunately, the same agency that enabled us to make the choices necessary to be privileged to come to earth and receive our bodies brings about a lot of misery while we are here. Choices we make bring about some of our own suffering. In a like manner, choices others make may also bring about suffering of the innocent. An earth had to be created where the righteous and wicked could exercise their agency. While choosing the correct course allows us to earn the right to live in the celestial kingdom, the same right must be given to those who choose evil to "earn their reward." In the process, inculpable people pay a temporary price for the wickedness of others. Unfortunately, there is no other way.

In the spirit world, teaching is going on that will eventually give every person who has ever lived upon the earth an opportunity to be reacquainted with those truths they learned at the feet of Heavenly

Parents. Each and every person will have an unfettered chance to accept and live those truths. Temples are being built all over the world that will give every person who has ever lived a chance to receive the ordinances necessary to bring the genes of godhood out of their embryo condition into their full omniscient, omnipotent, and omnipresent potential.

Help from beyond the Veil

Understanding our premortal condition is very beneficial when working in Africa, where we observe so much pain and suffering. When we consider Africa, it also helps to understand the postmortal world of our spirits. When I thought of the many millions of people who lived their mortal lives on the African continent and who are waiting for the full blessings of the gospel, my conscience was seared relative to the urgency of the work. Not only did I feel for the 400 million people currently living in the Africa West Area, but I also felt for their ancestors. I frequently felt the assurance that we were receiving help from beyond the veil. I often envisioned the marvelous missionary work going on in the spirit world with those who had been deprived for so long.

Of the work going on in the spirit world and the interest they have in us, President Joseph F. Smith said, "We begin to realize more and more fully, as we become acquainted with the principles of the gospel, as they have been revealed anew in this dispensation, that we are closely related to our kindred, to our ancestors, to our friends and associates and co-laborers who have preceded us into the spirit world. We cannot forget them; we do not cease to love them; we always hold them in our hearts, in memory, and thus we are associated and united to them by ties that we cannot break, that we cannot dissolve or free ourselves from. If this is the case with us in our finite condition, surrounded by our mortal weaknesses, shortsightedness, lack of inspiration and wisdom, from time to time, how much more certain it is, and reasonable and consistent, to believe that those who have been faithful, who have gone beyond, are still engaged in the work for the salvation of the souls of men, in the opening of the prison doors to them that are bound and proclaiming liberty to the captives, who can see us better than we can see them— that they know us better than we know them. They have advanced; we are advancing; we are growing as they have grown; we are reaching the goal that they have attained unto; and therefore, I claim that we live in their presence, they see us, they are solicitous for our welfare, they love us now more than ever" (*Gospel Doctrine*, 430).

We have been assured that those who have preceded us beyond the veil are given permission on occasion to assist us, to which Joseph F. Smith testifies: "Our fathers and mothers, brothers, sisters and friends who have passed away from this earth, having been faithful and worthy to enjoy these rights and privileges, may have a mission given them to visit their relatives and friends upon the earth again, bringing from the divine Presence messages of love, of warning, of reproof and instruction to those whom they had learned to love in the flesh" (*Journal of Discourses*, 22:351).

On numerous occasions, when we seemed to be facing overwhelming and staggering odds, I took comfort in the experience of Elisha when an army from Syria surrounded the city of Dothan to take Elisha prisoner. One of Elisha's young disciples discovered the trap that had been laid for the prophet and manifested great fear. "And when the servant of the man of God was risen early, and gone forth, behold, an host compassed the city both with horses and chariots. And his servant said unto him, Alas, my master! how shall we do?"

Elisha calmly responded to his question, "Fear not: for they that be with us are more than they that be with them.

"And Elisha prayed, and said, Lord, I pray thee, open his eyes, that he may see. And the Lord opened the eyes of the young man;

and he saw: and, behold, the mountain was full of horses and chariots of fire round about Elisha" (2 Kings 6:15–17).

Harold B. Lee taught, "Where is the spirit world? Is it away up in the heavens? That isn't what the scriptures and our brethren explain. They have told us the spirit world is right here round about us, and the only spirits who can live here are those who are assigned to fill their missions here on earth. This is the spirit world. And if our eyes could be opened we could see those who have departed from us—a father, mother, brother, a sister, a child. We could see them, and sometimes when our physical senses are asleep, sometimes our spiritual self—and we have ears, spiritual ears, and spiritual eyes—sometimes they will be very keen and awake, and a departed one may come while we are lying asleep and come into our consciousness. We'll feel an impression. We'll wake up. Where does it come from? It comes from the spirits of those whom we are sealed to. . . .

"The Prophet Joseph Smith taught: 'The spirits of the just are exalted to a greater and more glorious work; hence they are blessed in their departure to the world of spirits.' Now listen to this: 'Enveloped in flaming fire, they are not far from us, and know and understand our thoughts, feelings, and motions, and are often pained therewith.' (*Teachings of the Prophet Joseph Smith*, 326.)" (*The Teachings of Harold B. Lee*, 58, 60).

I am thankful that on several occasions, when things seemed hopeless, the veil was parted sufficiently to enable us to keep going in spite of the odds. In my mind's eye I could see millions of the ancestors of the African people in a vast army bringing to pass the Master's plan and patiently waiting to receive all that he has. It was on these occasions that I learned that the Lord has his own timetable, and I was powerless to speed it up—but I would be held responsible if I did anything to slow it down.

Rather than worrying too much about why these great people

had waited so long, I focused on the strong conviction I received that current African Saints must have been extremely valiant to have been reserved to come forth through their lineage at this time in the history of the Church in Africa. They had been blessed with the opportunity of spreading the gospel to the people currently living in Africa, as well as the opportunity and responsibility of making it possible for the ancestors of all Africans to receive all the Lord has to give. Those now living and those who have passed beyond the veil are to receive no less than anyone else who has been born under any circumstance or into any lineage. All of this is made possible through the Master's plan of salvation, which includes the work performed in the holy temples.

With these perspectives in place, please join me on my journey to the continent of Africa.

2

THE ETHIOPIAN FAMINE—
AN INITIATION

My personal introduction—or perhaps I should say *initiation*—to Africa occurred in 1985. It was before I was called as a General Authority. I was employed by the Church as the managing director of the Welfare Services Department. In 1984 a very historic tragedy caught the attention of the world and ultimately influenced humanitarian efforts by numerous charitable organizations. As far as the Church is concerned, the event became the springboard from which the current humanitarian program of the Church was launched, which includes the creation of LDS Charities.

The tragedy was a devastating famine in Ethiopia. A television crew from the British Broadcasting Corporation captured the human suffering in a documentary that was released in 1984 and was aired throughout the world. The compassion and concern generated by this program were unprecedented. Members of the Church saw these television productions and were understandably touched. Many wrote letters to Church headquarters asking what the Church planned to do to help the Ethiopian people. Stories had been published and broadcast about some humanitarian organizations whose administrative costs were allegedly too high, and this made some of our members skeptical about whether money donated to private organizations would reach the people in need. Our members wanted to send their contributions to Church headquarters and have the Brethren decide where to make the donation.

As they considered the scope and circumstances of this tragedy, the First Presidency and Quorum of the Twelve decided to invite members to participate in a special fast on January 27, 1985. This is a key date in the history of the Church's humanitarian efforts throughout the world as we know them today. While the Church has always responded to the suffering caused by various disasters, the Ethiopian famine triggered a more methodical and organized effort than had been experienced before. To announce their thinking, the First Presidency (Spencer W. Kimball, Marion G. Romney, and Gordon B. Hinckley) sent a letter to priesthood leaders in the United States and Canada on January 11, 1985. The letter noted:

"People throughout the world have been touched by the portrayal in the media of the plight of many thousands of starving people in Africa. There are others in similar circumstances in other areas. We have sent funds to assist those in need. We now feel that our people would like to participate more extensively in the great humanitarian effort to assist those in Ethiopia, other areas of Africa, and perhaps in other parts of the world.

"The First Presidency and the Council of the Twelve have accordingly determined that Sunday, January 27, should be designated as a special fast day when our people will be invited to refrain from partaking of two meals and contribute the equivalent value, or more, to the Church to assist those in need. All fast offering funds contributed on this day will be dedicated for the use of the victims of famine and other causes resulting in hunger and privation among people of Africa, and possibly in some other areas. They will be placed through agencies of unquestioned integrity.

"The regular February fast day will be held on the first Sunday of the month as usual and funds contributed on that day will be used in the customary way to assist those in need in the Church. We repeat, however, that all funds contributed on January 27 will be earmarked particularly to assist the hungry and needy in distressed areas regardless of Church membership.

"We shall appreciate your advising the people of your wards and stakes accordingly. This letter may be read in the sacrament meetings of all wards and branches. We are confident that there will be a great outpouring from this effort."

The response from members was not only "a great outpouring," but it exceeded all expectations. Six million dollars was raised on that one fast Sunday. The First Presidency was overwhelmed and humbled by the support of the members. I remember sitting in a welfare meeting where this was being discussed. President Hinckley, then second counselor in the First Presidency, spoke with great emotion about the goodness of the Saints. He said, "The Saints have placed a great trust in us. We cannot and will not let them down." Then he craned his neck and looked down toward me at the other end of the table and said, "Will we, Glenn?"

At that moment I felt the pressure of the trust of every member of the Church on my shoulders. I remember limping back to my office, sitting at my desk, and wondering how a naive boy from Provo who later became a certified public accountant had gotten himself into this assignment. I had been trained in auditing what other people did, not in making decisions myself. Perhaps you are familiar with the old joke about the definition of an auditor: it's the person who goes onto the battlefield after the battle is over—and shoots the wounded.

On the other hand, I knew I had received an assignment from the First Presidency of the Church. And I knew that *each of us has a role to play in the Master's plan and each of us can make a difference.* Little did I know, however, what was ahead with my continued work in Africa or what impact this point in history would have on the humanitarian work of the Church. Yet I knew enough to feel inadequate and stretched far beyond my own capacity. As is typical of most of us, I could see a high risk of failure because of my weaknesses. It is very difficult in the heat of a battle to remember that *the rolling out of the kingdom in accordance with the Master's plan cannot be stopped.*

It is likely the reader can relate to these feelings. Our challenges often don't come in ways that are this visible. Yet how many of us feel completely overwhelmed at being mothers and fathers as we think of the trust which has been placed in us? How many of us feel overwhelmed at teaching teenagers in a Sunday School class week after week or standing in front of the Relief Society or elders quorum to teach our peers? At that moment in my history, I was overwhelmed with the pressure of honoring the trust of the members and the First Presidency of the Church.

Humanitarian Partnerships

Thus began one of the most intense spiritual and emotional experiences of my life. I was given the assignment to make an extensive investigation into various humanitarian organizations administering aid and to make recommendations to the Brethren on those through whom we should work. Furthermore, time was of the essence. The Brethren made clear to me that members of the Church had not donated this money to let it sit in a bank account drawing interest. The money was contributed to immediately bless the lives of the suffering people.

At that time the Church did not have the infrastructure or license to deliver aid directly to people in various parts of the world; we were therefore dependent on using other organizations. It was several years later that LDS Charities was organized and we were able to do more things on our own.

I spent the first ten days after the special fast in New York City and Washington, D.C., learning all I could about the agencies involved in administering assistance. I then started to meet with those whose reputations seemed to draw the best reviews. Getting appointments on such short notice with people in high places in these agencies was one of many miracles. It was a very busy time for them, but they bent over backwards to make time for me. When they heard the "Mormon" Church had raised $6 million in one day, some began to knock on *my* door. The humanitarian community is a very tight community, and word gets around fast. The awe with which they viewed a church raising that much money in one day was genuine. When I explained that the letter from the First Presidency announcing the special fast had gone out just sixteen days before the fast, they were even more impressed.

I experienced a wide range of emotions, from wondering if it would ever work out to recognizing the Lord's hand at every turn. I often thought about the inconsistency of feeling on top of the world one day and thinking the sky was falling the next. I was on an airplane flying home from New York City when I recorded in my journal: "This has been the most difficult week I have spent in a long time. I generally function best under pressure, but the responsibility I have felt to the Church for this decision has stretched me to the limit."

Of course, the final decision would be made by the Brethren, but I knew they would rely heavily on my opinion. If I was wrong, there wouldn't be time to do the work over again.

One of the most unique recommendations I planned to make was that $1.4 million be donated to Catholic Relief Services. I wasn't looking forward to standing in front of the First Presidency and Quorum of the Twelve of The Church of Jesus Christ of Latter-day Saints and recommending that we give more than a million dollars to another church—but within hours I would be doing that very thing. When I did make that recommendation I observed several raised eyebrows, and I was asked to elaborate a little bit. I explained that my assignment had been to make sure the aid reached the people in need, and it was my opinion that the Catholic Church had the infrastructure to accomplish that. The response: "I have no further questions." Never have I been so proud to be a member of this church. Helping the people was all that mattered to the Brethren.

A Trip to Ethiopia

My next adventure was an assignment to go to Ethiopia for an up-close inspection prior to releasing the funds. I was assigned to travel with Elder M. Russell Ballard, who was then serving as a member of the presidency of the Seventy. We left on March 11, just two months after the letter on the special fast was written. My physical initiation to Africa was about to begin.

While we were in the Dulles Airport in Washington, D.C., awaiting our flight to London and then on to Addis Ababa, Ethiopia, I checked in with President Hinckley. He said something that would prove to be very comforting and reassuring during some tense moments in the weeks that followed. He said, "The First Presidency and Quorum of the Twelve will be praying for you and Elder Ballard, by name, that your mission will be successful." I knew we were on the Lord's errand and that *the Master's plan cannot be stopped.*

Later that evening, while flying somewhere over the Atlantic Ocean and still basking in the reassurance from President Hinckley, I recorded in my journal: "The Brethren praying for me, Glenn Pace? How did all this happen? I sometimes feel I am being swept along in a current of events beyond my control but to which I humbly and willingly submit, because at rare times such as this I have the conviction that the Lord is directing the course of the current."

Within minutes after landing in Addis Ababa, I had a rich spiritual experience. It had nothing to do with Africa per se, but with traveling and associating with one of the Lord's anointed. Prior to leaving on our trip, Elder Ballard had checked the Church membership records to see if any members of the Church were living in Ethiopia. He had located the name of one member, a man from Seattle, Washington, named Harry Hadlock. He was located in Addis Ababa temporarily while doing consulting work for Ethiopian Airlines.

I had been working on the humanitarian aid assignment for two months. We were finally on site in Ethiopia, and I was raring to go. We had appointments with government authorities as well as various representatives of humanitarian organizations. We had less than two weeks to make some very important decisions. But first, I was ready to check in to a hotel and freshen up—we had been traveling for more than twenty-four hours.

I soon discovered Elder Ballard had other ideas. His first priority was to locate this one member of the Church. I felt like a little boy who had been told I couldn't eat dessert until after I finished my spinach. I grudgingly acquiesced, and we began our search by talking to people at the airport to see if they had heard of him. Much to my surprise, we found out he actually worked at an office in the airport, and within minutes someone brought him to us.

We found out that he had been in Ethiopia for several months. His wife had not traveled with him because of the terrible conditions in the country, and he was very lonely. As far as he knew, there were no other members of the Church in Ethiopia at that time. Elder Ballard told him we would be holding a sacrament meeting the following Sunday and that we would love to come to his home for the meeting. Tears welled up in Brother Hadlock's eyes and he began to sob as he said, "I have not partaken of the sacrament in months." At this time, the shame I felt for being in such a hurry was exceeded only by the joy I felt that Elder Ballard had his priorities straight and was listening to the promptings of the Spirit. "Seeking after the one" took on a whole new meaning. I thought of the Savior's words about searching for the lost sheep: "How think ye? If a man have an hundred sheep, and one of them be gone astray, doth he not leave the ninety and nine, and goeth into the mountains, and seeketh that which is gone astray?" (Matthew 18:12).

Brother Hadlock wasn't lost, but he was very lonely, separated from the people he loved and living in a country where pain and suffering were all around him.

The joy of seeing how much this meant to Brother Hadlock was only a precursor to the outpouring of the Spirit we felt at the sacrament meeting we held in his home a couple of days later. In attendance were Elder Ballard, myself, and Brother Hadlock—three Melchizedek Priesthood holders in a sacrament meeting in a Marxist country. I gave the opening prayer, which was followed by testimonies and the sacrament. I said the blessing on the bread and Brother Hadlock said the blessing on the water. Brother Hadlock had a difficult time getting through the blessing because of the emotion he was feeling. In his testimony Elder Ballard expressed his feelings that the welfare program and the missionary program would work closely together as the gospel is spread throughout the world, and that it was no whim but inspiration that President Hinckley sent Elder Ballard, who then was executive director of the missionary department, with Brother Pace, who was the managing director of the Welfare Services Department of the Church, on that assignment together.

At the close of the meeting, Elder Ballard offered a most sacred prayer and blessing on Ethiopia, which I recall clearly but did not make record of at the time. In his supplication to our Heavenly Father, Elder Ballard noted that we were the only Melchizedek Priesthood holders then in the country and that we were there on assignment from the First Presidency of the Church. He expressed gratitude to the members of the Church who had contributed their means during the special fast and who had offered up individual and family prayers on behalf of the people of Ethiopia. Then, with as much power and boldness as I had ever witnessed, he called upon the power and authority of the holy Melchizedek Priesthood and commanded the elements to gather together to bring rain upon the land, thus to begin to relieve those who had been suffering for so many years. It hadn't rained in a year, and the prayer was offered on a clear and sunny Sunday morning.

We left the sacrament meeting for a luncheon with representatives of Catholic Relief Services and Africare, an African-American humanitarian organization. It was agreed in this meeting that our organizations would work together in partnership on some relief endeavors. It is noteworthy to mention the positive feelings I had in working with Catholics and African Americans on a common cause. I couldn't help but feel that there are wonderful, caring people throughout the world of every nation, creed, and color.

We returned to the hotel in the afternoon to rest up for the coming week, and I was sitting at a little desk writing in my journal when I heard a clap of thunder. I went to the patio just in time to see the beginning of a torrential downpour. People began to run out of their little huts and public buildings, looking up at the sky and reaching their arms toward the heavens. They were shouting and crying. The heavy downpour continued for some time. I was mesmerized as I watched the scene from the window. As the ground became saturated and began to puddle, children and adults alike began to frolic and splash on each other. They grabbed buckets and barrels to collect rain from the roofs. It was a celebration unlike any I've ever witnessed.

As I stood at the window watching the scene unfold, my emotions turned from great joy to exquisite thanksgiving. I began to weep. I knew there were only two other people in the entire country who understood what had happened. Once I had gained control of my emotions, I went down the hall and knocked on Elder Ballard's door. When he came to the door, I could tell he had been overwhelmed in a like manner. We said a prayer of thanksgiving and returned to the privacy of our own rooms and thoughts. From that day forward, wherever we traveled, it rained.

Leaps of Faith

This was the first of several miracles we were to witness. One of our major objectives was to visit several of the camps to observe the distribution of food firsthand, so we could see how the infrastructure was working. Our first major obstacle came as we tried to obtain permits to travel into these areas. At that time Ethiopia was under Soviet control, and movement from state to state was tightly restricted. In this way the government could tell where a person was at all times. You could not even buy gasoline without a permit. Waiting for a permit to help people seems like the epitome of lack of freedom.

We were shocked and horrified to learn it would take at least ten days to obtain all of the documents we needed. Elder Ballard did not have ten days—which meant we would not be able to accomplish our mission, or I would be left to do so alone.

As we discussed the dilemma, we came to the mutual feeling that we had not come this far to have our mission fail. I thought of the reassurance President Hinckley had given just before we left. We returned to the hotel, knelt in prayer, and literally asked the Lord for a miracle. We then went back to our hosts and asked them to do all they could to speed things up; meanwhile, we would proceed with our travel plans. They looked at each other with some skepticism but agreed. Three days later, on the eve of our planned field trip, we had the permits. The details of how we got them are not important, but the explanation of our hosts began with, "We just experienced the strangest coincidence." We just smiled and commended them for their ingenuity and diligence.

For the two months leading up to our site visit and during the two weeks on-site, we worked very closely with numerous humanitarian and governmental organizations. I gained a whole new appreciation for the goodness of people in general. I didn't see blacks and whites, capitalists and Marxists, or Catholics and Mormons. I saw children of our Father in Heaven helping children of our Father in Heaven.

In feeding stations we saw doctors and nurses who volunteered their time for months while living in deplorable conditions. They came from many different nations and organizations. There were no political debates in their foxholes. Instead there was mutual love and respect. All of their combined energy was directed toward the common goal of eliminating the suffering of strangers.

In Eritrea we heard of a Catholic priest from Italy who had been working there for seventeen years, long before international publicity had made helping Ethiopians fashionable. The people called him Father Caesar. This and many other examples taught me there was more than one Mother Teresa in the Catholic Church. I saw many Mother Teresas and Father Caesars in various churches, governments, corporations, foundations, and among the private citizenry.

Catholic Relief Services had been working in Ethiopia since 1958 and had been doing some development work to help the country. As the seriousness of the famine became apparent to them, they tried to bring world attention to the problem, but it was almost a year before the media captured the story and everything exploded. During that year and the year following, Catholic Relief Services concentrated most of their efforts on famine relief. By the time we visited, their best estimate was that 1.3 million people had died already and at least 2 million more were at serious risk. As I mentioned earlier, every day is 9/11 for many in Africa.

Very little humanitarian service in these countries is performed risk free. Humanitarian workers are exposed to all manner of diseases, not to mention the ever-present danger of war. In Ethiopia, it was often difficult to get supplies in because of problems related to their civil war. Trucks full of life-saving supplies and food were often attacked because one side or the other thought they were carrying military supplies. Drought was only a partial cause of the starvation. Civil war and mismanagement were others.

I received a much-appreciated personal lesson in the real life of a true humanitarian from one of the officials from Catholic Relief Services. As we were making plans for our trip to Ethiopia, I would often ask, "Is it safe to travel in that area?" The first few times I asked that question, my hosts would do all they could to reassure me that it was safe. But I guess I asked the question once too often, because at one point one of the seasoned veterans who had worked all over the world in some very desperate circumstances said, "No, Glenn, it isn't safe. In this business we cannot guarantee safety. We do all we can to stay away from danger and be wise in our planning. We are constantly vigilant to what is going on around us and don't take unnecessary risks. However, in some cases, it is necessary to risk a life to save one. If you are going to help desperate people, you sometimes find yourself in desperate circumstances."

I reflected on this many times while serving in West Africa thirteen years later. You live with risk everywhere you go. This was why it was particularly meaningful to us when our African friends wished us a *safe journey*.

When you pray for the Lord to protect you during your travels in Africa, you really mean it. During this two-week trip and the subsequent three-year tour of duty with my wife, we prayed for safety with a fervency never before felt. Of equal importance, when we returned safely, we knelt down and thanked our Father in Heaven profusely for his watching care. In the process, both faith and gratitude increased.

With this increased sensitivity, miracles become easier to recognize, and you see them all around you. I'm grateful to Africa for convincingly answering the question "Have miracles ceased?" As Mormon wrote:

"And now, my beloved brethren, if this be the case that these things are true which I have spoken unto you, and God will show unto you, with power and great glory at the last day, that they are true, and if they are true has the day of miracles ceased?

"Or have angels ceased to appear unto the children of men? Or has he withheld the power of the Holy Ghost from them? Or will he, so long as time shall last, or the earth shall stand, or there shall be one man upon the face thereof to be saved?

"Behold I say unto you, Nay; for it is by faith that miracles are wrought; and it is by faith that angels appear and minister unto men; wherefore, if these things have ceased wo be unto the children of men, for it is because of unbelief, and all is vain" (Moroni 7:35–37).

It is my observation that in places of relative comfort, safety, and prosperity, people gain a false sense of independence and often don't feel a need for their Maker. They don't feel a need for miracles, they don't believe in them, they don't ask for them, and, consequently, they don't get them. In places like Africa, the people recognize their dependence on the Lord just to live from day to day. They believe in miracles, they ask for them, and they receive them.

As we journeyed into the troubled areas of Ethiopia, it became necessary to take occasional leaps of faith. For example, on one trip we traveled to Makalle, a city in the north of the country. We knew how we were going to get there, but we didn't know how we would get back. We hitched a ride on a British Royal Air Force supply plane that was headed for one of the camps. At the camp we were met by officials who took us where we wanted to go and hosted us very well throughout the day. Then, late in the afternoon, we were dropped off at an airport consisting of a very primitive runway and nothing much more than a bench for a terminal. Our hosts informed us that humanitarian planes landed on this strip from time to time, but there was no particular schedule and certainly no updates. Our instruction was to wait until a plane landed; then, while they unloaded the cargo, we were to approach the pilot and find out if they were headed for Asmara. If they were, we were then to ask him if we could hitch a ride. If he agreed, the next step was to approach the Russian soldier who accompanied every flight and get his permission. We were completely at his mercy. He had the authority and the rifle. I have experienced better odds for life's little gambles than having two Americans approach a Russian soldier in 1985 asking for favors.

We saw several planes come and go. Some were not going our direction and others didn't have room for us. Finally a Swiss Air Force cargo plane came along. We asked the pilot for a ride, and he very willingly gave his consent and then nodded in the direction of a young soldier with a rifle and added, "The final decision is his." After staring us down for some time to let us know who was in control of the situation, the soldier gave his permission.

By now Elder Ballard and I were very weary, not to mention dehydrated. I can still see him sitting in the belly of that big, empty plane. It had brought flour to the camp, and there was a fine white dust everywhere, including on our clothes and faces. The scene was so humorous I snapped a picture of Elder Ballard sitting there looking forlorn. That was a mistake. The soldier ripped off his seat belt and headed for me with fire in his eye, pointed the rifle at me, and asked for my camera. I said something like, "If you saw your commanding officer looking like that, wouldn't you want a picture of him?" For the first time he smiled and sat back down. We arrived at our destination safe once again.

Hitching a ride on an airplane in the middle of nowhere is but one example of the numerous miracles, large and small, that followed us everywhere we went. Each scene unfolded as if it had been a script, and all we had to do was remember our lines.

The Savior's Love Is Universal

Many experiences illustrated to me that *the Savior's love for his children is universal.* I have never seen more despair and suffering than I observed on this trip. However, I also received a constant assurance that the Savior loved these people and that he was very near and well pleased that the members of his church were trying to help. My conviction of the Savior's love was accompanied by my own feelings of love for the people and the Savior.

In Makalle, feeding camps had been set up to house 120,000 people in tents. They were migrating to Makalle from several hundred miles away, with thousands dying on the journey. Those who arrived at the gate were devastated to learn there was a waiting list to get into the camps—some 30,000 were outside waiting to get in. I will never forget walking out into a sea of dingy, dirty, starving, diseased, and desperate men, women, and children. The children sat as if in a trance. They stared at us with sunken eyes and bloated, malnourished stomachs. Flies were crawling all over their faces and they didn't have enough energy to swat them away. There were thousands of children and no laughter. None of the children were playing. Our ears were met with a haunting, eery, deafening silence. Occasionally someone would get up and move toward us, followed by another. Our guides would begin to beat them back with a staff. We begged them not to do that, but the guides looked at us as if to say, "You don't understand the danger." We asked them to stop the beating anyway.

Elder Pace greeting children at the wall of the refugee camp.

A mass of people waiting to get into the camp.

Elder Ballard at the refugee camp.

A toddler and mother at the camp.

Three children in line for food at the camp. The last little girl is blind.

I have never felt so helpless. As we began mingling, some would approach us and say, "Doctor! Doctor!" They would thrust a baby into our arms and point to a skin infection or some other problem and ask us for medication to help heal the sores. Others would approach us and say, "Sister! Sister!" This stumped us until someone explained that the only other white person they had ever seen was a Catholic nun. The designation of "Sister" had come to mean a white person who was trying to help. Later on, Elder Ballard and I agreed that "Elder! Elder!" should become a part of the world's vocabulary. It brings me much peace to realize what has happened in our humanitarian work since 1985, which has placed the Church on the map as a major player.

I won't go into more detail about the scene of suffering people. But I was haunted as much by what I didn't see as what I did see. I made a journal entry about that on March 20, 1985:

"The sight I didn't see, but which has been well-documented by others, is what haunts me most—the people who haven't yet made it to the edge of the camps. A mother carrying a baby on her back and running out of hope and energy. People cold at night and hot in the day without food and water. The scenes we experienced personally have been depicted and documented well in the newspapers and on television. Television viewers have already seen much of it— but to that, one must add the repugnant odors that permeated the camps and the pleading eyes that looked directly into ours."

I felt an overwhelming love for the people. Despite their dire situation, their pride in their humanity showed through. As I noted in my journal, "They have a stately stature. They have compassion for each other. They are a bright, industrious people."

It was a relief to go back into the main camps and see what a difference a few days of food and water could make. There, living in the tents, were people who had regained their strength. Children were laughing and playing, although many of them were orphans or at least did not know where their parents were. They were curious about us, since many had never seen a white person before. They would follow us around. Elder Ballard looked like the Pied Piper. The children would approach us and reach out to touch our skin to see if it felt the same as theirs. It did—and they seemed surprised at that.

One of the most touching scenes was the long line of children coming to eat their dinner. We could pick out siblings helping each other. Many carried a brother or sister on their back or in their arms. Three-year-old children would walk with their arms around younger children and help them eat. Their love and concern for each other seemed to far outweigh their natural desire to be first in line.

I walked out into the tent city with an Ethiopian worker who translated for me. As we walked by the tents we would stop and talk to those sitting outside. I recall a mother sitting with her fifteen-year-old daughter, braiding her hair. In the midst of this poverty, sitting on the dirt, she was making her daughter look and feel as pretty as possible. I watched her tender fingers lovingly put the final touches on the hair. She then cupped her hands under the daughter's chin and raised her face toward me and said, "Isn't she pretty?" I smiled and said, "Yes, very!" but I thought to myself, "But she is not nearly as beautiful as you!" Oh, the African mothers! They are wonderful!

We continued our walk down the endless rows of tents. Toward sunset many were settling in for the night, and the prayers began. Some of the people were Muslim and others were Christian. Yet all seemed very religious and devoted to their God. We paused at one tent and eavesdropped on a prayer. My guide translated the prayer, which went something like this, "We thank you for our life. Some of our children have died. We are thankful some have lived. We pray for other family members who are missing. Our crops have failed for

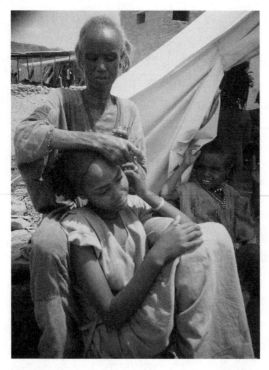

A mother fixing her daughter's hair at the refugee camp.

three years in a row. We are thankful for seed. We will plant again. We pray for rain."

I couldn't get over how thankful they were for what they had and for the faith they had in the future, in spite of the tragedies they had experienced. They had not turned bitter or lost their faith. Tears came to my eyes as I pictured the Savior listening to those prayers.

Another unforgettable experience occurred outside a hospital that was set up in the tent city. An old man stumbled into the camp carrying a baby. He had a look of desperation and disorientation on his face. We learned he had been walking for fifty to seventy-five miles to find refuge in the feeding camp. As he began his journey he heard a baby crying and, upon investigating, found an infant beside his dead mother. She had been trying to reach the camp but did not make it. He picked up the baby in his arms and carried him those many miles by himself. As he arrived, thirsty, hungry, and delirious,

An old man who carried an unrelated baby a long distance to the camp.

the first words he uttered were, "What can be done for this baby?" Can anyone doubt the love the Savior felt for this man? I have never loved a stranger more.

At the end of another field trip we were tired and hungry and drove to an isolated piece of road where we could eat our lunch. We handed out the sandwiches and took one bite when we looked up and saw the car was surrounded by children looking in the windows. We took one look at each other and started to hand out everything we had. The smiles took away our hunger in a hurry, but it seemed like such a drop in the bucket compared with the need. I was so grateful at that time for the donations of our members, which would keep hundreds of thousands of people alive for many weeks.

Desperation was everywhere. As we drove from one place to the next, people were out on the street begging or selling everything and anything. I later saw the same thing for three years in West Africa. We quickly learned that you can't help every person you see, and in some cases it would start a riot to help anyone. Nevertheless, we tried to follow the Spirit and act according to its direction. As we traveled down one of the roads outside Addis Ababa, we came upon a young woman, probably fifteen years of age, with a baby on her back. I don't know whether the baby was hers or if it was her sister. She was selling a bracelet that had belonged to her grandmother. The thought crossed my mind that selling that bracelet was like selling a book of remembrance. I had the impression to ask her what it would cost, give her the money, and let her keep the bracelet. But when she told me how much she wanted I felt she was asking too much, and so I didn't follow the impression and I didn't buy it. One of our associates purchased it instead.

I didn't sleep all night long. I was ashamed of myself. I felt the Lord was not pleased with me either. Unfortunately, I was leaving the next day and didn't have time to make up for it. Therefore, I gave our associate three times what he had paid for the bracelet and asked for a favor. "The next time you see something like that, give the money to the mother and don't take the heirloom." He promised he would do so and then presented the bracelet to me as a gift. That bracelet is one of my most prized possessions because of the reminder it gives me. I have tried to learn from that mistake.

The next day I left for home. My initiation to Africa had come to an end, but I have never forgotten what I saw and felt. In many ways I dreaded returning to Utah for fear I would fall into the entrapments of a comfortable life and start taking everything for granted again. I was also sad that the experience itself was over, because it had been so loaded with things of great spiritual import. I wondered if anything in my life would ever be able to match it. As I recorded in my journal:

"I guess the thing that has been on my mind the most today is what a spiritual experience I have had since January 27, 1985, the day the Church fasted for Africa. I have never experienced an unfolding of events like this. I have worked hard and given it my best, but the hand of the Lord has illuminated the way step by step. Without experiencing it personally, it is impossible to convey to others. This light I have experienced continuously since January 27 is far beyond what I ordinarily experience, and I cannot deny it. I have been blessed by the personal prayers of the First Presidency and the Quorum of the Twelve, plus the fasting of the members of the Church. I'm dreading the end of this week when a large part of the job will be complete and I will get back to normal, because I will not deserve the kind of guidance I've been privileged to enjoy on behalf of the Saints.

"I believe the Church will benefit greatly from the efforts we've made, let alone the benefit these poor destitute citizens of Ethiopia will receive. I have strong feelings this will be the beginning of greater involvement of the Church in Africa. I personally feel a spiritual love and connection to the people of Africa. I have never experienced anything like it before. I'm sad in many ways that the opportunity is gone."

One week later I was called to be a General Authority and asked to serve as second counselor to Bishop Robert D. Hales in the Presiding Bishopric. Six months later Elder Ballard was called to the Quorum of the Twelve.

"It Has Been Most Gratifying"

To top it all off, as I sat in the Sunday morning session of general conference on April 7, 1985, as a newly sustained General Authority, I heard President Hinckley recap the events I have just described. It provides an excellent summary of this chapter. Following are excerpts from President Hinckley's remarks:

"And now, I should like to turn to another matter, dealing with an expression of the gospel of our Lord of whom we have spoken.

"When the lawyer tempted Him, asking, 'Master, which is the great commandment in the law?

"'Jesus said unto him, Thou shalt love the Lord thy God with all thy heart, and with all thy soul, and with all thy mind.

"'This is the first and great commandment.

"'And the second is like unto it, Thou shalt love thy neighbour as thyself.

"'On these two commandments hang all the law and the prophets' (Matthew 22:36–40).

"When hearts across the world were touched by reports of starving populations in Africa, we invited members of the Church in the United States and Canada to observe a special fast day, abstaining from two meals and giving the equivalent value, or more, to aid these famine-stricken people. We at the time asked only those in North America because of a desire to move quickly, and we felt there was not sufficient time to put in place the program elsewhere. Many of you outside North America have asked that you be given a similar opportunity, and some have responded.

"The response of those who participated has been wonderful. It has been most gratifying. It was far more generous than at the regular monthly fast. We, as the trustees of your contributions, should like to give you an accounting of what we have done to date. Your contributions have reached the sum of $6,025,656. We indicated that any money so received would be handled through organizations of demonstrated integrity. We do not have members of the Church in the areas where the need is most acute. If we were to help quickly and effectively, we had to join hands with others, and this has been a most gratifying experience. We have come to know that there are many organizations that are doing great good in stemming the tide of hunger that threatens millions in that part of the world. We have associated ourselves in this endeavor with four of these, who have been most cooperative and helpful. . . .

"Some few have criticized us for extending aid to those who are the victims of the policies or mismanagement of their governments.

My response has been that where there is stark hunger, regardless of the cause, I will not let political considerations dull my sense of mercy or thwart my responsibility to the sons and daughters of God, wherever they may be or whatever their circumstances.

"Elder M. Russell Ballard, of the Presidency of the First Quorum of the Seventy, and Bishop Glenn L. Pace, who joined the Presiding Bishopric yesterday, have just returned from Africa, where they went out into the rural areas of Ethiopia. They saw firsthand how the funds you consecrated are literally saving the lives of many who otherwise would die of starvation, disease, and exposure. Your contributions not only have supplied food and medicine where they are so desperately needed, but your contributions also have furnished tents sufficient to put thirty thousand people under shelter from the blistering sun and the cold night winds, with blankets to comfort them. The food and other commodities are getting through to those who need them. There has been no interference with this, but only the best of cooperation.

"Elder Ballard and Bishop Pace have been with these suffering people. They say they are men and women of courage and character, but they are defeated and frightened by the terrifying circumstances in which they find themselves. Their lands are dry and naked. There is neither irrigation water nor food. They wander in desperation until they and their children die unless they are fed. A little cracked wheat literally spells the difference between life and death. . . .

"I, for one, am deeply grateful for the opportunity to assist in blessing those of our Father's children in that part of the earth who are in such desperate need. I am confident that there springs up in the heart of each of you a feeling of appreciation for what has come to pass and will yet further come to pass as the result of many of our people with one heart doing so small a thing as refraining from two meals and contributing the value thereof to a common effort. Think what might happen if there were such a fast day observed across the world. No one would be hurt, and many would be helped. How grateful we are for the inspiration of the Almighty in establishing so simple, yet so effective a program for relieving want and suffering.

"In the administration of African relief we have not used a single dollar for overhead, but every dollar you have contributed has gone or will go to help directly those in such urgent need, not one of whom is a member of the Church.

"May I read a few lines from two letters. The first is from the chairman of Catholic Relief Services:

"'I want to acknowledge the very generous contribution of The Church of Jesus Christ of Latter-day Saints . . . for relief efforts in Ethiopia and the Sudan. You can be sure that these funds will be put to rapid use to help alleviate the suffering that millions face in those countries.

"'We are pleased to participate in an interfaith action of this kind. Such ecumenical efforts underline the compassion and concern we hold in common when faced by such human tragedies as well as our common commitment to positive action.

"'This cooperation between us has a special character since the resources involved come directly from your individual members through a day of fasting. It is thus in a very heartening sense an example of people responding to people at a fundamental level of moral and practical concern. . . . Sincerely yours in Christ, [signed] Daniel P. Reilly, Bishop of Norwich, chairman of the board of directors'

"And now from the president of the American Red Cross:

"'I cannot thank you and your members in the U.S. and Canada enough for the outstanding support you have given the Red Cross relief effort in Africa. Your most recent contribution of $800,000 brings the total donations to $1,400,000. This support . . . has permitted us to provide 350,000 victims food for a month based upon the Red Cross estimate that $4 a month is needed to feed a child. . . .

"'In Ethiopia . . . on a daily average the Red Cross workers are feeding more than 500,000 people. . . . Red Cross assistance is being provided to the most vulnerable groups: children under 5 years of age, pregnant women, nursing mothers and the elderly. In northern Ethiopia where few other organizations are able to work, assistance is being given to the most needy. . . .

"'You may be assured the Red Cross is honored by the trust you have placed in our relief work. *All* contributions given through the American Red Cross are used in African Famine Relief. No overhead or fund raising costs are being deducted. I know your members have sacrificed to make this relief possible. The trust of your fellowship will be honored. God bless you all. [Signed] Richard Schubert, President'

"Thank you for what you have done. Many contributed far more than the value of two meals. You have cast bread upon the waters, and it will return to you as you experience the peace of generous hearts.

"You responded in a magnificent way in sharing of your plenty with those who are destitute. We can similarly respond to a score of other challenges we face as Latter-day Saints to move forward the work of God" ("The Victory over Death," *Ensign*, May 1985, 53–54, 59).

Words can't express the joy and gratitude I felt for the blessings and guidance of the Lord over the three months I was involved in the relief effort for the good people of Ethiopia. The humanitarian program of the Church as we know it today had been born. Ethiopian lives had been saved. And, on a personal note, my ministry as a General Authority had begun.

3

AN APPRENTICESHIP

A fter returning from Ethiopia in 1985, I thought my work in Africa had come to an end. My call to the Presiding Bishopric one week later put it right back on my radar scope. One of my geographic assignments as a member of that bishopric was Africa. I can't resist passing along a comment I received from Bishop Robert D. Hales when I received my assignments. I jokingly brought to his attention that all of my geographic assignments were in the less affluent countries. His comment was "Glenn, the second counselor in the Presiding Bishopric will never see Vienna." I might add, I still haven't seen Vienna.

As I have reviewed the incidents that make up this chapter, I have been inspired and humbled by the loving tutelage I received during these years. With 20/20 hindsight, it is impressive to observe how the experience gained during this seven years in the Presiding Bishopric would enhance my ability to be of service to the people many years later. This is but a small example of how the Master's plan is playing out with every one of us. It was also very moving, with this same hindsight, to observe the implementation of the Master's plan through the lives of the numerous people I grew to know and love. Another thing I observed as I reviewed these years was how quickly the African people worked their way deeply into my heart.

Space dictates that I can only record a tithe of the experiences I had during my service in Africa while a member of the Presiding Bishopric, but I believe those things I am recording do document the reality that there is a master plan. As I have prepared to write this book, it has been inspiring to me to see how the pieces of the plan have come together—including the pieces made up of events in my own personal life.

My first trip to Africa as a member of the Presiding Bishopric came in January 1986, one year after my Ethiopian adventure. I went to Ghana and Nigeria with an assignment to look into the building program, welfare, and a special project relating to primary health care. The Church was still in its infancy in Africa in 1986, although it was growing fast. We had one mission in Nigeria and another in Ghana.

For reasons unknown to me then, I was driven with a desire to receive a vision of the potential of that continent. As I looked at the problems of Africa, I found they were legion. There are wars, crime, corruption, disease, illiteracy, witchcraft, poor transportation, inadequate communication, poverty, unemployment, tribalism, multiple languages, and many other seemingly impossible impediments to the work. Could the gospel of Jesus Christ survive in that kind of an environment? The answer to that question began to emerge on this and subsequent trips.

On January 29, 1986, we went on a three-hour drive from Accra to Abomosu, Ghana, to visit one of the first welfare farms in Africa. Ghana is very green, and it seemed good to see healthy Africans, compared to the deprivation I saw in Ethiopia. Some of the priesthood leaders in Abomosu joined us for a long walk through the jungle to the site of four hectares of land on which they wanted to build a farm. There I saw about twenty men with machetes clearing

*One of the first welfare projects in West Africa. Members with
machetes are starting to clear the land.*

off a piece of land that was heavily covered with jungle foliage. The
leaders had called six eighteen-year-old young men to be farm
missionaries to serve for six months. Other members also helped,
volunteering their time. The plan was for the proceeds of the crop
to support local missionaries, welfare needs, and a building fund. I
was impressed with the people's enthusiasm, work ethic, and bright
smiling faces.

This experience gave me my first personal observation of how
hard-working the African people are and how they want to become
self-reliant. Their finely chiseled bodies are not the result of visiting weight rooms during a long lunch hour, but come from hard
labor from sunrise to sunset. Those labors are necessary in order for
them to be able to eat, as opposed to being able to buy a second car,
boat, or snowmobile. My respect for the African women was also
intensified. In addition to working for twelve hours in the fields or

markets, they care for the children, build the fires, and cook the meals. Seeing these things left me with the desire to help in some way. We were pioneers in the 1980s and were willing to try many things. This farm was one of our first organized efforts.

On the other hand, this and other experiences alerted me to some potential problems in administering a welfare project in Africa. When you turn over financial resources to priesthood leaders in desperate circumstances, some cultural challenges need to be considered. For example, it is possible for a ward to lapse into what I call a "chief" mentality, and a project can risk the possibility of being administered according to the chief culture rather than gospel principles. Jealousies may arise from real or imagined preferential treatment a bishop gives to one member of the ward over another. These conditions can be managed, and as principles are taught they can be overcome, but if we are blind to cultural issues big problems can develop. These early insights helped tremendously in later years, and I am thankful for the education I received at this point. Over the years we have tried many different approaches and are still trying to find the right combination.

We returned to the mission home in Accra just before dark. I was exhausted, but President Miles Cunningham had promised the new elders in the "missionary training center" that we would visit them. They looked more tired than I was. It was very impressive, however, to see fourteen coal-black missionaries dressed in white shirts and ties, getting ready to serve a mission in Ghana. Who would have believed it eight years earlier?

In those days the West African mission presidents had to create their own missionary training centers—travel to an established center was prohibitive, and the Church was too small in Africa to create a center there. In fact, this continued to be the case for the next sixteen years. In addition to not receiving the benefit of a complete

Beautiful Ghanaian girls attending a school that received materials from LDS Charities, May 1999.

Elder Pace and Elder Bob Linnell at a new water well provided by LDS Charities, December 1998.

The gas station where Elder Pace received bad gasoline.

MTC experience, none of the missionaries had been endowed. That situation also continued throughout the years of my involvement.

A few days later I traveled with President Cunningham to look at some possible chapel sites. We were still about an hour and a half from home when the car died, probably from some bad gasoline. I recalled we had earlier stopped at a station that had those old-fashioned bottles on the top of the pump through which the gasoline would flow on the way to your tank. I commented to President Cunningham at the time that it looked to me like there were a few too many solids in the liquid for my comfort. We just laughed it off because it was our only option right then. Apparently the fuel filter absorbed all it could, leaving us stranded.

We got out of the car and started walking. We were quite a spectacle as we walked along, two white men out in the bush of Africa with white shirts and ties, he carrying a briefcase and me a camera around my neck. But we had walked less than two blocks when we were able to flag down a car whose occupant was an African Methodist minister. He gave us a ride all the way to Accra.

I mention this little experience to demonstrate the kindness of the majority of the people in Africa. If a car is stalled, it isn't long before it is surrounded by people willing to push. I've been high-centered in ruts and ditches so deep there was no way out. Soon the car would be surrounded by people who would literally pick up the car and move it over on a firm footing.

Teaching Primary Health Care

One of my assignments in Nigeria was to visit the Thrasher Foundation primary health care project in Eket. On January 31 we went to the airport nearly three hours early to catch a flight to Calabar. Extra time is needed at the airport because you never know what kind of hassle you'll experience. In Nigeria, most flights are oversold. Therefore, when the time to board the plane arrives, the airport staff opens the gate and all the passengers stampede through the doors, onto the runway, and up the stairs of the plane. If you are among the first two-thirds to reach the plane, you stand a pretty good chance of getting on. If you are frail, very old, or very young, your odds are not so good. I don't know that I've ever felt less secure about an airplane ride.

When we arrived in Calabar we found a missionary couple waiting for us. We were anxious to continue our trip to Eket right away, because the Thrasher group was expecting us at 1:00 P.M., but the missionaries insisted that the mission president, J. Duffy Palmer, take time to see a visitor. When he asked what it was about, all they would say was, "You have got to attend to this problem because you created it."

We soon were introduced to a successful businessman in the area. President Palmer had earlier met this man at the mission home and had given him some pamphlets to read because he had been very interested in the Church. The president told the man he would visit him in Calabar towards the end of the month when he made his next trip there and would talk with him further at that time. As the month began to draw to a close, the man had traveled into Calabar from his village every day asking to see President Palmer. He had read every pamphlet and wanted very much to be baptized. He had also been talking to his friends and had 120 people who wanted to join the Church.

Apparently, this is not uncommon in the area. President Palmer made an appointment to visit them in the village, and said that prior to his visit he also would send two Nigerian missionaries to the village, providing they could find a place for them to stay. The businessman said, "I have a very nice place and an extra room and they can stay with me." The missionaries would begin to teach the people so that when President Palmer visited their village he would know if they were sincere.

I tried to discern spiritually and intellectually the man's motives, but I wasn't able to tell, although he did seem very sincere. I asked him why he wanted to be baptized, and he looked at me like I had just asked the most ridiculous question he had ever heard. He said, "Because it's the true church." His childlike faith was touching.

I had heard the stories of the early missionaries in Africa who baptized whole villages. I had always looked upon this success with a fair amount of skepticism. My work in welfare for ten years had opened my eyes to the potential of people joining the Church for the wrong reasons. I spoke to every missionary couple I met on this trip and asked them their feelings about the sincerity of the numerous converts. I asked questions like, "Do they really have testimonies, or is this just another supernatural story they find easy to believe because of their traditions?" One couple's response was an invitation to come to church on Sunday and see for myself. I decided it was about time to do that. Thus far I had never been to a Church service in Africa. I resolved I would do that in Aba the next Sunday.

After we'd visited with the businessman in Calabar, we traveled on to Eket. We spent the next day with the young men and women who were working on the Thrasher project, which was organized by Mary Ellen Edmunds to instruct the Nigerian people in primary health care. The experience with these young people is worth mentioning as an example of the many who have sacrificed much for their love of the African people. It also supplies an anecdote of the primitive conditions so many missionaries have lived under to bring the Church to its present maturity.

The Thrasher group lived in two homes in the same compound as the missionary couples. There was no air conditioning in the compound, and the air was heavy and hot. They had a generator that ran ceiling fans and lights, but it was turned off at 10:00 P.M., leaving the occupants without either.

Before breakfast we went to a meat market. I'm not sure it was a good idea on an empty stomach. They went early because there was a better chance of the meat being good. The meat market was quite a sight. There were tables holding slabs of meat set up under partial shade. In a corral were a number of cattle, and on the ground was the head of a steer. The proprietor sold every part of the cow, including the "insides" and hide. They were currently cutting open the skull. My hosts bought four pounds of meat. I asked them what part it was, and they didn't know. I asked them how in the world they dared eat it, and they said they didn't have any problems as long as they bought it early and made sure it was cooked thoroughly. I knew if they had meat for lunch, I wasn't going to eat it.

We then went into some of the little villages where the Thrasher volunteers were working. I was impressed with the reception the people gave them. It was easy to see they were trusted and loved. They knew the names of people walking down the street. I met a member family who were applying everything they were taught. They were very industrious and had a water filter, an outside bathroom, and a separate habitat for the animals. They had decorated their home as best they could, and it was evident from the pictures on the walls that they were members of the Church. I didn't meet the husband, but the wife's name was Cecilia. There was a striking difference between her family and others we visited. She had gained a much-needed twenty pounds in the previous five or six months and was thrilled about it. She was teaching a primary health care class in the branch.

Fifteen years later I met Cecilia again when I divided the Nigeria Eket Stake. She was serving as the stake Relief Society president. I was thrilled not only that she had learned primary health care but that she had been a faithful member of the Church for all those years.

Later that evening we had a meeting with some of the local members. I hadn't been expecting the meeting and certainly wasn't prepared for it. I said a few words to them but didn't feel very good about the impact of what I said. I knew this was the first time many of them had seen a General Authority and felt they deserved much better. On the long drive to Aba the next day President Palmer informed me that he had called a special meeting of the Aba District for Sunday night. This was unexpected as well, and I was a little disturbed that the meeting had been called. I felt ill prepared for such meetings, since my assignment was temporal affairs. In addition, I realized people would be coming from as far as fifty miles away to attend the meeting. This would mean several days' food money to some, or a long bicycle ride for those rich enough to own a bicycle, or a several mile walk by others.

When I thought of the sacrifice the people were making I turned to President Palmer and suggested he cancel the meeting. He gave me an incredulous look and said, "Cancel it! What do you suggest,

Thatched hut in rural Africa.

sending the message by drums? I can't cancel it! There is no way to reach the people at this late date. They have been planning on this meeting for several weeks. You don't need to come if you don't want to, but they'll be here. Also, let me remind you that they aren't coming to see you. They are coming to see a General Authority." While giving me this pep talk, he kept thumping me in the chest. I'm still sore. I appreciated the reminder that I was not just Glenn Pace anymore. I still hadn't quite become accustomed to the mantle of my call of nine months earlier. I felt better about having the meeting, but I felt awful about my responsibility in it. What was I going to tell them?

As we talked further, I learned that President Palmer had scheduled an hour and a half leadership meeting in the afternoon and a meeting of the general public after that. I felt inadequate and unprepared, and I kept thinking of how poorly our meeting in Eket had gone. I was troubled about what I could say that would have a positive impact on the people. President Palmer repeatedly reminded me how much the people wanted and needed to see a General Authority. But that didn't make me feel any more ready.

I began a fast as part of my preparation for the upcoming meeting. That night I remember praying, studying, and pondering about what I should say. I walked outside into a beautiful, warm, humid evening, with the moon in the middle of the sky. There was a gentle breeze blowing (although it was anything but cool), and I felt peaceful about many of the issues I had been carrying around. Although I still didn't know what I was going to tell the people, I retired for a good night's rest, looking forward to my first Sunday meeting with the Saints in Africa. I was going to attend Sunday services at the Nsirimo Branch of the Aba District. Aba later became the first stake in Nigeria and is the location of the first temple in Nigeria.

The Nsirimo Branch is one of those villages of 150 people who joined the Church all at once. When I visited, not one of the members of the congregation had been a member for more than six months. We drove up in a four-wheel-drive vehicle and then walked to their modest chapel. I observed a beautiful testimony meeting. I saw young Aaronic Priesthood men bless and pass the sacrament with reverence we would do well to emulate in Utah. I sat in a priesthood quorum meeting. There were only three or four manuals for twenty prospective elders. Because of the humidity and heavy usage, the manuals were coming apart. Every page was handled as if it was scripture or, perhaps a more apt comparison, a page from the golden plates themselves.

I saw a district president correct little technicalities when all the right words were not used in the confirmation of a new member of the Church. And, most of all, I felt a great, powerful spirit. My turmoil was ended.

Elder and Sister Pace with Samuel in 1992.

"I Am Samuel"

A young man named Samuel, who was fifteen years of age, caught my eye. He was leading the Primary in singing "I Am a Child of God." I struck up a conversation with him. Later, after I had returned home, I received a letter from him. Keep in mind this young man had been a member of the Church for only six months.

"Dear Bishop,

"Love and peace in Jesus name abide with you. It has taken quite a long time since you came to our branch. It was a joyous day and we would like to cherish your smiling face once more. How are things moving in the General Authorities of the Church and its administration? I know you have been doing your best for our branch. Our branch in the Aba District is increasing and progressing and we hope to become more than a branch someday."

Why does a fifteen-year-old boy care whether he is in a ward or a branch? After being in the Church for only six months, how does he even know the difference? The Nsirimo Branch is now a ward. Aba, Nigeria, became the first stake in West Africa on May 15, 1988.

"The true, heartwarming, strong testimonies that you gave in our branch are still alive. I enjoyed listening to your voice in the cassette when you were speaking at a conference meeting about the welfare program. I know your testimonies are true."

Here was a young man who had access to conference tapes because his father was the branch president. Imagine a fifteen-year-old boy being more excited about conference tapes than the newest DVD or CD. Just to make sure I knew he wasn't putting me on, he rehearsed back to me what I had said in conference, and then he went on:

"To introduce myself. I am Samuel, the second son of the branch president. I am a fifteen year old boy, a teacher in the Aaronic Priesthood and the branch investigator's teacher. I'm the secretary in the young adult program and one of the song leaders in our branch. I was the boy, if you remember, who picked [borrowed] your pen and returned it when you left it with me after giving me your address at our branch. Could you remember when you remarked that I have acted like a Mormon?"

He took this as the ultimate compliment. He had "acted like a Mormon." What I really had said was that he acted more like a young man who had been a member of the Church all of his life than one who had only been a member for just a few months.

"How is our president, seer, and revelator, Prophet Ezra Taft Benson, I know the Lord is improving his health condition and increasing his life span. Next time you feel his hands, tell him that I love him so much. Also ask him to remember me as he prays in the holy temple, inform him I need his blessings to progress in my studies and pass my examinations. The Lord who has chosen him will help him magnify his callings very well in this dispensation of fulness of time. I pray the Lord will guide you to deliver my message to him."

What beautiful, simple faith. I did share this letter with President Benson. He was touched.

"When are we going to have a stake in my country? I will like us to have a stake here in my country and missionaries to live with us so as to meet the demands of the growing Church, talk to the Prophet about this issue." He was no shrinking violet, this young man. He now has all of the above and a temple too.

"I very much like to open contact with you and your family and would like you to introduce me to your family members. I will meet you again and I know that." Again, he demonstrates his faith. His prophecy has come true; we have met on several occasions.

A couple of years later, I was in Africa again and tried to find Samuel. Just before going to the airport to return home, I talked to a man who was his home teacher. Samuel was living on his own, working and going to school. On the way to the airport, I wrote him a note explaining how I had tried to find him and hoped all was well. In response, I received a letter that included the following:

"Dear Beloved Bishop,

"It has been quite a long time now since I have written you, but I am with you in spirit and quite often I remember you in my prayers.

"It was a very sad moment when I met the assistant director of seminary at the stake center. He told me, 'Bishop Pace came to Nigeria and he very much wanted to see you but you were not at home.' It pained me in the heart so much that I missed you that day in the Sunday School, sacrament meeting, and quorum I kept remembering you. It would have been an opportunity to shake your hands, see your smiling face and talk to you once more. If it had occurred to me, I would have postponed my journey because I had prayed to see you but all the same, God has a way of doing his own thing, I know that.

"Bishop, this letter is not enough to contain my heart now, I will write to you again. I still remember the first day we met in our branch. After the meeting I requested your address. You were very kind to give me your address and you forgot your beautiful writing pen with me. I picked it up and ran and gave it to you. How you smiled and said to me 'You are a good Mormon.' That day was wonderful.

"I like to tell you that I love you, and the Church as a whole. Ezra Taft Benson is a true prophet of God. May our Heavenly Father continue to guide and protect you and your family till we meet again here or in the celestial kingdom in Christ, amen. Samuel."

A Little Visit from the Prophet

To return to my experiences in Nigeria in January 1986, as I thought about the leadership meeting I was to speak at, it occurred to me that the Church in Nigeria at that point was not unlike the Church in Joseph's time. In the early days of the Church, many people who joined the Church brought with them their own strong opinions and customs. I wanted a scripture to support that thought, and the Doctrine and Covenants fell open to section 49:2, which read, "Behold, I say unto you, that they desire to know the truth in part, but not all, for they are not right before me and must needs repent."

It was exactly what I was looking for, and yet it wasn't a scripture that had ever impressed me before. When I saw that passage, though, I knew what I was supposed to talk about. I knew my prayer had been answered.

Later in the day we returned to Aba for the leadership meeting. A large group of priesthood leaders had assembled, and some had traveled fifty miles to get there. The cost for the trip was more than they could afford, and it was a slow journey because the public transportation van constantly stops to pick people up and let them off. Sometimes the van breaks down. The district president, David Eka, was there. (President Eka later served as an Area Authority Seventy during my service in the Area Presidency in West Africa.) Some of the leaders were quite well educated. I was able to deliver my talk in English; the main theme was that when we accept the gospel we must accept all of it. I told them about the Shakers referred to in Doctrine and Covenants 49 in a way that I trust was not offensive to them, but I think they could see how others had dealt with the problems they were experiencing. They responded very well, giving both me and the leaders an entirely different experience from that I'd had in Eket.

In the general meeting I told some of my favorite Joseph Smith stories and could tell they were things these people had never heard.

The most inspirational and endearing experience of the whole trip came in the middle of my formal address in the general meeting. It came to me spontaneously, as is usually the case with those things that have the most impact. I had just finished a story about Joseph Smith and then asked, "Who is our prophet today?" That sounds like a simple question, but it hadn't been long since the death of President Spencer W. Kimball and I wondered if they would give me his name as opposed to President Benson. That question was laid to rest quickly as they responded with a thunderous, "Ezra Taft Benson." This was with that wonderful Queen's English/African accent I have learned to love so much.

I then said, "Do you know that as a member of the Presiding Bishopric I am privileged to meet with President Benson and the First Presidency every Friday morning?" Their eyes got as big as saucers. I went on to explain that about two weeks earlier in our Friday meeting I had reported to President Benson that I was going to Ghana and Nigeria. President Benson's response was, "Can I go?" I looked at President Hinckley and President Monson, and they were both shaking their heads, "No." He looked at them and replied, "Well, I guess not. But Bishop Pace, will you do me a favor? Will you tell them hello for me?" I promised I would, and to the congregation I said, "and so from the prophet I say to you 'hello.'"

I was not prepared for the response I received. Smiles came on their faces and tears streamed down their cheeks. They had received more than a verbal message. Through the power of the Holy Ghost they had received a little visit from the prophet. They felt his love and concern for them.

I was so touched it took me a few minutes to gain control of my emotions. Because of their reaction I went on and said, "I see that means a lot to you. I'll tell you what I'm going to do. At the conclusion of this meeting I'll go back to those doors and as you leave you can shake my hand and I will take your greeting and love back to President Benson with me."

I might as well have ended the meeting right then. Many of them went to the back of the room and started to line up. I bore a testimony and went to the back of the room where I remained shaking hands for almost an hour. They didn't just shake my hand; they all had a message. "Tell the prophet I read the Book of Mormon again." "Tell the prophet I don't smoke anymore." "Tell the prophet I have a temple recommend." One of them said, "Tell the prophet I don't hit my wife anymore." I said, "He will be most happy to hear that." They all had sweet childlike messages to give.

Incidentally, when I returned home I made a point of telling President Benson this experience, and he was very touched. He asked how many were there and when I said about fifty, he walked over to me and began shaking my hand, counting the handshakes, one, two, three . . . I couldn't wait to get back to my office and send a letter to President Eka to explain the president's reaction to their messages.

As I left those meetings, I rejoiced at how the Lord had helped me. I had been feeling completely lost and fully dependent on the Lord. Then, as every other time I've visited Africa, I was able to gain the confidence he was there and that I had the right to gain access to him through the Spirit. I had also been blessed with a vision of the potential of these people, when at first it was such a struggle for me. I concluded that there definitely were leaders there with true spiritual depth, and that the Church could thrive in spite of the numerous problems in Africa.

Prior to leaving for the airport we rode into downtown Lagos. The poverty and filth were hard to witness in the smaller towns, but in the big city it was even worse. People were living stacked on top of each other, with only a tin roof over their heads. It was depressing, and it made me think about the mass of humanity and how few of the earth's population the gospel reaches. I also thought about the great sacrifice the older missionary couples make to be there for twelve or eighteen months. I was physically and emotionally drained by just a short visit to that city. I couldn't imagine how I would feel after a year or so. (A dozen years later, though, I would get the answer to that wonderment.)

"The Unfolding Plan of the Lord"

My next visit to Africa was in November 1988. This was just six months prior to a devastating blow to the members of the Church in Ghana. In June 1989 the activities of the Church in Ghana were "frozen," which meant all expatriates needed to leave and the Church was no longer recognized or registered in the country. The government took over the meetinghouses and other buildings. Even more damaging was the fact that members could no longer meet as congregations.

On the positive side, my visit was just six months after the formation of the first stake in West Africa by Elder Neal A. Maxwell. Here is how the *Church News* reported this event:

"The first stake in western Africa—the Aba Nigeria Stake—was created May 15, emerging from an alliance of faith and work.

"The stake was created less than a month before the 10th anniversary of the June 9, 1978, revelation making it possible for all worthy male members to be ordained to the priesthood. The stake's formation is a milestone in Church history not only because it is the first stake in western Africa, but also because it is the first stake in which all priesthood leaders are black.

"More than 1,000 of the stake's 2,300 members filled the Aba meetinghouse and courtyard to sustain the nation's first stake presidency: David W. Eka, president; Ephraim S. Etete, first counselor; and Lazarus Onitchi, second counselor. The new stake has six wards and three branches, and some 300 Melchizedek Priesthood holders. Sacrament meeting attendance ranges from 44 to 75 percent.

"The first 12 members of the Church in Aba were baptized in January 1981. By the end of that year, there were 40 members. The Aba District was formed May 14, 1984.

"In the history-making conference to create the new stake, Elder Maxwell conveyed greetings from President Ezra Taft Benson and his counselors, President Gordon B. Hinckley and President Thomas S. Monson.

"He spoke of the 'timing and planning of the Lord' and then quoted Alma 29:8, which says, 'The Lord doth grant unto all nations, of their own nation and tongue, to teach his word . . . all that he seeth fit that they should have.'

"Of the creation of the first stake in western Africa, Elder Maxwell said, 'On this day, for this nation, there now comes more of the gospel's fulness in the unfolding plan of the Lord.' [The complete fulness could not come until a temple is built.]

"He expressed 'deep gratitude to all past mission presidents and their wives; missionary couples; full-time missionaries; local priesthood leaders and sisters who have labored so hard for this day, which is a historic day in the Church in this dispensation, and in any dispensation.'

"Elder Maxwell told the congregation that news of the stake's creation 'would flash around the world of the Church and be received with great rejoicing.' [I certainly rejoiced.]

"'I was present in the upper room of the temple that early June day in 1978 when all the General Authorities gathered to receive the revelation and decision from President Spencer W. Kimball,' he recounted. 'I wept with joy that day. The handkerchief I wiped my tears with I took home and told my wife not to wash it. I put it in my book of remembrance, still bearing the marks of my tears of joy.

"'On this Sunday, I have a second handkerchief that has wiped more tears of joy. I will take it home and place it in my book of remembrance next to the other handkerchief.'

"As Elder Maxwell told the story of the handkerchiefs, the congregation appeared visibly touched.

"The members had come to the conference on a typically hot Nigerian spring morning from throughout the stake, some on buses, others on bicycles. Many walked.

"Elder Maxwell told the Church News he was impressed with the 'intent—almost enraptured—listening by the members. There was a great feeling of reverence and quietness, even with a great number of children present'" ("New 'First' for Western Africa: Stake Is Formed in Aba, Nigeria," *Church News*, May 21, 1988).

I must admit to having glistening eyes as well when I read of this great event. The thrill of it all was still ringing in the voices of the members six months later. Of course, Ghanaians were wondering when they also would have their first stake. It was being seriously

Sister missionaries in Ghana.

considered; however, those plans were placed on hold with the events that occurred in June 1989.

Freezing the Activities of the Church

During my visit in 1988 I had an experience that led to a friendship with a sixteen-year-old priest. The subsequent correspondence with him helped give human perspective to the faithfulness of these early members, who were forced to stand on their own two feet during the eighteen-month freeze. This experience began with a visit to a little branch in Koforidua, Ghana, which met in an old schoolhouse. That morning, I roved from the Melchizedek Priesthood to the Young Men, Young Women, and Primary meetings. I took pictures of the deacons, teachers, and priests separately. I spent the Sunday School time with the Primary, where they were playing out the Alma the Younger conversion story and then they sang "Popcorn Popping on the Apricot Tree" (none of them had ever seen an apricot tree). They included a verse that was new to me: "I looked

Michael (with usher badge) and his priests quorum.

out the window and what did I see? Two Mormon missionaries looking in at me!" Another highlight was meeting two sister missionaries, the first black sisters I had seen.

Almost a year later I received a letter from a young sixteen-year-old priest. This was six months after the government froze the activities of the Church. The letter is dated Christmas Eve, 1989. Some excerpts follow:

"Dear Bishop Pace,

"I am very glad to write you this humble letter. My name is Michael, I have black hair, black eyes, and fair in complexion."

Somehow, thus far, I was unable to place him. However, he continued: "Now, if I could remember [remind] you, you came to Ghana sometime ago and visited our branch. You took a lot of pictures that day and if you have got those of the priests, I am the boy wearing the black suit with an usher tag."

He went on to comment about the government's decision to freeze the Church's activities:

"I think you know what has happened in Ghana, but all the same I can assure you that it has been a blessing. It is good to give you my version of the story. It all happened on the 14th of June 1989. It was on Wednesday. I had just returned from school for holidays, and I was preparing myself for choir practice, which I enjoy very much.

"So, it came to pass [he obviously had done some reading of the Book of Mormon] that I was resting in my father's car when he called, 'Michael! Have you heard what has happened?' I said, 'No,' he then went on to tell me that the government has frozen the activities of the Church. From this, I just got up and said, 'They are joking, for no power on this earth can stop this church.'"

He went on to explain how the topic was debated very heatedly in their community. The Church was made to look very ugly and evil.

"From that time onwards in the newspapers, and news bulletins and even in town it was a topic for discussion. We had two sides: those against and those in favor. In one occasion, a riot broke out between a member of a Pentecostal church and a non-church goer. According to the Pentecostal man, he was happy that the Church's activities had been frozen and this was the reply he got from the other man, 'Mr., don't be happy. I know this church very well, I have been to Britain so I know what the Church stands for. It is the only true church on earth, and I tell you that I will be the first person to be baptized when their activity is unfrozen.' Bishop, these are the words of a nonmember. Due to what has happened, people have got to know about the Church."

With the persecution it must have been very difficult for Michael to go back to school:

"In my high school, on a Sunday, some students came to me and said brother Michael, are you a Mormon?" This sounds like Peter's test during the crucifixion. If so, Michael passed the test.

"I said, 'Yes,' they then said tell us more about this church and the Book of Mormon. After hearing this, I said to myself, 'This is the hour.' So I explained everything to them and after knowing something about the Church, they became happy. Many people have been inquiring about the Church and after telling them something they pledge to join the Church when it starts to operate again.

"Bishop, all members here in our branch greet you and your family. We like to tell you that our faith is now even stronger than before, we are praying and waiting patiently for the day we will return."

I was so touched and impressed, I immediately wrote to Michael and soon received a reply. At the date of the next letter, the Church had been closed in Ghana for over nine months.

"Dear Bishop Pace,

I was very grateful and humble when I received your letter dated 21 January 1990. A young boy and coming from a poor home was not expecting this sort of respect. My parents were filled with tears of joy when they heard that you have written. As I am now writing, in the dormitory of my school, I am in deep humility with tears all over my eyes."

The humble tears shed had little to do with Bishop Pace, but more of the overwhelming desire to be in complete contact with the Brethren and to be able to have the kingdom continue to grow in his land.

"For I feel for the Church and its activities, I feel for the voice of the prophet and all general authorities. But all is not lost yet. For I know that one day we shall meet again."

He then gave us an idea of how the members were coping and how his family was reaching out to those who were stumbling. This is home teaching and visiting teaching in their purest form.

"Concerning the members, most families hold their sacrament meetings and family home evenings but as you would expect, unfortunately, some have fallen. We usually pay frequent visits to members to strengthen their faith in the gospel due to rising persecutions especially from other churches."

Next, we find how his own testimony was standing up under the barrage of attacks from the government and other churches.

"Bishop, I attend a Catholic school where all go to worship as the Catholics do. One Sunday, a Catholic priest was invited to come and preach, but in his preaching he totally condemned the 'Mormons.' I was there and heard it, which immediately strengthened my faith. After closing, I left the church laughing and saying, 'Lord forgive him, for he does not know what he is doing.' To tell you the honest truth, I know that the Church is true and nothing can separate me and my family from it."

I had asked him in my letter what message he would like me to deliver at a reunion of the missionary couples who had served in Ghana. He wrote:

"This is my message for the returned missionaries. We in Ghana know perfectly well that one day we will resume activities in unity and love to build Zion for as one prophet said, the Church is moving according to the timetable of heaven. But tell them that they should be of good cheer and work hard for he who endures to the end shall be saved."

How about that! Seventeen-year-old Michael, who was living in a country where the Church could not operate in its fulness, had a testimony of one of the primary premises of this book: *The rolling out of the kingdom in accordance with the Master's plan cannot be stopped.* He continues:

"I would like to end with a quotation I usually share with my family members to strengthen ourselves and this can be found in Doctrine and Covenants 122:6–7, which states: 'If thou art accused with all manner of false accusations; if thine enemies fall upon thee; if they tear thee from the society of thy father and mother and brethren and sisters; and if with a drawn sword thine enemies tear thee from the bosom of thy wife . . . And if thou shouldst be cast into the pit, or into the hands of murderers, and the sentence of death passed upon thee . . . , if the very jaws of hell shall gape open the mouth wide after thee, know thou, my son, that all these things shall give thee experience, and shall be for thy good.'

"This is what I leave with you, hoping to get your reply very soon in the hallowed name of our Lord and Saviour Jesus Christ. Amen. [signed] Your Son, Michael."

The Tapestry of God's Master Plan

While on that same trip in November 1988, I had several satisfying experiences that hearkened back to the spiritual meeting we had had in Aba when I spoke of President Benson. At one point, for example, we went to a member's home for the key to one of the new chapels. When this brother came out with his family, his eleven-year-old son approached me. I extended my hand and started to introduce myself. Before I could, he said, "You are Bishop Glenn L. Pace." I responded, "How did you know that?" He replied, "I recognized your picture from the magazines, and I was at the meeting in 1986."

Later in the day I met many members who said, "Yes, I know you. I was at the meeting. The story of the prophet and your shaking my hand made a lasting impression." My faith is strengthened when I remember how they sacrificed to come to that meeting, how worried I was, how I almost canceled it, and how sincerely I had fasted and prayed that I might say something to make it worth their sacrifice. I am continuously reminded of how the most simple things can make a lasting impression when conveyed by the Spirit of the Holy Ghost.

I decided early that if I could maintain my sense of humor, my African experiences would be much more enjoyable than otherwise. The problems encountered in those early days, both temporally and spiritually, could have led to cynicism or depression. Getting the temporal affairs set up in countries full of corruption was no small feat. A simple example was being in Lagos when a long-anticipated safe was delivered to the area office. Rudy VanderHoeven, another man I admire and respect for his service, and his wife, Tonja, were waiting for the delivery of the safe, which would become his prized possession. He had been like a kid on Christmas Eve awaiting its arrival. It would replace the gym bag full of the Church's money that he kept under his bed. When the big day arrived there was an army of men trying to figure out how to get the safe up to the second floor. Rudy glowed with pride as he showed us his new acquisition.

There is a certain ironic humor in what happened next: within a short period of time someone came in during the night and stole both the money and the new safe. We suspect it was one of those who helped us figure out how to get it up there in the first place.

On that same trip something else occurred that was not funny at all. One of our employees in Aba was hauled off to prison after a sub-contractor had bribed the police to arrest him on false charges. Nigeria is not a place where you want to do prison time. He was being kept in a small cell with twelve other people and no sanitary privileges. He had been incarcerated for three days. The husband in one of our mission-ary couples, Lars Bishop, spent twenty-four hours a day for three days, without sleep during that entire period, trying to get him out. Elder Bishop was successful on the third day. How I love and appreciate these missionary couples, who could be home tending grandchildren but choose instead to serve the Lord and the people of Africa.

In May 1990 I visited Zaire, Nigeria, and Kenya. I was disappointed not to be able to go into Ghana, but the freeze on Church activities was still in effect until June of that year.

This was my first trip to Kenya and Zaire (now known as the Democratic Republic of Congo). My main reason for traveling to Kenya was to determine where the new area office should be located. It is hard to believe that up until that time (1990) the continent of Africa was administered from the British Isles, with offices in Solihull, England. The work in Africa was moving so rapidly the Brethren decided to set up a new area office on the continent of Africa. The big decision was whether to locate it in Johannesburg, South Africa, or Nairobi, Kenya. Arguments for Johannesburg included its modern amenities including communication and travel. The argument for Nairobi was that the growth of the Church was coming from "black Africa," and it made some sense to live among the culture from which the growth was coming.

In reflecting back on this moment I have chuckled to myself. I remember going through the reasoning that in order to understand a culture, you are better off living around the people with that culture. Even as I said that I thought, "That's easy for you to say, since you won't be the one who will live in these primitive conditions." Sometimes in life when we make another person's bed, we end up sleeping in it.

For various reasons it was decided the office should be set up in Johannesburg for the time being. Eight years later the Church was growing so fast in West Africa that an office was set up in Accra, Ghana, and I became a member of the first Area Presidency to serve in that new area.

In Nairobi I attended a special evening meeting with members of the Church. We had to obtain special permission from the government to meet with a congregation exceeding twenty-five people, and we had more than fifty in attendance. Because of these restrictions, the Church was piloting a "family-centered church." It was interesting to talk to the members about what they missed in not having the full program of the Church. They said they missed getting together in large groups, especially the youth, but as far as the regular meetings of the Church are concerned, they felt that they participated more frequently and got more out of the meetings when it was just a family or two. It was an unsolicited testimony of what we were hoping to accomplish.

This is only one example of the many different approaches the Brethren have allowed members to take to accomplish the mission of the Church, depending on local circumstances.

On this same trip I met members of the Church in the Congo for the first time. Their problems were and are immense. The wars they have suffered caused many to question whether the Church could possibly survive there, let alone flourish. I personally had many doubts about that during my visit with a small group of converts. At that time our membership was about five hundred.

Years later, during my service in the Area Presidency in 1999, I created the third stake there. Time and time again I have been proven wrong in my pessimism about the Church surviving in some very primitive and dangerous conditions. It reminds me of hiking high in the mountains and seeing flowers growing out of rocks above the tree line where nothing else grows. The members in Africa are equally hardy and beautiful.

I returned to Africa less than one year later in February 1991, flying into Lagos, Nigeria. The Lagos, Nigeria, airport is a fairly modern airport—except the air conditioning doesn't work and the heat is unbearable. The lights in the hallways are not lit, and it is like walking through a tunnel. You feel certain you are going to get mugged at any moment—and the one who robs you will most likely be wearing a uniform. Unlike my previous visits, no one met me inside the gate to help me through passport clearance, and so I had to do it by myself. It is a very uncomfortable and intimidating experience. You hand an official your passport, he'll start to look at it, and then someone else will come with about five more passports and reach over the glass to put them on top of yours, because he is working for someone who has given him a bribe. Eventually, when the agent gets to yours again, he looks at it for awhile and asks you if you "have anything for him." Of course he means dash (or a bribe). He then passes it to the person next to him, who looks at it awhile and then asks you the same question.

In all the traveling I have done in Africa, I have never "dashed" anybody at an airport. I don't know whether it is because I am cheap or stubborn—certainly the Church wouldn't approve. Most of the time it takes longer, but you eventually get through.

When I finally made it out of the airport, I found Georges Bonnet, the director of temporal affairs, waiting for me. As we walked to the car, we were surrounded by nine large Nigerians, all of whom were claiming they had helped me get through customs and passport clearance; they therefore thought they should receive a tip. Others explained they had been watching the car so nothing bad would happen to it. They also wanted a tip. We kept explaining that nobody helped me and that we didn't owe anything. It was dark, and the experience was very intimidating. These young men were obviously desperate for any kind of a tip. When we got to the car, I jumped in and locked the door. When Georges got in they were still putting their hands through the window, wanting us to give them something. It was one of the more threatening arrivals I have experienced.

We drove to the Lagos mission home, where President and Sister Douglas Alston gave us a very nice dinner. They were very hospitable and fun. As we talked, they mentioned that they had been robbed once by three men who came right into the house and took a large sum of money. They were almost nonchalant about it, as if they were telling us the home teachers had dropped by.

In Africa being robbed is like a badge of honor the couples wear. You aren't really accepted as a first-string player until you've been robbed.

It seems to naturally follow that spiritual experiences accompany intense sacrifice. My experiences in Africa are the most spiritual of my life, but the dangers and discomfort have also been the highest. I did discover, however, that adjustments came easier when I was assigned to stay for a full three years rather than going in and out via a decompression chamber each year.

On this particular trip I met with many priesthood leaders about members' welfare needs. It was agonizing to me to see the huge need and not be able to come up with solutions. The needs were definitely infinite and could potentially swallow up the resources of the Church in future years as the Church in Africa grew into the millions. What resources will be needed when the Church begins to grow in China, India, and other similar locations? Typical of my spiritual and intellectual agony and stupor of thought were my feelings expressed after a full day of meetings with members on February 22, 1991:

"As you look around at the need, one comes away frustrated that there aren't easier answers. I cannot figure out how I could have spent almost ten years in the Welfare Services Department and not have a clear answer. Sometimes I wonder if that is because we are trying to do too much. Maybe it is as simple as using the priesthood amongst our members and letting them, in effect, take care of each other after teaching them correct principles, and then responding to emergencies when they cannot help themselves. I can't seem to get a solid confirmation as to what we ought to be doing."

I believe the feelings and thoughts I went through on this issue while in the Presiding Bishopric were helpful when my responsibilities increased as a member of the Area Presidency. In hindsight, I probably learned more about what not to do than what to do. This is just another example of how the Master gently weaves the tapestry of his master plan, using each of us as individual threads. We are all dependent on him and each other to succeed in this work. I'm so grateful for all the people I have worked with in the African experience.

After the Freeze

On this trip I was able to go to Ghana again. One Sunday we attended services in Koforidua, Ghana. This is the same congregation I had attended in 1989 just before the freeze and the branch to which the young priest, Michael, belonged. It had been only two months since the freeze imposed by the government had been lifted. I was curious about what happened to the Church in the interim, so I wanted to attend the same branch.

When we arrived, I was pleased to see that the members had worked together to paint their rented facility so it looked even nicer than it had two years earlier. We were greeted warmly, and I hadn't been there two minutes before the president brought Michael to me. He had grown into a very handsome and strong nineteen-year-old. He went with me to the different classes in order to interpret for me. I was impressed to see that the investigator class had an attendance of twenty-six.

After classes, I was informed that I was the only sacrament meeting speaker. As I looked at the congregation, it appeared there had been no reduction in the number of members since my last visit. I was impressed with the spirit in the meeting. I have never seen more reverence of children while the sacrament was being blessed and passed. The Primary made a presentation and each child had memorized something. One child had memorized all of the Articles of Faith; others quoted various passages from the Bible and Book of Mormon. They also sang a musical number. The choir sang about three numbers, all of which were excellent. After the meetings, I went over to Michael's home. The Boatengs have ten children, with eight still living at home. Michael is in the middle of the group. It appears that this family was the first to join the Church in Koforidua in 1985.

I asked Michael about the time during the freeze when the boys in school asked him if he was a Mormon. I wanted to know if he was afraid to admit that he was a member of the Church. He said he wasn't because it was a Catholic school and he was used to being kidded about being a member of the Church. I personally thought it took a lot of courage, or even more important, conviction of the gospel. It was humbling to see the faith of such people as Michael and his family.

These kinds of experiences continued to build my testimony about the potential of the Church in Africa. The single most inspiring event of this trip occurred when I was privileged to participate in interviews with some missionaries at Cape Coast. When the government decreed that the Church could no longer function in Ghana, more than seventy Ghanaian elders and sisters were serving as full-time missionaries. Without any notice, their missions were over. A few of them were thrown into jail for several days. All of them eventually returned home to take up their lives of school, work, and dating.

Eighteen months later, again without notice, the Church was back. These missionaries were all contacted to see if they wanted to finish their missions.

I was privileged to sit in on several interviews of those missionaries to determine whether they were worthy and desirous of finishing their missions. As we pulled up to the chapel at Cape Coast, excitement was in the air. Those young men and women were involved in a cross between a missionary reunion and a spiritual revival. To give you a flavor of it, I am going to share a few interviews with you.

The first elder had eighteen months left of his mission at the time of the freeze, and he said, "I want to continue to serve." After the freeze he had gone to live with his family in Liberia and was there when civil unrest broke out and massive killings began. The family escaped without being hurt and had returned to Ghana. They were active in the Church in Liberia. When we asked if he was living a chaste life, and then asked to explain what chastity means, he said, "You don't do certain things with women that are reserved for marriage." I thought that was an innocent and very appropriate answer to the question. He was worthy and anxious to resume his mission, even though his life had just settled down.

The next elder also had eighteen months left of his mission. His brother, who is not a member of the Church, had offered to send him money so he could travel to London, where he could find a job and go to school. He was the only member of the Church in his family and lived with his sister. He was asked to express his testimony and he said, "When I used to read the Bible, I read it more like a story book. After I joined the Church, I have begun to ponder every word. When I heard about the Church, I felt like I had come home. I felt joy that I had never really felt before. I don't want to do anything wrong to spoil the joy I feel. I always knew that the Church would come back because I felt it in my heart. I have written to my brother and asked if he will consider keeping the offer open for eighteen months."

The next young man was twelve years old when he joined the Church and was therefore one of the early members of the Church in Ghana. During the freeze, he often wore his missionary badge so that people would ask him questions and he could defend the Church for what it really is. He was also one of the elders who had been thrown into jail at the beginning of the freeze.

Another elder had acquired a taxi. The members of his family and some of the members of the branch were counseling him not to go back on his mission because he would lose the car. He said simply, "Heavenly Father helped me get this taxi. If I finish my commitment to him, he is very capable of getting me another car when I get back, if that is what he wants me to do."

Next we interviewed a sister who had twelve months of her mission left to serve. When the Church activities were frozen, she was persecuted harshly by her family, as well as the members of her village. She had some concern about returning to the mission field for fear that after her mission she would receive the same treatment. When we asked if she had been living the standards of the Church, she said she had, except for one thing. "I was sick. The doctor recommended for my low blood pressure that I have a little bit of alcohol each day. I did that for a few days and then decided that I would rather have low blood pressure than break the Word of Wisdom, so I stopped taking it. Am I still worthy to serve?"

Of the seventy-seven missionaries serving at the time of the freeze, the mission president had interviewed forty by the time I left, and only three decided not to return. Two of those three had nearly completed their missions and had opportunities for education that likely wouldn't come along again. The third one was the only one who was unworthy to finish his mission. I wondered, If we were interviewing missionaries from the United States, what percentage of them would be worthy and desirous of finishing their missions under similar circumstances? After being home for eighteen months, would they have a desire or be worthy to resume their missions? It was a very humbling and faith-promoting experience to see the faith and faithfulness of the young missionaries in Ghana.

"Want to Come Again Next Year?"

My last visit to Africa as a member of the Presiding Bishopric took place in March 1992. This trip took on additional meaning because my wife, Jolene, went with me for the first time. For several years she had been wanting to go, and this time she almost insisted. This turned out to be very providential. First, although we didn't know it at the time, I was released from the Presiding Bishopric in October of that year and this would have been her last chance to accompany me under such circumstances. Second, this experience gave her an invaluable perspective six years later when we were asked to serve in Africa. Her spiritual and emotional preparation for our service in Africa was infinitely enhanced by these earlier experiences.

It wasn't long into the trip before Jolene could relate to the negative aspects of traveling in Africa. We waited for twenty-four hours to catch one flight and spent long days in meetings in heat and humidity. Neither did it take long, however, for her to be able to understand why I love Africa in spite of the discomfort and frustrations of traveling. While in Lagos, I had been assigned to meet with Brother and Sister Christopher Chukwurah and Brother and Sister John A. Ehanire to interview them to become the first black Africans to serve as mission presidents. Ato Dadson of Ghana was also among this elite and historic threesome. This was one of the most spiritual experiences of the trip. I was so glad Jolene was with me and able to give and receive the woman's perspective on the issue. President Chukwurah was assigned to serve in Ghana and President Dadson and President Ehanire in Nigeria.

Neither couple had been endowed because there was no temple nearby, nor had any of them received their patriarchal blessings. I will never forget hearing President Chukwurah on the phone in the area office trying to sell all of their possessions so he and his wife could take all of their children with them to Salt Lake City when they went to the Missionary Training Center so they could be sealed as a family. For them to attend a temple otherwise, they would have been required to travel to Europe or Johannesburg, both of which are prohibitive because of the cost. (Both temples are the same distance from Nigeria.) These two couples had a lasting effect on Jolene as she began her lifelong love affair with the African culture and especially the African women. I might add that the contribution Jolene made to our later ministry in West Africa was infinite.

On June 17, 1992, I was able to witness the sealing of the Dadsons performed by President James E. Faust, and on June 18, I was

A crowded busload of Saints traveling to the Koforidua District in November 2000.

privileged to perform the sealings of the Chukwurahs and Ehanires. It was a privilege to have Jolene with us in the temple as well. At that time I was able to seal only one of the Chukwurahs' children to them (in the end, they could afford to bring only one with them), but I am thrilled to say that all members of their family have subsequently been sealed. As I stood at the head of the altar in the Salt Lake Temple and performed those sealings, I was overwhelmed with the beauty of those handsome and beautiful black faces and longed for the day a temple would be closer to the people of West Africa so they wouldn't have to sell all of their possessions just to have one child sealed. In fact, this was probably the beginning of my absolute obsession with wanting to see a temple built in West Africa.

For Jolene, one of the highlights of the trip was going to Koforidua, Ghana, to the little branch I had visited several times in the past. She had asked the Primary in our Bountiful ward to write letters to give to the Primary children in Ghana. The Ghanaians

Sister Pace on a beach in Ghana teaching children how to count.

returned the favor and we brought those letters and pictures back to Bountiful with us.

In the sacrament meeting a sister gave the history of Relief Society, a recently returned missionary sang a beautiful solo, and we heard a choir number. In between, Jolene and I spoke. Jolene talked about sisterhood, and I could tell by the looks on the sisters' faces that they thoroughly enjoyed having her participate. I spoke of my history with the Koforidua Ward and how proud we are of their development and how we looked forward to the time that they might have a temple.

After sacrament meeting, they made a presentation of some native costumes to both Jolene and me. They asked her to cut the sesquicentennial cake for the Relief Society. They also had a little cake in the shape of a chapel, inasmuch as they had broken ground for a new chapel. I realized that the next time I visited Koforidua they wouldn't be meeting in the schoolhouse. What I didn't realize was that on that next visit the Koforidua Ward of the Accra Ghana Stake would be the Koforidua District working toward becoming a stake of their own.

After a grueling two weeks, we left Africa on March 18, 1992, taking off for London. On the plane I recorded: "As usual, it has been a rewarding but exhausting trip. I'm glad Jolene was able to come and see the things that I have talked so much about. We will have to wait until next year to see if this will be her final trip."

Jolene looked as exhausted as I felt. With no small amount of mischievousness in my eye I turned to her and said, "Mama, want to come again next year?" to which she responded, "I think that will do."

I observed her staring out the window for some time after that, and just before I dozed off she turned to me and said, "I have a strong feeling we are going to end up living in Africa sometime in the future." Why are our wives always right about these things?

4

THE CALL

In October 1992 I was released as a member of the Presiding Bishopric and called to serve as a Seventy. Within a few weeks I received a call to serve as the mission president of the Australia Sydney North Mission. I am very grateful to the Brethren for giving me that experience. After that assignment we returned to the United States in 1995 to serve in the North America Northwest Area. This was also a wonderful assignment, and we learned to love the great people of the beautiful Northwest. We served in that area until 1998. It had been six years since we had traveled to Africa, and we were kept so busy our memories were fading. They may have faded completely except for my wife's reminders about her feelings regarding an eventual assignment in Africa.

My distant memories received a jump start in February 1998. This was when President Hinckley traveled to Africa and made an announcement that brought inexplicable joy and excitement into my heart.

A few excerpts from the *Church News* article covering this historic trip will add to the reader's perspective and memory:

"ACCRA, GHANA—President Gordon B. Hinckley announced plans Feb. 16 for a temple to be built in Ghana. . . . Earlier that morning, President Hinckley had visited a prospective temple site in Accra with Elder Jeffrey R. Holland of the Quorum of the Twelve and Elder James O. Mason of the Seventy and president of the Africa Area.

"Then, at an outdoor gathering of some 6,700 members assembled in Accra's Independence Square that afternoon, President Hinckley said: 'You've gone a long time without a temple. When I was here five years ago [as a member of the First Presidency], we tried to find a place to build a temple. We didn't find anything and we didn't say anything to anybody.'

"But efforts Monday, Feb. 16, were more fruitful. 'This morning we approved the purchase of a beautiful piece of ground,' President Hinckley announced. The 3.6-acre site is in a residential neighborhood on one of Accra's main thoroughfares.

"The first person to hear the news was Ghanaian President Jerry Rawlings, who met with President Hinckley shortly after noon at the presidential home in Accra. 'We're going to do more building here to accommodate our people. We'll likely build a temple,' the Church leader told President Rawlings.

"The Ghanaian president told President Hinckley that he was supportive of the Church and its objectives. The remarks were particularly meaningful because the Ghanaian government shut the Church down in 1989 after it was wrongfully reported that Latter-day Saints were working against the government. Church buildings were locked and guarded by police, members could hold Church meetings only in the privacy of their own homes, and foreign missionaries were expelled from the country.

"The ban was lifted Dec. 1, 1990. However, the meeting on Feb. 16, 1998, between Ghana's national leader and the Church leader officially closed the 1989 matter. 'I must take back some of the conflicting signals,' President Rawlings said.

"The new temple will take several years to complete, President Hinckley told the congregation assembled in Independence Square.

'When it's completed you won't have to travel all the way to London, or all the way to Johannesburg, to have the blessings of the Lord.'

"President Hinckley encouraged members, in the meantime, to ready themselves by obtaining temple recommends.

"For Joseph W. B. Johnson, news of the temple is something he has waited 15 years for. He is one of the Church's pioneers in west Africa, having in 1964 started a congregation patterned after the Church after he read LDS literature and the Book of Mormon. He and others in his unofficial congregation were baptized after the missionaries arrived in Ghana in 1978. Brother Johnson said that he had a dream several years after he was baptized that the spirits of people who had died asked him what he was doing for them. 'What could I do?' he pondered, not having access to a temple. 'Now we can start doing the temple work for those of our ancestors,' he said after President Hinckley announced the temple.

"On Nov. 8, 1978, the Church's first official delegation to visit west Africa brought news of the priesthood and the pending establishment of the Church in Nigeria and Ghana. It was news entire congregations, most of them unbaptized followers, had been fasting and praying for.

"Now nearly 20 years later, on Monday, Feb. 16, President Hinckley brought news that a temple would soon be built in Ghana. This is also news for which Latter-day Saint congregations here have been specifically fasting and praying" ("A Temple to Be Built in Ghana," *LDS Church News*, February 21, 1998).

"The Church Will Grow As You Grow"

Prior to this announcement President Hinckley visited Nigeria and made some significant comments to those Saints:

"'A magnificent moment in the unfolding drama of the

Restoration of the Gospel of Jesus Christ.' This aptly describes the arrival of the first Church president ever to set foot in West Africa.

"Soon after he arrived in Nigeria, President Hinckley said, 'The great nation of Nigeria needs the gospel of Jesus Christ in the hearts of its people.' Members here said that his visit to this city exceeded their high expectations. They were in awe to see with their own eyes the face behind the familiar picture they've seen so many times.

"As President Hinckley arrived at the priesthood leadership meeting, held at the Port Harcourt Civic Center, a group of Primary children sang for him. One youngster, almost overcome to be in the presence of the Church leader, shyly presented him with a bouquet of flowers. Women with bright silken headdresses stood outside the center to catch a glimpse of President Hinckley as he arrived.

"At the meeting, attended by 1,150 priesthood leaders, President Hinckley encouraged them to stay abreast of new developments in Church policy and curriculum. 'You can't stay in the past and be a good leader of the Church,' he said. [Later in this book I will call these problems of the past 'golden calves.'] . . .

"Further, he said, 'Think of the great opportunity we have in building the kingdom of God in this part of the world. Help the kingdom grow and shine in this land of Nigeria.'

"He also suggested that leaders find a quiet place and meditate about their responsibilities. 'And there will come into your lives a great sense of satisfaction. The Church will grow as you grow. If you don't do anything, nothing very much will happen with the Church. But if you are anxiously engaged in assisting those for whom you are responsible, the Church will grow and blossom in strength. . . .'

"At the regional conference session on Feb. 15, a total of 12,417 members from throughout the nation gathered hours before the appointed time of the meeting. Some spent two days aboard buses traveling through villages and tropical forests to attend. Many of the women dressed for the special occasion in traditional bright colored dresses with turban-like head ties. The reverent congregation stilled as President Hinckley stood, and hardly a sound was heard from the members until he concluded his address.

"In his address, President Hinckley noted the anniversary of the priesthood revelation of 1978. 'I express deep appreciation for the revelation that came to President Spencer W. Kimball 20 years ago in which all the opportunities and blessings of the priesthood would be made available to every worthy male,' President Hinckley said. 'What a marvelous thing that was! I was present when it happened. I am an eyewitness that it happened. . . . How grateful we are—how thankful we are.' . . .

"'I hope you will remember this day when we came among you to give you our love and our blessing,' President Hinckley declared. 'May you have food on your tables, clothing on your backs and a roof over your head. May you love the Lord with all your heart, might, mind and strength.'

"As President Hinckley concluded speaking, a quick but heavy rain crackled on the roof, prompting him to say, 'Be thankful for the rain—the moisture of the earth. The heavens have smiled upon us.'

"Elder Holland, who noted that he has been in Nigeria before, underscored the significance of President Hinckley's visit.

"'Sometimes we are so close to history we don't know we are making it,' he said. 'You are making it in a profound way,' he told the conference-goers.

"He asked members to record and pass on to future generations their account of 'when a prophet of God was in Port Harcourt for the first time in the history of this dispensation—the first time, I suppose, in the work of the Lord through all the world from the beginning. We declare the beauty and wonder of this moment'" ("Nigeria Needs Gospel in Hearts of Its People," *LDS Church News*, February 21, 1998).

As I read this account I couldn't help but think of the spiritual experience we had in Aba in 1986 just fifty miles away from Port Harcourt, where many of that congregation were able to have a visit with President Ezra Taft Benson by proxy. Now another prophet was there in person. The account in the *Church News* could not adequately explain how much this visit meant to the Saints of Nigeria. They are still talking about it.

During my three-year ministry in Africa, which was about to begin, as we faced seemingly insurmountable challenges, I always had a deep conviction that we were living in one of the most unique, historical periods of all time on the African continent. I knew this was a pristine country as far as the Church was concerned. I felt a kinship with the Saints, including my own forefathers, of the Kirtland and Nauvoo periods of the Church. The future temples in Ghana and Nigeria will be to the African Saints as the Kirtland and Nauvoo temples were to the American Saints.

The *Church News* article continued: "At the end of the meeting, as President Hinckley and the other Church leaders left the podium area, members surged forward in hopes of adding touch, through a handshake or other contact, to the sights and sounds of being in the presence of the Church president. [Once more I thought of the people surging to shake my hand in Aba, so I could return that handshake to President Benson. Now, another prophet was there in person.] Outside, people converged at his car.

"'Everybody was praying President Hinckley would come,' said Nduka B. Ojaide, president of the Port Harcourt Nigeria Stake and a member of the regional conference planning committee. 'When I read the letter saying President Gordon B. Hinckley and Elder Jeffrey R. Holland were coming, I was so excited. As I drove through a junction on the way home, I almost crashed because of my happiness. When I broke the news to the children, everybody was happy and jumping around. We felt the Lord had answered our prayers.'

"During a drive to the nearby city of Aba on Sunday, Feb. 15, members, their neighbors and friends waving Nigerian flags lined the road in President Hinckley's honor" ("Nigeria Needs Gospel in Hearts of Its People," *LDS Church News*, February 21, 1998).

One thing that was not referred to or announced is that President Hinckley looked at a potential temple site in Aba, Nigeria, on this visit. The decision to build on this site was not made or announced until April 2000.

A "Green Beret" Assignment

As I read these historic accounts in February 1998, all of the spiritual experiences I had received on my various trips to Africa came flooding back into my mind and heart. My wife's "premonition" was also triggered in my memory.

I was not left in a speculative position for long. It was only a few days later that I received a visit in my office from one of the senior Brethren. He asked if I had a few minutes. He then proceeded to remind me that I had been home for three years and the Brethren were doing a little planning. He asked if I would accept a "green beret" assignment. I told him I would do whatever the Lord wanted me to do. He asked where I would like to go next and I said I wanted to go wherever I was needed (that's always the safest answer at times like that).

He said, "So if you found yourself asked to go to a place like outer Mongolia you would go?" I said yes. I wondered why he went back to the well so many times. In my memory I have always done what I was asked to do. On the other hand, I very much appreciated the sensitivity of the Brethren. He had not mentioned one thing about Africa, but at this point there was no need.

I went home that night and asked Jolene if I had given the right answers. While we were both feeling sad about leaving home, we both were at peace and feeling we would end up in Africa. The hardest part was waiting a month before we would know for sure.

After that visit to my office, Africa was constantly on our minds. Jolene even gave me a book on West Africa for my birthday. Life was not the same after that visit.

We had an appointment with President Monson on Wednesday, March 25, where any question was erased. He checked his notes several times to make certain he was issuing the right call. I had to chuckle at Jolene, who meant no disrespect when she said, "President Monson, you can just tell us where you want us to go." He issued the call and we accepted.

From there we broke the news to the kids, who weren't too surprised but were holding out some hope we would stay home another year. We had very mixed emotions about the whole thing. We didn't want to leave. We were at a perfect time of our life, enjoying our home and posterity, but we had the conviction that for some unknown reason we had been handpicked by the Lord for this call. Of course, the announcement that there would be a temple in West Africa for the first time brought an extra excitement and focus to the call as well.

General conference took on an entirely different tone once we knew we would be going to Africa. I heard all of the General Authority training with different ears. The Brethren were very supportive and even solicitous of our welfare and appreciative of our acceptance. For example, Elder Neal A. Maxwell saw Jolene some distance away in the parking lot and walked all the way over to her car to ask how she felt about it.

As we walked from the parking lot to conference the next morning a security man pulled up beside us in his vehicle, and I heard the familiar voice of President James E. Faust say, "Glenn, come and join us." At first we declined, but he insisted, so we got in. He immediately turned to Jolene and with much feeling and sincerity asked her, "How do you really feel about this call to Africa?" She said she felt fine as long as she had her curling iron and blow dryer. He laughed and said, "We will make you as comfortable as we can while you are there." He was speaking in that session of conference, and I was impressed that, given the pressures of the moment, he was still concerned and sensitive to her feelings and welfare. All of the Brethren were very supportive.

However, the biggest help was the inner peace we had felt during the previous month, as well as the impressions we had felt six years earlier. When you know you are on the Lord's errand, everything is easier. As is often the case, this was just the calm before the storm, and I was oblivious to a test of faith that was just around the bend.

The next few months were spent on my current assignments, as well as working on all the papers necessary to obtain a visa for Ghana. It was a simple process compared to Australia. Ghana did require some strange things like a high school graduation certificate, priesthood ordination certificates, marriage certificate, and a letter from the bank saying you have been a good boy. Surprisingly, they didn't ask for a physical exam.

"Critical but Stable"

For my own protection I felt I ought to get a thorough medical checkup. I had been using a treadmill for several months and had lost about twenty pounds. I was even able to waddle about five miles. However, I felt I was never really able to hit my stride. I remembered in previous years when I was running a lot my body would shift into overdrive at about three miles, and I felt like I could run forever. In 1998, however, it seemed like I was laboring for the full five miles.

On May 21, I went to the Salt Lake Clinic for a physical. Our departure date for Africa was set for August 15. Everything seemed to be all right except I registered high blood pressure. That has happened in doctor's exams for as long as I can remember. I told him my symptoms while running and we decided I would come in the next week for a stress test.

On June 1, I went to the doctor's office for a stress test, something I hadn't had for over ten years. As the incline got steeper and my pulse rate faster, all of a sudden the doctor turned off the machine. I just thought the test was over. He had me lie down and asked if I was all right. I told him I was fine. He disappeared, and the next thing I knew he was standing there with a cardiologist, who began his own set of questions: "Are you in any pain?" and "Why did you stop running?" I explained I had stopped running because they turned off the machine.

Soon I began to pick up the fact that they were very worried. The cardiologist said, "You have shown the classic symptoms of someone who has just suffered a heart attack." He then asked me in detail about how I had been feeling. He kept coming back to whether I had pain during exercise. I said I only felt fatigue and couldn't figure out why my body wouldn't shift into overdrive. He was always disappointed in my answers.

When I explained I had come in for an examination prior to going to Africa, he all but laughed in my face and said, "Well, we'll talk about that later, but we need to go in and see what is going on in there." I asked, "What does 'we need to go in there' mean?" I was shocked when he said he would like to set up an appointment to perform an angiography.

I was told they would make an incision in my thigh, insert a tube, shoot some dye into my heart, and follow the course of the dye through the heart. He told me he was all but certain they would find some serious heart disease. Depending on how serious it was, they would follow up with an angioplasty or open-heart surgery. Needless to say, I was stunned and shocked. The last thing he said was that he would be hard pressed to recommend to the Brethren that they send me to Africa.

He wanted to set up the test for that Thursday, but I told him I had a stake reorganization that weekend so we set it up for Monday, June 8. I did have a stake reorganization, but what I really wanted was some time to process this! In addition to the shock of the possibility of not being able to accept a call I felt the Lord had been preparing me for, I recalled the death of my father while I was serving in Australia. He died following open-heart surgery. I had a lot to think about.

I went home and talked it over with Jolene. We decided not to panic until we saw what was wrong. We also talked it over with our children during the week. They decided to fast about it that Sunday, and then our sons would give me a blessing. To see our call in jeopardy for this reason was a little hard to take. How could all the deep spiritual feelings we had received about Africa have been bogus?

I knew I should call the Brethren and let them know of this development. In anticipation of that I called the cardiologist so I could give the best information possible to the Brethren. I was to go in at 8:00 A.M. and, assuming no problems, would be out at 6:00 P.M. The best case was that there would be no problems, but he didn't think that too likely. The worst case would be open-heart surgery. They would do the surgery right away, and it would be about six months before my normal schedule could resume. He was very doubtful about Africa based on what he had seen to that point, but he said, "Let's get in there and see what we're dealing with."

With that cheery news, I went to get my passport and visa pictures taken. It seemed strange, and I was wondering if I was just going through the motions.

On June 4, I sat down and talked with Elder L. Aldin Porter about the possibility of not being able to fulfill the assignment to Africa, but I requested that he not do anything until I had the angiography next week. I then called President Packer. After explaining my situation to him I said, "With the strong feelings we have had for years about Africa, it is hard for me to understand this." He said, in a very sensitive way, "Well, maybe it just means you won't be going now." He was very supportive and anxious to get the results. On June 5, I recorded the following:

"I chose to drive to Idaho Falls and stay overnight prior to the assigned stake reorganization in Rexburg. I wanted to be alone and think things through. It was quite a drive. In fact it was quite a weekend, knowing I would be going in for the test Monday. It was a beautiful June day. I love June. When I arrived I checked into the Ameritel near the falls.

"This place always reminds me of Dad and Mom and our childhood vacations. I went for a walk around the loop, past the temple, falls, and river and thought things through. I was feeling extra close to Dad, partly because of the location but mostly because of the situation. He died three years ago after open-heart surgery of the same type I might be having. Even though he was twenty-seven years older at the time, it did give me some sobering thoughts.

"I experienced the full spectrum of possibilities, from their not finding anything (which doesn't seem very likely because of the problems I've been experiencing when I exercise) to the reality that I might die on the operating table. I dwelt on that for quite some time and was astonished at the peace I felt. There was no panic. I had the peace that if that was in the plan, I was ready. Never in my life had I faced the reality of that possibility. The hardest was thinking about the children and grandchildren and not being an influence in their lives like Dad has been in mine for twenty-seven years longer than I might be in theirs. I chastised myself for thinking of the worst because the operation is so common and usually successful, but when you just lost your dad that way you can't ignore it.

"The feelings that stand out the most as I went for my walk was a closeness to Dad and yet a loneliness for him and trying to reconcile the Africa connection. I'm not anxious to leave home, nor am I anxious to go to Africa. However, if I had to be reassigned for this reason, I would be very disappointed and somewhat confused about the spiritual impressions we have received over the last several years regarding Africa. I also marveled at how fast things can change. All in all I came through it deciding 'whatever, it's out of my hands.'"

Subsequent to the conference on June 7, 1998 (which was our thirty-fifth wedding anniversary), I wrote: "In spite of considerable stress, I was able to bury it during the conference and enjoyed the stake reorganization. The hardest thing was having people ask me how I felt about my upcoming assignment and to talk about it as if it was a done deal.

"On the drive home, a new emotion came over me, which had to do with anxiety about the operation itself. It is an eery feeling to realize that in eighteen hours someone is going to have a knife in your heart. It also bothered me to think of walking into a place feeling reasonably healthy and have them wheel you out of a room in 'critical but stable' condition and then have to be fairly inactive for a while. Still, I was at peace."

When I got home I discovered that Jolene and all of the children were there. I took the opportunity to tell them all about the possibilities. They had all been fasting and praying that my heart condition would not be serious and that we would be able to fulfill our call to Africa. Their support and love were very touching to me. At the conclusion of the evening I had my sons administer to me. I had Darin be voice since he was the oldest of those present. He gave me a beautiful and encouraging blessing. It was a celestial moment with the family.

The next day was the day of the operation. Jolene and I were up first thing and on our way to LDS Hospital. I don't like hospitals. I felt like a lamb going to the slaughter. The cardiologist was there on time, which was a blessing because I didn't have to sit and stew. Before I knew it I was on a table rolling down the hall, watching the ceiling lights go by one by one. As they rolled me out of the room, I overheard the doctor tell Jolene we could be back in an hour or more, depending on what they found. His last comment was, "I'll tell you one thing for sure. With the test results we've already received, you will not be going to Africa. Someone else will have to go in your place."

The procedure was surprisingly simple and I was awake through it all, watching the little tube sitting next to my heart on the X-ray screen. It stung when they made the incision in the thigh and put the tube in, but from then on it was relatively painless. I experienced a burning feeling as the dye was shot into my system. I listened carefully, trying to discern if the "uhumms" and "ahaas" represented good or bad news, but I couldn't really tell. Then the doctor put the tape on instant replay and showed me the arteries he had been concerned with. They showed about a 30 percent blockage, which he said was normal for someone my age. He said they don't even think about doing an angioplasty unless it is close to 70 percent.

They wheeled me back to the recovery room, and Jolene was ecstatic. The doctor was a little puzzled because of what they'd seen when I was doing the stress test. He scheduled another stress test involving a CAT scan and some dye. That second test also proved negative. In fact, the last words the cardiologist said were "Elder Pace, you're clean as a whistle." I've never seen him again and hope I never do. (Nothing personal, of course!)

The day after the angiography, Elders L. Aldin Porter and Joe J. Christensen were waiting at the doorway to my office, asking for my report. They were genuinely pleased and relieved. Their final expression was "Well, I guess the Lord wants you in Africa." I called President Packer and gave him the same report and got the same reaction.

We had experienced the first of many miracles relating to our service in Africa. We give all credit to the Lord and the power of the priesthood.

Partings

The next few weeks were full of preparations and adjustments. General Authorities don't often speak personally about the challenges of their callings, but I would like to disclose certain personal details to pay tribute to my brethren of the Seventy and their wives for the numerous sacrifices they make for the kingdom. Some of my brethren and their wives have spent fifteen to twenty years away from their families on various assignments. Currently the average Seventy can plan on three to five years away for every three years he is at home. I say "at home," but I really should say in Salt Lake City. Many of the Seventies aren't "home" even while living in Salt Lake City, since they are called from all over the world. Therefore, for some of our number, being called as a General Authority means leaving home until they reach the age of seventy. All of them do it willingly and would not want me to bring attention to them, but I think the members should know of the dedication and sacrifice involved.

In their honor I wish to share some of the feelings we have when we know we are going to be gone from home for some time. We also know it won't be the last time we will leave. In my case, when I returned from this African assignment I had been away from home for six of the last nine years. This is not unusual for my brethren of the Seventy. I love and respect them very much. The Seventies are the officers in the field with the troops, in the line of fire, and often in harm's way.

We made arrangements the last of June to bring our whole family together. This was the first time we had all been together in six years. We have six married children and we have been blessed to see them all married in the temple. In fact, I have had the privilege of performing all of those marriages. I pay tribute to them for the lives they are living in spite of the frequent absences of their father and mother.

One golden moment sticks out above all others during this reunion. We were in the celestial room of the Bountiful Temple, standing together. Then, without anyone saying anything, we realized at the same time we were all together in the house of the Lord in the celestial room. We were standing with our arms around each other and the Spirit hit us all and brought tears to our eyes as we just kept looking from individual to individual. I will always remember that split second. Nothing needed to be said, and if anything had been said it would have detracted from the sacred moment.

Within a couple of days our oldest daughter and her husband were moving to Little Rock, Arkansas, to begin a medical residency there. This brought our reunion to an abrupt halt. Reality had to set in sooner or later. We had a family prayer, gave some tearful farewells, and then saw them drive off with their three sweet daughters. We knew we wouldn't see them again for three years. Before we knew we were going to Africa, we had planned on them coming to visit us in Bountiful from time to time while our son-in-law Ryan was in medical residency. Now that possibility was gone—and so were they.

I remember one poignant visit to our widowed mothers in Provo. We stayed overnight on July 3, each of us with our respective mothers. I wrote in my journal, "Staying in Dad's room always brings back a certain melancholy as I look around at the Holiday Bowl picture, BYU memorabilia, the hat I sent him from Australia, and just the smell of the house. When I awoke on the Fourth of July I missed him hustling around and getting the ice cream machine turning. I missed Mom not being able to be out barbecuing the chickens. How fast it all went and how much for granted we took it. When the children were young and we made trips to Provo, it seemed like it would last forever. Now in about a month we will be out of the country again."

About a week later we spent a few days at Grand Teton National Park, which is one of our family's traditional vacation spots. We will always remember a testimony meeting we held around the campfire on Sunday, July 12. I wish I had a recording of all the words on tape because it was a beautiful moment. Our children were absolutely supportive. The biggest impression I had that evening was that the Lord would bless them more with our being gone than they would be blessed by our presence if we were here. It's not that we wouldn't all miss each other, but in the long run we all would be better off. I also felt a very strong impression, which I shared, that the Lord would fill in the blank years as far as our missing out on the lives of the grandchildren and that our overall closeness would not suffer because of this assignment. It was a heavenly night around the fire.

June and July of 1998 were essentially a two-month reunion or going-away party. We spent every possible minute with the children, but even that didn't seem long enough. We kept trying to get a three-year supply of experiences to tide us over, but we all knew that just doesn't work any more than trying to drink in a three-year supply of water. No matter how much you drink, you are thirsty the next day.

Our last official assignment in the North America Northwest Area was to accompany the Hinckleys and the Packers on a trip to Canada. One morning during breakfast President Hinckley looked across the table at my wife and asked, "Well, Jolene, are you excited about going to Africa?" She pondered that question briefly and then said, "I'm ready." President Hinckley got a big chuckle out of that.

On August 14 we had one last chance to see our mothers. My feelings were close to the surface as I thought that my mother might not still be alive when we returned. Leaving parents who may not be there when you get back is one of the hardest parts of these assignments. Of course, the memory of losing my father while I was away on my previous assignment in Australia didn't help. I walked around the inside and outside of the house and remembered happy times that will never return in this life as far as my father is concerned and perhaps my mother. On the other hand, you have to look forward to different times rather than wallow in the fact that old times won't return. The visit with my mother was very special, and we were able to communicate on the "what ifs." My fears proved to be correct—she passed away eighteen months later.

We then had one final day to see our children and grandchildren. On August 15, I wrote:

"We began the final packing today, which means our suitcases. The day was captured in a photograph of Jaden (an eighteen-month-old grandson) sitting on my suitcase in our empty master bedroom watching me pack and not having a clue as to the separation ahead. I ached at not being able to explain what was going on. The only thing that keeps you from shriveling up and blowing away at times like this is the knowledge that children are so resilient. Adults should be so lucky.

"In the afternoon the wake began. Most of the kids came by and it was like the last twenty-four hours before an execution. We were all just waiting around for the ax to fall. It was not one of my happier days. This is not the way it is meant to be and cannot be the way it will be in the eternities."

Off to Africa

The next day (August 16, 1998), we left for Africa. We took the car to the parking lot at the Church office building to drop it off and security drove us to the airport. Jolene told the driver she felt like he was taking us to the dog pound. We had hinted to the kids not to come to the airport, but they felt they wanted or needed to. We had only about twenty minutes at the gate, and there was so much

Jaden Lindquist, one of the Paces' grandsons, sitting on their luggage.

confusion we couldn't really have appropriate farewells. It was frustrating because there were things we wanted to say but couldn't. Jo'ell Lindquist, our youngest daughter, came over to me just before I got on the plane. She needed to say one more thing—or perhaps she needed to hear words of comfort—but it was time to board. I'll never forget the look in her eyes. Her expression said, "Daddy can't make this one all better, can he?"

Please excuse these sentimental details, but it is all part of the story. I often think how sad it would be if the heart didn't ache during farewells. If we don't miss someone, do we really love them? If we don't long for the time we can all be together forever, what is the purpose of eternity? If we don't feel incomplete when we aren't together, is it possible to feel complete when we eventually are all united? Nevertheless, we can't wallow in homesickness, and one of the testimonies I have gained is that the Lord blesses us and allows us to function in spite of this temporary void. He also blesses us with a finite amount of omnipresence while on this earth. By this I mean that through the Spirit it is possible to feel of each other's presence and "company" even while apart.

There is also a positive side. When going through trials and tribulations, we gain a focus we often lack during times of plenty and contentment. We develop a healthy dependence on our Father in Heaven and draw closer to the Spirit, which enables us to find and do his will sometimes in a superhuman fashion. We stay connected to supernal things. Even healthy feelings of inadequacy lead to a total dependence on the Lord, and those feelings pave the way to revelation from him.

As the plane took off and flew over Bountiful, I felt both lonely and empty for the past and inadequate for the future. And yet, with all these feelings of loss and with the pain of separation, we went willingly, desiring above all things to do the will of the Lord and to serve him in his kingdom—even in sacrifice.

5

MAKING ADJUSTMENTS

————

I spent a lot of time on the airplane fantasizing about what was ahead. One of the primary thoughts on my mind was an excitement about the temple that had been announced in Ghana. I thought about what a joy it was going to be to help prepare the people for the temple, as well as to watch it be built. Before we left, our biggest apprehension about the temple was that we would miss the groundbreaking. Upon our arrival we learned it had been scheduled for October 31, 1998. This was a very exciting prospect for us. We couldn't have been more oblivious to what challenges lay ahead concerning the temple. (These are discussed in some detail in chapters 6, 7, and 8.)

We were met by President James O. Mason, his wife, Marie, and some employees from the Church. The Masons are two more of my heroes. They had been living in South Africa for four years, and I'm sure they had some hope they would be returning home. Instead, they were asked to spend an additional year in West Africa to help get the new area office started. Previously, all of Africa was administered out of Johannesburg, South Africa. President Mason became the first president of the area, and I was his first counselor. Our second counselor was Emmanuel Ohenre Opare, who was a newly called Ghanaian Area Authority Seventy.

Culture Shock

Our home in Accra was beautiful and as comfortable as one could make it. I came to refer to it as the world's most expensive camper. The reason for this is that water had to be stored in tanks outside. We had a three-filter system for our water. The first one took out the solids, the second iodized the water, and the third took the taste of iodine out of the water. We had a septic tank that would back up once in a while. Tanks of butane gas were brought in to run the stove. We had a diesel generator for electricity, since the city's power was on a cycle where it was on for twelve hours and then off for twelve. However, the generator was strong enough to run the home's air conditioners and our comfort level was therefore high. As long as all of those things were working, life was very pleasant—until you left the house. And yet repairs were constant. The biggest frustration was the telephone. Whenever it rained, the phones wouldn't work. Heavy rains brought floods inside the house and septic tanks backed up. The construction of the house left much to be desired. Nevertheless, we felt guilty living in such opulence as we started to mingle with the locals.

We brought several appliances from home, which ran on 110 volts instead of the 220 that is common in Africa. To get along we therefore had to purchase several converters. We brought a hot-air popcorn popper, which shook our confidence in being very creative with converters. Every time we plugged it in it would blow a fuse and send out sparks. One of the first things we bought was a fire extinguisher for each floor. We had been told that if a fire broke out, the house would burn down before the fire department could arrive. We came to believe that because of what we saw with the police department. If you have a problem requiring police attention you have to go pick them up.

It is not my intention to make fun of the country but just to state the facts. It is common to hear outsiders berate these countries for

Market in downtown Accra, Ghana.

Sister Pace at a rural market in Ghana.

their lack of services. The truth of the matter is that they do very well despite their poverty, and they are extremely creative in meeting challenges to the best of their ability and circumstances.

The day after we arrived some Church employees took us to the market. That was a culture shock. As soon as you get out of the car you are besieged by people either looking for a handout or selling something. You have to fight your way into the store. Once you are inside another shock awaits you. These are not Super Targets. They are about the size of a Seven Eleven. They have quite a few imported commodities, and you are thankful to see something familiar once in awhile, even though it is very expensive. Occasionally you will discover something like Aunt Jemima's pancake flour and shout for joy. You shout until you get it home and discover that the weevil have invaded it before you got your chance.

On the positive side, the pineapple is plentiful, inexpensive, and the best I have ever tasted. They also have large, wonderful avocados, and a fairly large variety of fruits and vegetables. The thing I missed most is milk. The only milk they have is imported and sterilized. It was bearable on cereal or for cooking purposes but I simply couldn't enjoy just drinking it. I found some Nestle's Quik chocolate, but even with a heavy concentration of chocolate in it, I couldn't drink the milk down.

The cash system was also difficult to get used to. Most places don't take a check or a credit card, and therefore it is a cash economy. To complicate matters further, the *highest* denomination of currency is about the equivalent of $1.50, which means you have to carry around a stack of money several inches thick, bound up in rubber bands. It won't fit in your pocket, and you get very concerned about having it in plain sight. Paying for our goods was embarrassing at first, because it took us so long to count out the proper amount. The clerks count the money very quickly and got out of patience with our lack of experience.

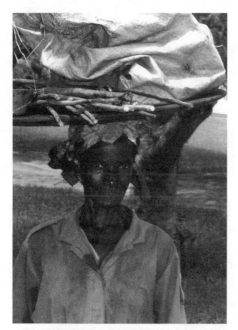

Hard-working African woman.

A woman with a sewing machine on her head, posing with Sister Pace.

Shopping was a continuous adventure. We had to go to several places with a shopping list of only eight items. When buying fruits, vegetables, or even eggs you have to take them home and sanitize them, which means scrubbing everything with bleach. If you purchase anything leafy, you have to take each leaf and scrub it thoroughly. We didn't risk leafy greens very often. The couples learn through trial and error where to buy meats. Sometimes, the error results in a very large trial.

We had heard from the couple missionaries about a great fish market in Tema. One morning we went to Tema to check it out. We were swarmed over by peddlers the minute we got out of the car. They all had metal tubs of fish with flies all over them. The smell of fish and other things persuaded us we didn't really want fish after all. We chalked it up to another cultural experience and went back home and ordered fish and chips at one of the nice hotels—which probably bought their fish at the same place we just left.

Relative to the peddlers and beggars, I always felt torn between feelings of annoyance and compassion when I was approached by beggars and vendors. People in West Africa are so desperate. You can't give to everyone, but none of them take no for an answer. They won't stop trying to sell to you until you get angry or rude, and then you feel bad. It was difficult to find the balance between being generous and just being an easy target. Part of my solution was to follow my feelings, and to give when it felt right. But even that can be complicated. I once gave something to a young man who thanked me by telling me it wasn't enough. I asked him to let me see the money I'd given him. He gave it back and I put it in my pocket. He said, "I didn't say I wouldn't take it!" I doubled it and returned it to him.

There are other trials. Getting a mosquito bite puts you into a panic about malaria. We would all take medicine to prevent malaria. The most common was Larium, but many of us had a bad reaction to it. The minimum reaction was crazy dreams, which almost all of us had. We could entertain each other for hours talking about Larium dreams. I would estimate that about 50 percent of us got malaria sometime during our service. The locals shrug it off like the common cold.

Another difficult problem you learn to live with but never quite get used to is the stifling heat and humidity. All the people have to keep the chapels cool are fans, but they don't usually work because the electrical power fails. This results in dehydration. When you are traveling there is always a constant dilemma before leaving for the day. You have basically two choices. You can drink a lot of water and risk not being able to find a rest room or you don't drink much water and risk dehydration. The lack of private facilities is such that there are no decisions in between. The more "rest rooms" you visit

The first area presidency of the Africa West Area, on a windy day in 1998. From left: *Elder Pace, Elder Mason, and Elder Opare.*

on the way, the more prone you are to choose dehydration the next time. Facilities are few and far between, and their quality leaves much to be desired. Gas stations will advertise "rest rooms," but when you get there the room will often consist of four walls with no roof, and a trough running down the middle. There are no separate facilities for men or women. I will leave it to your imagination as to other problems encountered, and I assure you even the most vivid imagination will fall short.

I am neither criticizing nor ridiculing the culture. When we live in the opulence of America, it is difficult to understand how something as basic as rest rooms cannot be a top priority. It is difficult to understand many problems when you have never had to go without anything. When you are a West African, you may be so concerned about getting enough food for your family each day that nice rest rooms don't seem like such a high priority.

The weekend we arrived we held the first area council of the Africa West Area. The three Area Authority Seventies were all familiar to me. Our second counselor, Elder Ohenre Opare, had

Area Authority Seventies in the Africa West Area. From left:
Elders Christopher Chukwurah, David W. Eka, and Ohenre Opare.

been serving as a stake president when I visited on a few occasions when I was in the Presiding Bishopric. Elder David W. Eka from Port Harcourt, Nigeria, had been the district president when I gave my first leadership training in 1986, and he later became the first stake president in Nigeria. Elder Christopher Chukwurah from Lagos, Nigeria, had been the regional manager when I visited as Bishop Pace. He was called as one of the first African mission presidents, and I later was honored to seal him and his wife in the Salt Lake Temple in June 1992. I thought it was more than coincidence that I had these previous relationships. It was good to see them all again, and the timing for the area council couldn't have been better to get us involved early.

The next few weeks were very exciting and educational as we got acclimatized to our new environment. The frustrations of the living conditions were quickly overridden by the immense love we felt for the people. I was completely overwhelmed by how fast I fell in love with a culture so different from my own. I've never experienced anything like it.

The Ghanaians are a gentle, loving, and friendly people. The first day I tried to drive to the office by myself I got lost. In desperation I pulled into a service station to ask directions. Between the accent and the unfamiliar names, I didn't understand a word the attendant said. Another man was filling up his tank and could see how perplexed I looked. He turned to me and said, "Follow me, I will show you." This was a perfect stranger, and he took ten minutes out of his day to show me how to get to the office. That was the first of three years' worth of experiences that have deeply endeared that people to me.

As a rule, the people have very little in possessions but are very happy. They are also a very religious people. Almost all of their little shops have sayings from the Bible or some statement about Jesus. Most aren't open on Sundays. All smile and are friendly to us when we give the least indication that we want to be friendly to them. It is strange to be the only white person among thousands and realize they are very curious. They are also very accepting.

Even at the end of the three years I never lost the wonder and fascination of it all. We traveled in many African countries, and negative experiences with the people in general were extremely rare—much more rare than the rudeness and insensitivity we sometimes experience in our own country.

Plain Speaking

Our first official assignment was a mission tour of the Nigeria Enugu Mission and a conference with the Abak Nigeria District. Trying to prepare for those was an exercise in futility. Each attempt ended in a stupor of thought. I would try to write an outline and decide what to do but would come up empty because I couldn't really envision the audience. I finally decided I would just have to rely on the Lord for instant, spontaneous inspiration and be completely extemporaneous. There is nothing more humbling to me than to stand before an audience completely foreign to my own culture, knowing they are looking to me as a General Authority of the Church. They have complete confidence that the General Authority will lead them where they need to go. I therefore left on this first assignment with much trepidation.

And yet my concerns turned out to be unfounded.

When I visited the mission, I was very impressed by the intelligence, inquisitiveness, and attentiveness of the missionaries. I was speaking to them about foreordination when one of them asked whether we would be black or white after the resurrection. Another wanted to know if we were individuals when we existed as intelligences. One thing I learned from that experience is while you have to be pretty basic in teaching procedures and policies, you don't have to hold back a minute when teaching doctrine. On this first assignment I received a certain knowledge that *the doctrines of the kingdom have a universal appeal.* I'm thankful for that early recognition because it gave me the confidence I needed for "straight talk" throughout our ministry.

One of the most pleasant surprises was meeting three siblings of the young man, Samuel Arungwa, whom I had met in 1986, when he was fourteen years old. A brother and sister were serving as missionaries in that mission and another sister was going to law school nearby. We met with her at the mission home. It was touching to hear her say she remembered very clearly the day I came to their home in Nsirimo. She had been only nine or ten and yet had been extremely impressed that a General Authority would come to their humble home. She seemed to think that my visit has had quite a lasting effect on the family, even though I didn't do much more than show up at the house of the branch president in 1986.

I was also thrilled when I met the stake president of the Port Harcourt Stake, President Nduka Ojaide. As we were riding around looking at chapel sites, he reminded me that he had been at that district training meeting in Aba in 1986 when I brought the greetings of President Benson. That had been twelve years earlier, but the Spirit had been so strong in that meeting it became a highlight of his life.

These two experiences resulted in a recognition of the beauty of the tapestry the Lord weaves with each of our lives. Connections are formed early; then they come back into play later. The pattern in the tapestry becomes recognizable as it comes into focus through 20/20 hindsight.

On the way to the district conference in Abak we passed two human bodies along the side of the road. This is one thing I never got used to, though I saw it fairly frequently. Unfortunately, the local authorities must find a family member to claim a body before moving it. Anyone who tries to do so prior to locating the family must take responsibility for it. Several days must pass before the authorities can finally dispose of a corpse without involvement from the family. I never adjusted to that cultural fact of life.

As I visited the Abak District I could see there was a great need for basic training, but the Spirit was strong in all meetings. I spoke extensively and plainly on men, women, and the priesthood and explained how they should interact in the home and units of the Church. For this culture my teachings call for some changes in thinking, but they accepted the counsel very well. After giving them some pretty strong counsel on the subject I asked, "How do you know I'm telling you the truth and not just trying to impose an American custom on you?" They simply said, "The Spirit tells us you are speaking the truth." As simple as that statement is, I found it to hold true throughout my ministry, and I'm thankful for that early teaching they gave me. It gave me the courage to continue to speak to them in plain terms about delicate subjects.

In the general session of district conference the next day I spent a lot of time talking about the temple and our need to be worthy of it. Jolene did exceptionally well in all meetings. In Africa at this time (in contrast to many other General Authority assignments), our wives are able to travel with us on most assignments. We don't want to leave them home alone, but even more important, they are needed in the field to help teach the women and children, and for that matter, the men. My most lasting memory of this first conference in Nigeria was my wife standing outside after the meeting surrounded by women and children. One of the women was holding an umbrella over Jolene's head so she wouldn't get wet. Jolene was glowing as she expressed her love, and the smiles on the faces of the Saints were priceless.

As I expressed earlier, I could fill a book on experiences and frustrations of travel. This season in Africa was no different. The first difficulty awaited us as we returned from this district conference. We had been gone for more than a week and were completely drained and anxious to get back to our cocoon in Accra. We drove back to Port Harcourt, rested a couple of hours, and then were driven to the airport. There we waited one hour, two hours, three hours, at which time we were told the plane couldn't get into the airport because of the rain and they had no radar. Come back tomorrow. I'll never forget the disappointment on Jolene's face. We returned the next morning and waited one hour, two hours, three hours, and our plane didn't come in. Finally a plane from a local airline arrived. We had avoided flying on this airline, but since this was the only option at the moment, we decided to go for it. It was easy to see the plane was not well maintained. The armrests were coming off, some of the oxygen masks were hanging down, the seats needed repair, and the inside was very dirty. To add to our concern,

Sister Pace being protected from the rain by an African sister after a conference at Abak District, Nigeria.

a local Catholic man in the seat next to us kept crossing himself from takeoff to touchdown.

In the middle of the flight it dawned on me that we would be flying into an airport different from what we had expected, so we didn't know what adventure lay ahead. Lagos, Nigeria, is not a place to be when you don't know what you are doing. When we arrived, our first priority was getting our luggage. Just as the luggage started coming off the plane, we were met by an employee of the Church. I don't know what we would have done if he hadn't been there. This was one of an endless number of experiences where little miracles were provided for our safety and well-being. I have spent days trying to reach someone by phone in Nigeria, without success, but in less than an hour President Jerry Kirk was able to reach the employee who came and rescued us.

"This Is the Day of Africa"

On September 20 I was asked to dedicate the Lartebiokorshie Stake Center. This was the first Church-owned building ever to be dedicated in Accra, Ghana. This seemed strange, since the Church had been there for twenty years and there are two stakes in Accra, but most of the buildings were leased.

Just as I got up to speak during the dedication the lights all went out. They immediately started up the generator and put two portable lights on each side of the pulpit. The audience could then see me, but I couldn't see a thing.

In my talk I testified to the reality of the Lord's plan. Words cannot express the intensity of feelings I had for these wonderful people that evening. I had been in the country only one month and yet I already felt an eternal bond with them. The love and trust they extended to this white man from Bountiful, Utah, was simply overwhelming.

Here is part of what I told them on that occasion: "This is a very historic day for Accra, Ghana! . . . The dedication of this building tonight and the groundbreaking of the temple next month [at this point in time we were still laboring under the delusion that the temple groundbreaking would be October 31] are physical manifestations of something very spiritual stirring in this nation and other parts of West Africa. It is my opinion that the Spirit is brooding over this nation, and it is time to move the work forward in a major way.

"Part of my testimony about this matter comes from instructions I received from members of the First Presidency and Quorum of the Twelve over the last few months since I received my call to come here. These prophets, seers, and revelators call Seventies to form Area Presidencies throughout the world. About eight years ago all of Africa was supervised from the British Isles. The Church grew to the point where they found it necessary to locate an Area Presidency in South Africa. However, beginning August 15 of this year these prophets, seers, and revelators felt it was time to bring a presidency closer to the people in West Africa.

"Prior to receiving this call I was president of an area that covered the northwest United States. In that area we had 200 stakes and 700,000 members. Here, we have 16 stakes and 70,000 members. Why would an Area Presidency be called to preside over just 70,000 members? Through personal conversations with some of these apostles and prophets I can tell you it is because the Brethren feel we are on the verge of great growth. In the words of one of the Brethren, 'This is the day of Africa.'

"This is a very critical time in the development of the Church here. We need to make certain that the doctrine being taught is pure and that the administration of the Church is in harmony with that which has been revealed in this dispensation of the fulness of times. I will illustrate this by speaking of a tree we planted in the backyard of our home in Bountiful, Utah. When the tree was very young and tender, the trunk would bend in any direction. We had a strong east wind where we live, which resulted in the tree constantly leaning under the power of the wind. Gradually, as the tree grew older, the trunk got thicker and less pliable, and the roots were sent deep. Because we gave it no support it grew up in a leaning position, and the trunk would no longer bend. While it was young, all we would have had to do is attach some support to it until it could stand alone with deep roots and solid trunk, and it wouldn't matter how hard the wind blew, it would have stood straight and tall of its own strength. But we didn't do that, and we had to dig it up and start all over again.

"We are here to help train the leadership so that you can become self-reliant. Africa should be led by Africans. I was thrilled when President Opare was called as a Seventy and assigned as a counselor in this Area Presidency.

"It is my opinion that the work will grow no faster in Ghana than leadership is prepared from among Ghanaians. It will also grow no faster than the current members of the Church grow into their spiritual potential. Buildings such as this are dedicated to bringing that about. However, a building is just materials unless the Spirit is there. Even a dedicated building is dependent upon the spirituality of those who enter it. It is my plea to you that tonight you will rededicate yourselves to living the things you will be taught in this building. I also challenge you to turn your homes into sacred buildings by the way you live your lives therein.

"Tonight we need to see beyond the dedication of this building alone and realize this is just one part of a big picture. We need to grasp the vision of our own potential and dedicate our lives to bringing about the purposes for which we were born."

After speaking about the Master's plan in terms similar to those used in chapter 1 of this book, I applied that doctrine specifically to them.

"Sometime after the Savior's plan was accepted and he was foreordained to become the Savior of the world, you stood before the Lord to get your assignment. In my mind I can hear him say, 'We need someone to go to the earth and live in Ghana, Africa, and join the Church prior to 1978. They will be subjected to persecution for belonging to the Church. They won't even be able to hold the priesthood at first. They will need to be true to the teachings, even though the Church won't be organized in Ghana when they join.'

"Who here joined the Church prior to 1978? Please stand. When the Lord said, 'Whom shall I send to Ghana?' these people stood up and said, 'Here am I, send me.'

"Then I think the Lord may have said, 'I need some children to be born in Ghana who will join the Church between 1978 and 1988 and start building the Church. You will see it grow, and then at the end of that time, because of some criticism about the Church, its activities will be frozen and you will need to worship for a time in your own homes. Your neighbors will think you belong to an evil church. However, you will need to be faithful and have the faith that the Church will return to Ghana.'

"How many joined the Church prior to 1989? Please stand. The Lord said, 'Whom shall I send?' All of you standing said, 'Here am I, send me.'

"I think that the Lord may have said, 'I need some to serve missions who are willing to have their missions interrupted for almost one and one half years and then return to the mission field to finish their missions after the freeze is eliminated.' Those who did that, please stand.

"The Lord said, 'Whom shall I send?' and you said, 'Here am I, send me.'

"Perhaps he then said, "We need more to join the Church between 1988 and 1998, and you will join all the others to help build the kingdom and prepare each other for a temple, which will be announced in February 1998.'

"How many have joined the Church since 1988? All members stand. And the Lord said, 'Whom shall I send?' and you answered, 'Here am I, send me.'

"Perhaps the Lord then said, 'During this critical time we will need some couples from the United States to leave their children and grandchildren for a few years and serve the people of Ghana.' All missionary couples stand. The Lord said, 'Whom shall I send?' and you answered, 'Here am I, send me.'

"Now tonight we find ourselves all together under the direction of the Lord bringing to pass his prophecies and fulfilling our assignments. I suspect we embraced each other in our premortal abode and said, 'We will see you at the dedication of the Lartebiokorshie chapel on September 20, 1998. More important, we will see you at the groundbreaking and dedication of the first temple in West

Africa.' And here we are together, with ties deeper than any of us know, which go back to our premortal existence.

"As we dedicate this building tonight I call upon each and every one of us to rededicate our lives to living the gospel so the Lord can reveal to us the things we must do to bring about his plan for Ghana. We made some promises to the Lord before we were born into our situation, and all of us want to keep those promises."

"The Clouds Are Dispersing"

Two weeks later, back in Salt Lake City for general conference, Elder Mason and I gave a report of our progress to a committee of the Twelve. It was hard to believe we had only been gone six weeks. My remarks to the Twelve at that time were as follows:

"I am going to be very brief so you can hear from the expert, as opposed to someone with just six weeks' experience. I went to Ghana and Nigeria for the first time in about 1986 as a member of the Presiding Bishopric. . . . I returned each year until 1992, which was my last trip until now.

"I am amazed at the progress that has been made in seven years. . . . I feel the clouds are dispersing and these nations are emerging out of the Third World. There are mammoth problems, but there is forward movement. The change is even more dramatic in the Church. We have some very strong leadership. There are stakes of Zion. I have a strong conviction that the nations are being blessed as our critical mass of Saints increases. As the nations change it becomes easier to do the work, and as the work increases the Lord blesses the nations.

"There is so much training to be done, it is overwhelming. In the little experience I have had in a mission tour and district conference, I have concluded that the people need very basic training in administration, but when it comes to teaching doctrine, you don't have to hold back. If there is a caution, it is to be able to teach the new handbooks in such a way that we don't start to give an impression that we feel the handbooks are more important than the doctrine and ordinances. Even with so much to be done in teaching the order of the Church, we still must keep them focused on the doctrines of the kingdom. I believe we can do one without letting the other remain undone.

" . . . I have never been anyplace where the nonmembers are so open to being taught. With the new temple that is about to be started we have a great opportunity to see geometric growth.

"With all the problems, and there are many, I feel this is truly the time for West Africa, and the Lord's hand is very evident in the work. It is 1850 in the history of the Church there, and people are having spiritual experiences much the same as in the beginning of the Church. There are miracles everywhere."

Hope in a War-Torn Land

Shortly after our return to Ghana we were reminded that Africa provides a roller coaster of extremes. After enjoying spiritual experiences one day, the next day you will hear horrible news, such as a missionary being killed. On October 21 this very thing happened when we got news that a young elder from Liberia had been killed in an accident in Nigeria. He and his companion had been in an accident while riding on a "taxi." The taxi was a motorbike. In some parts of Nigeria motorbike taxis are the only transportation available. Thus, they were not breaking mission rules. This tragedy was not the last we would see. I don't like to dwell on it, but danger is a fact of life in Africa. This was vividly brought to my consciousness again when we visited two districts in Liberia in November 1998.

On November 6 we arrived in Monrovia, Liberia. It reminded me of the airports as they had earlier been in Accra and Lagos. It was very intimidating and chaotic. We had to check our luggage in Abidjan, Ivory Coast, and just as we were about to land in Monrovia

Bombed-out apartment, Monrovia, Liberia.

the pilot made a matter-of-fact announcement that some of the luggage had been left behind. "We are sorry," he said. I couldn't imagine ever being able to locate luggage left in Abidjan while you are staying in Monrovia. Thankfully, our luggage made the cut and got on the plane. We felt bad as we looked around and saw several disappointed and irate customers who had not been so blessed.

Driving into the city of Monrovia was an education. Monrovia had been in a seven-year civil war that devastated the country. All of the electrical and phone lines were missing and had been melted down for the copper. There was still no electricity in the city unless it came through a generator. We drove by building after building that had been gutted, some of them many stories tall. Almost all buildings were pockmarked and strafed by bullets. More than 100,000 people had been killed out of a 3 million population. This was in a civil war, not from an outside bully. The waste was incredible, and I could see no spoils remaining for the victor.

About a month earlier the U.S. embassy had been under siege because it was rumored that the former leader of Monrovia was hiding out there. Many evacuations took place, and U.S. citizens were warned to be careful. Our hotel was about one block from the embassy. But we didn't feel threatened, so apparently things had settled down.

The next morning we began the leadership meetings of our conference. We met in a school hall. Big heavy benches had to be hauled in from the other chapels. It required a lot of work, but I heard no complaints. There were no fans, and the heat became stifling. However, the spirit of the people was inspiring. With all they had been through, they remained true and full of hope. I hadn't witnessed such deprivation since Ethiopia. Yet with all that, the attendance at all meetings was greater in number and percentage than any I had held in the northwest United States.

On Sunday we held two general sessions of conference in Monrovia and Bushrod. Between them, these two districts have about 2,500 members. There was an 80 percent attendance at the Monrovia session, where we met in a municipal building. Again, there were no fans. Occasionally we would feel a little movement of air through one set of windows and out the other. Two other denominations were meeting concurrently. One was directly across the hall, and they were singing, clapping, and having a good time. It didn't really trouble me—instead, I was simply impressed that the community was so religious.

In both sessions the members were reverent, attentive, and responsive. Perhaps the most surprising thing to me was most people were in their seats a half hour early. I was pleased when these two districts became a stake in June 2000.

The next weekend after this conference was spent in Nigeria and the week after that in the Democratic Republic of Congo (formerly Zaire). The work can be grueling when you have a number of

Elder and Sister Pace and President and Sister Banyan Dadson.

conferences and mission tours back to back. Travel alone drains you completely, but the frequent spiritual experiences rejuvenate you more than usual.

Keeping a sense of humor also helps get you through some tough times. This next experience illustrates that point. On November 12 my wife and I traveled to a district conference in Ibadan, Nigeria, where I dedicated another chapel. We left for the airport at 5:30 P.M. only to find they wouldn't start checking us in for two hours. By then our ride had gone. We waited for hours in the stifling and stuffy room packed with people. I was feeling rather impatient. Then I noticed how patient everyone else seemed to be.

The delays were compounded until we finally took off four hours late. We arrived at 1:15 A.M. Nigerian time. It was after 2:00 A.M. before we made it to the hotel.

Our Ghanaian mission president, Banyan Dadson, and his wife picked us up at 7:00 A.M., and we drove to Ibadan for the district conference. Jolene had forgotten her hair spray, so the first thing on her agenda was to find a place to buy some. Sister Dadson took her to the local beautician, where they went to work on her. African women have the opposite problem from white women. White women want to spray their hair to keep the curls in, while African women straighten their hair and spray it on very thick to keep the curls out. They wanted to please Jolene so much that they insisted on demonstrating how good the local hair spray was and how well it held. With her kicking and screaming, they pinned her in the chair and began spraying at point-blank range. The result was that her hair was soaked, matted down, and hard as a rock. She came to the conference looking like a football player wearing a helmet with hair pasted on it. Of course, her helpful husband met her as she came in, took one look, laughed, and said, "So did you find any hair spray?" It went downhill from there for her.

The Spirit in the meetings was strong. I am continually amazed at how much the Lord magnifies his servants when they stand up to speak. It happens in such a way that there is no doubt left in the minds of those who listen. Even when you are quite direct about things that need to be changed in their lives or culture to make it consistent with gospel principles, they just nod their heads in agreement. Periodically I would stop and ask, "Do you really believe that?" And they would say, "Yes." I would then ask, "Why?" Invariably a chorus of voices would say, "Because of the Spirit."

I couldn't help but express to them how grateful we should be for the Spirit of the Holy Ghost. How else could someone come to their country with a completely different background and be believed? Because of their believing hearts, the witness was magnified more than I had ever seen before.

In the general session the next day, the fun continued for both me and my wife. The general session was full of the Spirit in spite of some circumstances that would probably be disastrous back home.

The counselor started to sustain all the officers of the Church, even though it is supposed to be done only in the first conference of the year. When I told him it wasn't necessary, he just skipped to the district officers. I decided to let it go. Then he started recognizing all the branch presidents and everyone on the stand. At least ten minutes later the other counselor began his talk, and he went twice as long as he was assigned. Then another speaker was interjected, which I had not approved. By the time we were to speak we had less than half the time we had planned on. I thought Jolene ought to take some time anyway. In the middle of her talk the electricity went off, so she was speaking without a microphone to 920 people. To add to the problem, a chair collapsed in the back of the hall, sending an older gentleman to the ground. Of course everyone began to turn around. Poor Jolene looked at me and asked, "What should I do?" I just said, "Finish your talk." I think it would be safe to say this was not one of her favorite conferences.

The Blessing of Magnification

Less than a week later I was on my way to Kinshasa, Congo, for a stake conference and mission tour. We had been in our assignment for three months. The experiences that kept coming at us were all so unique that I felt my equilibrium was off. Thankfully, this was not true with spiritual feelings, because they remained constant. I had been to Kinshasa ten years earlier; this was my first trip back. There are about 10,000 members in the Democratic Republic of Congo, which has a population of 50 million. We have one mission there, but the Church is growing very fast.

If you're in Accra, Ghana (where we lived), you don't just get on a plane and fly to Kinshasa. Instead, you go to Nigeria, stay overnight and then fly to Douala, Cameroon, and then on to Kinshasa—if all goes well.

As I was flying to the Congo on that assignment, I kept thinking,

"What am I doing on an airplane called Cameroon Airlines headed for war-torn Kinshasa? I asked the question a little more seriously when we flew into the airport and I spotted tanks and soldiers scattered along the runway.

I was the only first-class passenger to get off. The rest of the cabin was filled with white men headed for South Africa. When I crawled over the person in the aisle seat next to me, he said, "I guess you know this is the Congo?" When I answered in the affirmative he said, "Do you really want to get off here?" With that vote of confidence I walked toward the airport terminal. Everyone was speaking French, which added to my disorientation a little.

My slight apprehension was outweighed by an inner peace I had enjoyed since arriving in Africa. That peace was born out of the reality that I had been called to serve by prophets, seers, and revelators, and as long as I did those things that needed to be done and took no unnecessary risks, my life would be in the Lord's hands. The answer to the danger and difficulty, then, is that you just swallow hard and keep going. I was completely at peace as I looked outside the customs area through a glass window and saw the smiling face of the acting mission president (Elder Langevin). He came toward me a little closer than he should have, and the police angrily escorted him back out. Da Tar, our regional manager, got the police settled down while we headed for the car. Then we were surrounded by the usual eight men wanting to carry my one bag, and another handful who claimed they had been protecting the car. Da Tar arrived again to take care of them. But I felt sad at how desperate everyone seemed to be.

The next morning I went to a zone conference in Kinshasa. The missionaries had been serving for six weeks without a mission president (President Merwyn Waite had had to return home for health reasons) but they handled the situation well. Adding to their difficulty, they couldn't do their work because of the civil war. They were still projecting baptisms in spite of it all.

As I spoke in the different meetings, I was touched at the magnification I received. That was a blessing I noticed over and over again during my three years in Africa—the Lord magnified me. It is hard to talk about it, because I worry about being misunderstood. But it was one of the most inspiring things about my assignment. That magnification was for them and not because of me. I had never before experienced it to that degree, nor have I experienced it to that level since. I was also repeatedly impressed at how I could speak of sensitive things and have the Spirit confirm my words. This blessing does indeed illustrate that *the doctrines of the kingdom have a universal appeal.*

After four hours of spiritually intense meetings, it seemed good to return to the hotel, have a good meal, and relax. I was very tired. For some reason, just before I drifted off to sleep, I remembered that some place very far away at that very hour the BYU versus Utah football game was in progress. It seemed very distant and very unimportant at the time.

I thought of the many games I had watched with seeming life-or-death emotions. In Africa, I was witness to life-or-death scenarios every day, and the people I was serving knew nothing else. Circumstances like these give you a different perspective on priorities.

Teaching and Training

Our general session was held the next day in "the palace," a huge building used by the government. It would have been comparable to holding one of our meetings in a wing of the capitol in Washington. There were 1,650 people present, which was 70 percent of the membership. The place was air conditioned with auditorium seats. It was by far the best physical setting I'd experienced in Africa. I was impressed that so many would sacrifice so much to be there. They came from all over the city of Kinshasa at real expense and sacrifice. Afterward, they all stuck around for a couple of hours mingling with each other, while I was escorted outside for many photo opportunities.

While we were in Kinshasa we attended a missionary zone conference. An interesting sight along the way was a fenced-in zoo. The vegetation was beautiful, but I was informed that it was empty of animals. During the tough times, some of the animals began to starve to death because their food was being stolen and eaten by the zookeepers. Eventually, the animals themselves were killed and eaten. Strange things happen in times of hunger.

When we were home in Accra, the Area Presidency would visit different wards in the vicinity to get a feel for how things were going. For the most part I was astonished at the maturity of the wards; however, there were many opportunities to teach and train. I had one particularly big opportunity in a December meeting I attended in one of the wards—although it didn't turn out as well as I would have liked.

We attended all of the meetings, and I went from class to class to see what I could observe. Overall, I was very impressed with the preparation of the teachers and the participation of the members. I was especially impressed with the children's knowledge of the scriptures and the doctrine. In the Primary, however, I was disappointed to see that one of the mothers had brought her picnic basket and was feeding her kids a sandwich. This was on a fast Sunday.

The fast and testimony meeting was as good as you would see anywhere. The people's expressions were short and concise and were testimonies, not just talks.

During the passing of the sacrament I noticed one "deacon" who seemed to be fairly young. I approached him after the meeting and asked how long he had been a deacon. His response was, "I'm not a deacon." I went to the bishop and brought it to his attention, and he explained he hadn't been able to "get to it yet."

The next week I went to the same meeting and the bishop asked the young man to stand up, asked for a sustaining vote, and informed the congregation that he would be ordained a deacon immediately after the meeting. Then the boy went down, stood next to the deacons on the front row, and proceeded to pass the sacrament. Patience and a sense of humor. A sense of humor and patience. You are dead in the water in Africa without both.

During December we were able to drive to Cape Coast and Elmina, where two castles exist that once housed the slaves prior to their being shipped to various countries. The Elmina castle is four hundred years old. I didn't realize how prominent a role Ghana played in the slave trade. This is a place where they would bring hundreds of people at a time and place them on hold under horrific conditions until the ships came in to take them off to another country. Depictions in movies are probably mild compared to what really happened there. It is impossible to believe men could treat other human beings like that. One thing that surprised me was that 70 percent of the "capturing" and selling was done by Africans themselves, and their own people therefore contributed heavily to the atrocities. Obviously, however, this would never have occurred if there had not been a market in countries like the United States for slaves. A fair amount of sorrow lingered with me throughout the entire day.

The Christmas season was upon us before we knew it. That first Christmas I had a thought-provoking experience with the seventeen-year-old young man who washed our car twice a week. Just before Christmas I put the bucket of soap, water, and sponge outside by the car so Douglas could wash it. (It is a fascinating detail that you have to provide tools to people who visit your house to fix things. It was very common to have a repairman come to our house and ask to borrow a screwdriver or ladder before he could make the repair.)

Before Douglas washed the car, I placed some money in a

Christmas card and left it on the seat. When he saw me later, he greeted me with a big smile and said, "Thank you for what you gave me this morning. It made me very happy." Of course I thought he was talking about the $5 I had given him. But he continued by saying, "That is the first Christmas card anyone has ever given me. I have hung it above my bed."

My journal reads: "He is seventeen years old. I think of my frustration yesterday with email, washing machines, and other problems with the house and realize the people we have come to serve have never even received a Christmas card. It makes me think through my priorities and blessings. We have so much."

I've said far too little about the missionary couples in Africa. Whenever we got a chance we would do something together. I have never experienced camaraderie like it. I think our bond grew partly from the fact that we were all in harm's way, but more of it had to do with enjoying spiritual experiences together and loving the people so much. I won't mention names except when discussing specific experiences because I'd leave someone out. However, the love and respect I have for all those who served with us is akin to what I feel for my own family.

Thus came to an end 1998 in Africa. We looked forward to 1999, which we were certain would bring the construction of the temple. After being in Africa for five months, the time of adjustment was past and a time of focused action was upon us.

6

DISSOLVED IN THE WORK

I once read a quote by Willa Cather that said, "This is happiness: to be dissolved into something completely great." During the next few months we became dissolved in the work to a degree that exceeded anything I had ever before experienced. I'm not sure why this was, but suspect it had a lot to do with how desperately the African people need the blessings of the gospel. In an assignment like this, you get down to bedrock on the purpose of life. The frills and fluff of prosperity are forgotten, and there are no distractions. Every day you observe a society immersed in raw physical and spiritual survival.

As the new year began, my greatest concern was the status of the temple. The groundbreaking had been delayed again and again because the temple had not yet been approved by the city planning commission.

Also of paramount concern was the building of the missionary training center. As noted earlier, African missionaries don't go to a central MTC. They receive that training in their own mission field. In fact, African missionaries aren't even endowed. We had 550 missionaries serving there and none of them had been endowed. (By the time we left Africa the missionaries numbered closer to 900.)

Less than 1 percent of our members had been endowed. That

meant none of them had temple clothes and in the small temples you can't rent them. But a bigger challenge was getting everyone spiritually prepared. The members were excited about a temple, but as a general rule I didn't feel they had a clue as to the magnitude of what was about to happen.

Related to delay in the temple approval process were other manifestations of opposition. The papers were preparing to run an article entitled "The Mormons Are Coming." One of the subsections of the article was "Why the Mormons teach against Christianity and how." We marshaled our public affairs people and tried to have it nipped in the bud, but in the end we were unsuccessful.

The civil unrest in West Africa was very troublesome, and I felt it also was related to our desires to build a temple. Sierra Leone had enough members to become a stake, but the country was in commotion and very unstable. It was in the same condition as Liberia in the time of its destruction. It seemed clear to me that the only thing that would save the African continent was the gospel—and I continued to be amazed at how the Church could grow in the middle of all the chaos.

"At War with the Adversary"

Early in the year I delivered a talk to the Church employees at our first devotional of the year. I spoke of the opposition we were facing, saying, "We have been at war with the adversary as far back as our premortal existence. We are in a war now. Opposition to the work continues." I then quoted President Wilford Woodruff:

"There are two powers on the earth and in the midst of the inhabitants of the earth—the power of God and the power of the devil. In our history we have had some very peculiar experiences. When God has had a people on the earth, it matters not in what age, Lucifer, the son of the morning, and the millions of fallen spirits that were cast out of heaven, have warred against God, against Christ, against the work of God, and against the people of God. And they are not backward in doing it in our day and generation. Whenever the Lord set His hand to perform any work, those powers labored to overthrow it" (*Deseret Evening News*, 17 Oct. 1896).

I also quoted at length from George Q. Cannon, who spoke on the same theme:

"Temple building brings increased power. Every foundation stone that is laid for a temple, and every Temple completed according to the order the Lord has revealed for His Holy Priesthood, lessens the power of Satan on the earth and increases the power of God and Godliness, moves the heavens in mighty power in our behalf, invokes and calls down upon us the blessings of the Eternal Gods and those who reside in Their presence.

"I fully believe that when that temple [Salt Lake Temple] is once finished there will be a power and manifestations of the goodness of God unto this people such as they have never before experienced. Every work of this kind that we have accomplished has been attended with increased and wonderful results unto us as a people—an increase of power and of God's blessings upon us. It was so in Kirtland and at Nauvoo; at both places the Elders had an increase of power, and the Saints, since the completion of and the administration of ordinances in those buildings, have had a power they never possessed previously. . . .

"Every temple that we build excites additional hatred, increases the volume of opposition, the volume of hostility and the threatenings of the wicked. Every temple that we have thus far completed—and every temple of which we lay the foundation—has been another testimony in favor of God and has brought strength to the people of God in enlisting the hosts in the eternal world upon our side; but at the same time there has been stirred up, from the very depths of hell, all the damned.

"Satan and his legions unite with their agents upon the earth in an endeavor to destroy this work and to do everything in their power to obliterate it from the face of the earth; hell is enraged at the work we are doing; hell is stirred up at that which we are accomplishing. Satan sees that which he dreads, . . . and seeing this he is determined to exert every power, every influence that he can muster for the purpose of preventing the spread and growth of this work.

"Satan rages as he views his domain trenched upon, his captives delivered, and the souls of men wrenched from his grasp by the labors of the living for the dead in and through those sacred ordinances that belong alone to the Gospel of the Son of God, administered in holy places by His chosen servants and handmaidens. And it must not surprise us if the rage of the arch-enemy of mankind increases and his emissaries grow more relentless and cruel, more brutal and inhuman in their efforts to stay this work, as the number of temples increases and the thousands of Israel go in thereto to minister the ordinances of salvation for their ancestors and departed friends.

"He [Satan] understands very well that if the children of men will enter into such holy buildings and receive the ordinances there administered and be faithful thereto, his power over them is lost forever, and his kingdom must go down. The struggle with him is a desperate one. He wishes to retain his supremacy on the earth—the territory he has usurped and over which he held dominion, by all the trickery and violence of which he is capable, for so many generations. God designs to overthrow him, to break his power and to have His children live for one thousand years free from his domination. Great issues are involved in this struggle; but God's Kingdom will triumph, and His people will be freed from the thraldom which Satan seeks to impose" (*Gospel Truth*, 366).

After sharing those statements, I said: "I wonder if we realize the magnitude of this time and this place. We come to work each day and get into a certain routine. Soon we will see the ground broken for the temple and we will watch it go up. Will we fully appreciate and comprehend the magnitude of the moment?

"When that temple on Independence Avenue is dedicated it will be like an atomic bomb has been dropped right in the middle of Satan's stronghold in West Africa. It will be the most significant thing that has affected West Africa since the atonement and resurrection of Christ. It will be the beginning of the end of Satan's hold on these countries.

"In addition, think of the thousands of years some of your ancestors have been waiting to have their temple work done. I can assure you there are those on the other side of the veil who are more excited than we are.

"I hope we understand what a pivotal time in the history of West Africa this is. For some reason we have been chosen to be laboring in the vineyard at this significant time. We need to make certain we remain worthy of the trust. Those in this room have been blessed for the time being to spend nearly every waking hour in bringing to pass the Lord's purposes. I hope we will never lose sight of that eternal perspective, even when we are in the middle of some duties that may seem a little mundane. We should be the happiest employees in all of Africa."

That presentation was the genesis of talks I would give throughout all of West Africa in 1999. It became a battle cry to the Saints to make certain we were all awakened to the magnitude of our responsibilities as members of the Church in Africa.

"Sir, I Need Some Spiritual Helps"

On one end of the member spectrum were those who were looking forward to the temple. But there was another end to that spectrum. While we were beside ourselves in Ghana trying to get a temple in Accra, other members would have been satisfied simply to have a Sunday School where they could associate with other members.

We received many letters from isolated members begging to have some contact with the Church and trying to find out if other members lived in the area. For example, we had a flurry of letters from people living in the little country of Gabon, which has a population of 1.3 million. We were not registered as a recognized religion in Gabon, but some citizens from Gabon had joined the Church while visiting other countries and soon little pockets of members sprang up. We also had Church members working for embassies or corporations in these countries. They would talk to people about the Church and then write to see if they could baptize them. This resulted in members all dressed up with no place to go and investigators excited about joining a church that wasn't organized in their homeland.

There is no shortage of fertile places to take the gospel in West Africa. Our problem is being able to service it all. We are having all the growth we can possibly handle. When we arrived in 1998 there were 75,000 members and when we left three years later there were 125,000. When we arrived there were 550 African missionaries serving in West Africa; when we left there were nearly 900. There is no place in the world where we need to be more careful about growing from centers of strength.

Nevertheless, the letters tear at your heartstrings. Here are a few examples:

"December 19, 1998

"Sir,

"I am a Nigerian living in Gabon, but the problems I am encountering here is the Church of Jesus Christ of Latter-Day Saints is not here and I can't cope with the method of the worship of other churches, and I can't attend church and I remain home on Sundays.

"Sir, I need some spiritual helps like spiritual books, Bible, Book of Mormon, magazines. I am in bondage here because no word of

God for me and I am here in darkness with Satanic power all around and I also need hymns in cassettes to help me.

"Please help me and advise me more on what to do."

This letter caused me to do a little research on Gabon. I spent a whole day reviewing all of the correspondence on the country. I was especially touched by a letter from a young father desiring to have the Melchizedek Priesthood. This particular young father had been a priest in the Aaronic Priesthood for ten years and has been teaching his family in their home. Recently another member and his family moved in, so the first brother wrote a letter wanting to know if they could have an official meeting. I can't comprehend his patience. It would seem he would feel so isolated and abandoned that he would just walk away. But he didn't. I received the assignment from President Mason to visit their little group and see what was going on.

A similar letter was received from Gambia, another country where we are not registered. Its population is also 1.3 million.

"Dear President,

"I am a Sierra Leonean living in Gambia. Since I was in Sierra Leone your members were preaching to me but I did not take it seriously. They tried but couldn't but they tried my girl lover whom they got. Later on my lover started preaching to me and I warned her to stop and said I will not worship Mormon, which I always meant be a Mormon. I lately understand the difference when I have got the difference I started listening to her preaching. When there is a trouble in our Country my stepfather whom I am staying with said we should travel to Gambia. I told her and she insisted that I should take a book along entitled *Our Heritage*. I was forced to read this book because I was idle. I later found the Church a leading way and a true way to heaven.

"I was discouraged when I finally know that this church is not in

The Gambia and I don't know the year I would return to Sierra Leone. Please, I want to be baptized in your church. I will like you to find me a way so that I can be baptized for I find the history of your church worthy. Please send me further books and a Bible.

"Your reply is highly needed."

I was constantly reminded of the pioneering aspect of our service. We worked with the first members who will join the Church in some of these countries. It is inspirational to see how the Lord is moving ahead to create a little seedbed of members for when the time is right to open a country to missionary work.

It took a few months before I was able to travel to Gabon, but it was a fascinating adventure and a story that should be told as an example of the continuing pioneering that goes on within the Church. The potential of the Church in Africa is still relatively untapped.

In March 1999 our regional temporal affairs manager in Kinshasa, Da Tar, visited Gabon to do some preliminary legwork for our upcoming trip. He spent a week there trying to find our members. They don't have telephones and their addresses are all post office boxes. We also knew there could be many additional members living there of whom we had no record. In Africa you must be creative, and Africans are very creative. Da Tar came up with the idea of going to a local radio station and making a public announcement asking for any member of the Church to call the station. It worked and was the beginning of his ability to locate our members. It was not until May that I was able to travel to Gabon; that trip will be covered later in this chapter.

Bad Press and Good

Unfortunately, the teaching we wanted to be doing in West Africa was constantly interrupted by emergencies. January brought much concern for our Saints in Sierra Leone. The war was heating up and atrocities were rampant. Many of our members had to flee from their homes. We began to receive pleas for help. My journal reads: "Our biggest concern here has been Sierra Leone. We have not been able to reach our members and we know they must be in bad shape. I keep asking if we have made contact and the answer is always 'not yet.'"

On the next day: "We got word that a couple of our members in Sierra Leone have been killed in the war, but the communications are back up. We hope to be able to house people in some of our chapels and get them some food and emergency supplies."

It was another week before we finally got through to the district presidents. On January 26 I wrote: "The members are in a terrible situation. Many are living in a soccer stadium with forty thousand other people. Some are in our chapels and others are hiding in the bush. Evidently they can get food if we can get them some money. We made the arrangements to get some funds wired to them, and that should happen this afternoon."

No sooner did we get that taken care of than we saw a copy of a local newspaper that said the editors were going to start publishing articles on the Church. The first article appeared the next day. It was the typical anti-Mormon article: 50 percent truth, 25 percent lies, and 25 percent just plain viciousness. We tried to reach the newspaper for a fair hearing, but it was too late. We had to move into the damage-control mode.

My biggest concern was for our members. There were rumors throughout the city that the temple plan was not going to be approved. Now they were going to have to face neighbors who were reading how evil the Church was. As I wrote at the time, "I'm certain this can be overcome, but the members have been through so much. Oh well, this too shall pass."

After two or three articles had appeared we issued a series of rebuttals. I wrote about six of them but will include only the introduction to the first:

"We appreciate the interest *The Ghanaian Chronicle* has taken recently in the doctrine of The Church of Jesus Christ of Latter-day Saints. We further appreciate the publisher and editor of this paper for allowing us to respond.

"Unfortunately it seems to be human nature to mistrust anything that departs from our own perception of normalcy, focusing so much attention on the things that divide us that we lose track of the many things we hold in common that should unite us.

"Few things in life can be more potentially divisive than a different interpretation of religious truth. One needn't search far to find historical verification of that fact, or to find someone willing to provide a litany of various atrocities committed by people in the name of religion. According to early American clergyman Samuel Davies, 'Intolerance has been the curse of every age and state.'

"We are not offended when other religions disagree with the doctrines taught in our Church. One of the chief tenets of our religion is 'We claim the privilege of worshiping Almighty God according to the dictates of our own conscience, and allow all men the same privilege, let them worship how, where, or what they may' (11th Article of Faith of The Church of Jesus Christ of Latter-day Saints).

"While we take no offense with anyone disagreeing with our doctrine, we feel it is unfair journalism to have those who disagree with us be the ones to state what our doctrine is. It would seem much more fair and constructive to allow members of The Church of Jesus Christ of Latter-day Saints to explain the official position of the Church. Therefore, we appreciate this opportunity to share some of our beliefs with the readers."

As is usually the case, this little storm blew over and probably ended up doing more good to the image of the Church than bad.

Even nonmembers came to our defense. Meanwhile, it was time to get back into the field, doing the work of the Lord there. In February we reorganized a stake in Owerri, Nigeria. Once again we found a combination of faith, humor, and challenging differences in culture.

We checked into a "hotel" on Friday night so we could arise early and begin interviews to find a new stake president. We were tired, hot, and hungry and decided to get room service rather than spend the two hours it usually takes to eat out. While we were waiting, Jolene decided she would take a bath—but there was no water. Not just no hot water. No water. The towels in the room looked dark and dingy and were as stiff as a board. They looked like the worst rags Jolene had hanging in her washroom closet at home. After an hour the room service finally came. We had asked for ketchup, and they did bring a bottle of Heinz. I gave him a tip and he continued to stand there. I had already tipped him generously. It finally dawned on me that he wasn't waiting for more money; he was waiting to get the bottle of ketchup back. Apparently another guest had ordered it too, and it was their only bottle, so he needed it back. He watched us dump the ketchup on our plate with a pained look of agony for every drop that left the bottle, and then he took it away. We ate our dinner with much fear and trembling, wondering if we would be sick within three hours, but we had no problems.

The next morning Elder Chris Chukwurah and I began our meetings with the stake presidency at 7:30 A.M. (Actually, we visited only one member of the presidency and the stake clerk. The other members didn't arrive until 8:00 A.M.) By noon we still had five left on the interview list, but these five never appeared. Nevertheless, I was very impressed with the priesthood leadership in the stake. There were three or four men who could have been called. President Declan O. Madu was called. He is a thirty-six-year-old attorney who is very much respected in the Church and community. He will be a great leader.

Prior to issuing calls, we are instructed to interview the wives as well as the leaders. But in Africa the wives are not usually "available." They are at the market and can't be reached. This left us with the undesirable option of issuing a tentative call and telling the priesthood leader it wouldn't be official until the next morning, when he was to bring his wife for her interview. While this is extremely unorthodox, in West Africa you are either flexible or dead in the water.

"When Is the Church Going to . . . ?"

In the priesthood leadership meeting I talked about vision, temple preparation, priesthood government, and a few other things. The African people are tremendously responsive. I was always amazed at their attentiveness. They were so much fun to teach because they would respond out loud and really participate in the presentation—even when I hadn't asked them to!

In the combined stake and ward council leadership training meeting, I spent all my time speaking on self-reliance. That is not the easiest thing to teach when people are so poor and see no way out. As a result, I was forced to come up with a unique approach to teaching this vital principle of self-reliance. Here is a portion of the self-reliance talk I gave in various forms during the three years we lived in Africa:

"I have been coming to Africa for about thirteen years now. My first visit was to Ethiopia in 1985. I came with Elder Ballard to deliver relief that had been donated by our members in the United States to that suffering country. Since that time I have visited Western Africa on about six occasions.

"On those visits the most commonly asked question was 'When is the Church going to . . . ?' You can fill in the blank with almost anything you want. It comprised of things like providing hospitals, medicines, buses to take the people to church, schools, and so on. The list is endless. It was a natural question, because other churches do many things like these. With your indulgence, I would like to tell you a couple of personal experiences I had that helped me better understand the doctrine of self-reliance.

"As managing director of the Church Welfare Services Department in 1981, I was faced with the challenge of recommending to the Brethren changes that could be made to the program to accommodate an international church. One of the key questions was what the Church must do to become independent. The key scripture was Doctrine and Covenants 78:14: "That through my providence, notwithstanding the tribulation which shall descend upon you, that the church may stand independent above all other creatures beneath the celestial world."

"How can the 'Church' become independent? How many farms did we need? How many storehouses and canneries? After months of studying the situation, I was blessed to run across a quote from Albert E. Bowen that changed my whole outlook on the task ahead. He said, 'The only way the church can stand independent is for its members to stand independent because the church is its members. It is not possible to conceive of an independent Church made up of dependent members' (*The Church Welfare Plan*, 76–77).

"I concluded from this that no church can be more independent than the collective independence of its individual members.

"On one occasion I was visiting with President Marion G. Romney not too long before his death. I was talking with him about farms, canneries, and storehouses. He listened and then said, 'Glenn, you are making things much too complicated. The only reason we set up the welfare system was to help people become self-reliant, because the more self-reliant they are the more they are able to serve and the more they serve the more sanctified they become.'

"He referred to this principle in a general conference address shortly thereafter: 'Can we see how critical self-reliance becomes when looked upon as the prerequisite to service, when we also know service is what Godhood is all about? Without self-reliance one cannot exercise these innate desires to serve. How can we give if there is nothing there? Food for the hungry cannot come from empty shelves. Money to assist the needy cannot come from an empty purse. Support and understanding cannot come from the emotionally starved. Teaching cannot come from the unlearned. And most important of all, spiritual guidance cannot come from the spiritually weak" ("The Celestial Nature of Self-Reliance," *Ensign*, Nov. 1982, 93).

"President Romney has also taught, 'It would be a simple thing for the Lord to reveal to President Kimball where the deposits of oil and precious ores are. We could then hire someone to dig them out and we could float in wealth—and we would float in wealth right down to Hades. No, the Lord doesn't really need us to take care of the poor, but we need this experience; for it is only through our learning how to take care of each other that we develop within us the Christlike love and disposition necessary to qualify us to return to his presence' ("Living Welfare Principles," *Ensign*, Nov. 1981, 92).

"If the Lord made it possible for us to come around every stake conference and hand each member a year's supply of money, we would give the money to you with one hand but rob you with the other. What would we be stealing from you? We would be depriving you of the opportunity and necessity of helping each other, which would in turn deprive you of sanctifying experiences.

"This is true of Americans, and it is true of Africans. It is as you take care of one another that sanctification comes. Even if the Church had the resources to buy hospitals and schools and to double the living standard of every member, it could not because by so doing it would seriously delay your purification process. In answer to 'When is the Church going to . . . ?' I would say, it already has. What has the Church given you that is of the greatest significance? The fulness of the gospel of Jesus Christ.

"The real long-term gift to Africa will be the changes that come about in local members of the Church who live the teachings of the restored gospel of Jesus Christ. Some feel that changing the environment is all that is needed to help people. Our doctrine is stated by President Ezra Taft Benson, who said: 'The Lord works from the inside out. The world works from the outside in. The world would mold men by changing their environment. Christ changes men, who then change their [own] environment' ("Born of God," *Ensign*, Nov. 1985, 6).

"The Church will continue to help in emergency situations such as are now being experienced in the Congo, Ivory Coast, Liberia, and Sierra Leone, but even there the members need to do all they can to help themselves and each other. We will also continue to do some humanitarian work. However, the greatest gift the Church will ever give you is the gospel itself."

After I gave a version of this address in Owerri, Nigeria, a brother raised his hand and started asking me a "When is the Church going to . . . ?" question. I didn't have to say a thing. The whole meeting erupted with people saying, "Haven't you been listening? We have to solve these problems ourselves." I was grateful most had gotten the message.

African Zion's Camp

A couple of weeks later we had a productive and interesting mission tour to the Port Harcourt Nigeria Mission, which includes the city of Aba, where the temple site is located. As we traveled to the Aba zone conference, we stopped on the way to visit the recommended site for the first temple in Nigeria. It is a stunning location,

Elder Pace and President Jerry Kirk at the temple site in Aba, Nigeria.

and it felt so good to walk on it and ponder the possibility. At that point a temple hadn't been authorized by President Hinckley, but preliminary plans were being made. Across the ravine from the potential temple site was the stake center where we held the zone conference. Before the conference started I walked out to the lane and looked at the site again, this time from about one mile away, and thought what a magnificent sight it would be to see a temple sitting on top of that hill.

Aba is a tough town. We don't even put sister missionaries there. The roughness of the social environment gave me some pause, but then I thought of seeing the temple in Las Vegas sitting as a beacon in that community, where it coexists with other buildings where all manner of wickedness takes place, and I thought of the influence the temple can have even in tough areas.

At the zone conference, I felt impressed to direct some of my remarks to the issue of preparing for the temple. "As soon as the

Mission tour with President and Sister Kirk in Nigeria, February 1999.

members are worthy, the temple will be built," I said. I was also having some very strong feelings about their ancestors waiting and pleading with them to become worthy and to do their temple work for them. At first I felt these were strange feelings to be having in regard to missionaries, but then the reality hit me that I was looking into the faces of those who would be the future of the Church in Nigeria.

I had my most spiritual experience of the trip just as I was concluding my remarks. I had been talking to them about commitments they made in the premortal existence and how crucial they were to the history of the Church at that time in Nigeria. I told them they were similar to Zion's Camp, because they were the ones who would be leading the Church in Nigeria as it goes from a local membership of thirty thousand to a hundred thousand, and then to a million within their lifetime. I started to leave them with my testimony; as I did so, I looked into the eyes of a handsome missionary sitting right at my feet. As I looked into his eyes I received a powerful personal insight that I tried to express.

I told them that as an especial witness I could testify that they were very dear to the Savior and that he loved them very much. "I can't tell you how vital and important you are, not only to the people you are teaching, but to millions of your ancestors who have waited for so long for the blessings a temple can bring them. I don't know why your ancestors have suffered so long and have been deprived of the fulness of the gospel this long. When we get on the other side we'll ask the Lord about that. In the meantime I can tell you that you must have been a choice spirit to be reserved to come forth at this critical time in Africa's history and be entrusted with the responsibility to liberate so many people. There is a dam holding back your ancestors from receiving all the Lord has, and when the temple is dedicated that dam will break and there will be a flood of millions of Africans flowing into the temple so they can receive of the fulness."

The next morning, as we made a two-hour drive to Owerri for our next zone conference, we had a very humorous experience. In Africa the driving is crazy, chaotic, bizarre. There are few rules, and those that exist are not followed and seldom enforced, which includes the speed limit. It is every man for himself. People cut in front of you, and you have to be very alert. Every car you see is all dented up, which means you always have more to lose than they do. Military personnel are spaced every few miles. I think we got stopped by the military six or seven times on this two-hour drive.

On one occasion President Jerry V. Kirk started to pass a car just as he saw the road block, which meant he had to come to an abrupt stop. The officer walked over to the car with his rifle and asked us to roll down the window. With a glare of ice, this mountain of a Nigerian man said, "Is this the way you drive in your country?" The irony was too much; we all started to laugh. To me, President Kirk had just received the ultimate insult. He had been accused of being a bad driver in Nigeria. I simply responded, "No sir, it has taken him six months to learn how to drive like this." The officer smiled for the first time and waved us on.

On our flight back to Accra we were joined by a missionary who had completed his mission and was returning to his home in Sierra Leone. I asked the elder if he knew if his family was all right and he said, "I don't know." I asked what he would do when he got home. He said, "I will take a taxi to my home and see if it is still standing, and then I will try to find my family." That was a sobering conversation. I thought of the hero's welcome our missionaries from the States get at the airport. As far as I am concerned, the blessings of those who were faithful in Zion's Camp belong to these missionary pioneers.

Apparently, there was a reason for my strong feelings about the temple in Nigeria. Upon our return to Accra we had some meetings with representatives from the temple department, who asked our opinion about the timing of building a temple in Nigeria. They expressed some big concerns about the stability of the country and said they were nervous about recommending we go forward until the country stabilized. I told them their concerns were well-founded, but if we are going to wait until Nigeria is stable we will have a long wait. Instead, we may need to take a giant step into the unknown.

In March we had a meeting with the mayor of Accra, Ghana. It had now been one year since President Hinckley had announced the temple. We had been working with the planning commission since arriving the previous August, only to meet constant stumbling blocks. We came to suspect the problem must be with the mayor of the city, who chaired the planning committee, because the resistance we were receiving just didn't make sense. The meeting didn't resolve our problem, but we were glad to get on his radar screen as people, and not just as an organization.

I learned something interesting while we waited to see the mayor. We waited for a full hour before we were able to see him, even though we had an appointment. During that wait, a constant stream of officials went in and out of his office, including the city attorney, treasurer, and several assemblymen. One of our four members knew every single person who came through. It was interesting to see that the hand of the Lord had been quietly at work. Though we had only fifteen thousand members in a country of 12 million, it was gratifying to see our members are of the stature to be respected. This was especially comforting in light of the adverse publicity we had been receiving.

Besieged with Emergencies

It was hard for our Area Presidency to keep its equilibrium because we were constantly besieged with emergencies. One of us needed to remain in the office at all times. What would be viewed as little emergencies in most places are big emergencies there.

Here's an example of this truth: About one day after our meeting with the mayor, I got an emergency phone call from the missionary couple in Kumasi about an elder with appendicitis. Kumasi is a large city, but our medical officer had not yet cleared the medical facilities for our use. I spent an hour phoning around to see if an appendectomy in Ghana could be safe. I considered flying him to Abidjan, Ivory Coast, but there was no flight for two days. I finally got through to Elder Hales (our medical doctor) in Johannesburg, seeking his counsel, but there wasn't much he could do thousands of miles away. I had to make a decision to get the missionary attended to in Kumasi or risk the four or five hours it would take to have the couple drive him to Accra to a better facility there.

There is nothing you can do at a time like this but do as much homework as you can, drop to your knees, and pray for help. You have to rely on miracles, and you get them.

Another example. We had a conference in Benin City, Nigeria, a week later, which required driving a stretch of road that is known for being very dangerous. We were traveling with President and Sister Dadson, our Ghanaian mission president serving in Lagos, Nigeria, and his two assistants.

They were all very anxious that we leave early enough to arrive before dark. The long road from Ijebu-Ode to Benin City was notorious for thieves after dark. Our traveling companions described how the thieves would block the road or climb trees and throw rocks through the windshields of cars to force them to stop, and then they would rob them. Several of our African employees had been robbed and carjacked on that road over the years. We had been listening to these horror stories for more than an hour when the van started to sputter. We felt it was either bad gas or some problem with the fuel pump. The next town was about twenty minutes away; we limped along until we arrived in Ijebu-Ode, where we have a district of the Church. It was about 3:30 in the afternoon, which was three hours before dark.

We drove straight to the district president's home. He was away, but his young returned missionary son was there and said he would take us to his father's mechanic. We drove through the city, with rain pouring down, navigating through potholes that almost high-centered us on several occasions, to the mechanic's place. The mechanic said he didn't have the right parts (by then we suspected it was the fuel filter), and so he sent us to the "Toyota dealer."

We found the Toyota dealer, went through the gate, and drove up to a shack about ten by twenty feet where ten men were standing over one engine. The owner walked over to our van, pulled out the fuel filter, tipped it upside down, and showed us the mud coming out into his hand. He didn't have a filter, so he sent the district president's son on a motorbike five minutes away to buy one. When he came back he handed the filter to the mechanic, who turned up his nose and said, "It isn't the same." When we asked, "Now what do we do?" he answered, "I'll make it fit." Jolene and I looked at each other dubiously. The mission president, his wife, and the two assistants who were with us are all native Africans, so this scene was not as unfamiliar to them as it was to us.

He "made it fit" within about five minutes and then suggested we buy a spare in case this one also got dirty from bad gas. The assistants then went over in a corner with the mechanic and started negotiating the price. At this point, I was much more interested in getting on our way so we could arrive before dark than I was in getting a bargain. They came back several precious minutes later, after much arm waving, and said he wanted us to pay too much. I asked, "How much did you pay?" The missionary said $2.50. I inquired as to how much the mechanic wanted and he said $3.00.

The next decision was whether to continue the journey or stay in Ijebu-Ode. It was now 5:30 P.M., one hour before dark, which meant the last hour or two of our journey would be in the dark. After a quick prayer we decided to go for it. Otherwise we would have a whole congregation of disappointed Saints in Benin City. With memories of the stories about thieves, it wasn't the easiest decision, but it felt right. Never have I felt so dependent upon instant revelation as I did during my years in Africa.

Thankfully, it must have been an off night for thieves, but we did have some very heart-wrenching moments. The road is lined not only with thieves but also with lepers. They slow traffic down in the same way as thieves—by creating potholes. When a pothole starts to develop, both beggars and thieves will help the hole along. As Sister Dadson put it, "The hole will be small when you go to bed, but when you get up in the morning it has grown much bigger." The large potholes allow the lepers and/or thieves to approach you while you are slowed down. Even though we didn't confront any thieves that night, the sight of the many desperate lepers was sad beyond description.

"The Spirit Says You Speak the Truth"

The meetings of the weekend made any risk worth it. The out-pouring of the Spirit and the love we felt from the people were refreshed every time we were with them. We had been somewhat worried about being able to accommodate the members who would be in attendance in Benin City. Our chapel wasn't very big and would hold only about five or six hundred people. They brought in extra chairs for the patio area, covered it with a canvas shelter, and set up a closed-circuit television. Some sixteen hundred people came, which represented 70 percent of the stake. The members were practically hanging from the rafters.

I've learned that the Spirit is always the strongest when you speak to the people from your heart. In Benin City, I expressed my feelings about trying to understand why I felt such an affinity towards them. I suggested that perhaps we lived in the same neigh-borhood for a period of time in the premortal existence. With that association, perhaps I asked if I could be assigned to work in Africa during this most exciting time of African history. I told them I didn't know what I had done to be so lucky as to be right there right then. They just loved that, and the love I felt coming from the audience was powerful. With the Spirit in the room at that time, they were prepared to accept whatever counsel I gave them.

I then spoke to them about families and especially how we should treat our spouses and children. Before doing so, I reminded them that some cultural traditions sometimes need to give way to gospel-oriented traditions. I then asked everyone to make sure there were no stones within reach because I was going to be very direct. They were extremely receptive. They were very generous in voicing their agreement because "the Spirit says you speak the truth." I have

Sisters at an auxiliary leadership training meeting in Nigeria.

learned that what is said in such meetings ultimately makes little difference; it is the powerful Spirit that is present that does make the difference. A successful meeting has nothing to do with my rhetoric.

Jolene, preceding me, spoke from the heart and the people hung on every word. It was one of her best moments. I could see the people, especially the sisters, were just eating her up. These people are wonderful.

I have never felt so at ease in being extemporaneous as I did in Africa. It seemed like the needs of the people flowed into my consciousness in a very powerful way, as did ideas on how to present the doctrine.

After the meeting, we remained for almost an hour afterward, visiting with the members outside. There was a little seven-month-old baby girl with a pretty little dress and hat whom Jolene took into her arms. As she held her, the baby kept looking into Jolene's face, seemingly knowing something was different. Then the baby slowly reached out her finger and touched Jolene's cheek so gently. It appeared that in the baby's little mind she was curious about the white face. I will always remember that little black hand placed so tenderly on my wife's white cheek. The baby didn't know black or white, but she knew something was different and had the most quizzical, but sweet, look on her face. Jolene was reduced to tears.

For three years of conferences in Sierra Leone, Liberia, Ivory Coast, Ghana, Togo, Nigeria, Cameroon, Gabon, Democratic Republic of Congo, and the Republic of Congo, these types of experiences were abundant. I've agonized over how many to include as I recount some of our experiences, and in the end I know I can include only a fraction of them. I am so grateful to the Savior for allowing me to see the Spirit work with these people and to have felt in a finite way the love he has for them.

As frustrated as we were getting about the delay in getting the temple approved, at one point we received a stark example of what would happen if proper governmental approvals were not received. A new motel was constructed between the airport and our homes. As I drove by the location one day, I was astounded to see that it had been leveled by dynamite. We discovered the owners had gone forward with the building project prior to getting proper approvals. The rubble was being gone through by the populace, who were packing off everything from rebar to cement blocks to boards. They looked like a bunch of ants around the carcass of a dead bug. Within days there wasn't much left at all. It was fascinating to watch as well as to ponder why the motel would be demolished like that. The government officials didn't give the owners time to take out televisions or furniture or anything else. Instead, the government seemed to have an attitude of "We'll show you!" With that visual aid in mind, we continued our quest for proper approvals.

Demolished motel.

Tithing As a Key to the Temple

About this time we learned that I would become the president of the Africa West Area in August of that year. The calling brought an extra weight to my shoulders. I also felt sad that President Mason, who had been serving as area president for five years, would not see the groundbreaking of the temple he had worked so hard to bring to pass. Now the responsibility for government approval of the temple shifted to me, and I didn't know what I could do that hadn't already been done.

We had a conference coming up in April for all of the mission, stake, and district presidents of the Africa West Area. With my upcoming responsibilities on my mind, I prayed and pondered about what my major address should be. A few months earlier I had come to a conclusion that I recorded in my journal: "I'm convinced we don't really have a planning commission problem as much as a problem with the complete commitment of enough members. In some way we've got to get through to them the importance of spiritual preparation *now* rather than waiting until the dedication of the temple."

With that in mind, I decided to speak to the priesthood leaders about tithing. In hindsight, I believe it was the beginning of the major step necessary to enable the Lord's blessings to come.

I started by giving a fairly comprehensive history of tithing, drawing from the Old Testament, Book of Mormon, and Doctrine and Covenants. I then tried to liken the scriptures unto the current circumstances of the Africans.

"Africa is in a situation similar to that which the early members of the Church found themselves in after arriving in Utah. However, the early Utah church did not have anything they didn't earn themselves. No money came to help them build chapels. No one gave them money to build the Salt Lake, St. George, Logan, or Manti temples. No one provided jobs, food, clothing, or medicines. If they had anything, they produced it or earned it by the sweat of their own brow. In the midst of this poverty, apparently the Saints became a little lax in the payment of their tithes, and so the prophet Lorenzo Snow stood tall and boldly taught the law of the tithe to our people. Here is some of what he said:

"'Part tithing is no tithing at all any more than immersing only half a person's body is baptism. I do not know how bishops can justify themselves in giving [temple] recommends to such persons—they cannot after they hear what we have to say to them. When persons do not conform to the law, how can we be justified in conferring upon them the highest blessings that God ever bestowed upon man since the world began?

"'Brethren, I want you to think of these things; for the Lord has manifested to us most clearly that these things cannot go along in this way. It is now time for us to wake up, turn our attention to the Lord, and do our duty.

"'The Lord will not protect those who neglect tithing. Through our nonobservance of this principle we have no promise but that we shall be driven from here as were the people in Jackson County. We cannot claim an inheritance in Zion. It is only through the wonderful mercies of the Lord that we have been protected and blessed with food, raiment, and shelter as we have been for many years past. But now I tell you, in the name of the Lord, the time has come when it will not do for you and me to neglect our duties any longer in this respect' (*Teachings of Lorenzo Snow*, 156).

"The Church was basically bankrupt at this point, and this was the beginning of blessings being poured out upon the Church in general and the members in particular.

"In our General Authority training last October President James E. Faust said, 'Temples will be in all places, and it is a consuming interest of President Hinckley. This is a time of temple building. Those receiving recommends must pay tithing. We cannot afford to lower our standards.'"

I continued, "The Saints in Africa are receiving a return on the tithing they pay over a hundredfold compared to that which they are contributing. This is coming in the form of chapels, missionary funds, the temple endowment fund, and many more temporal blessings.

"And yet as I have traveled around the continent this last eight months the most common question I receive is 'When is the Church going to do more?'

"To paraphrase what Lorenzo Snow told the Saints in Utah in the late 1800s, it is time we as the Area Presidency, speaking on behalf of the First Presidency and Quorum of the Twelve, say to the Saints in Africa:

"Part tithing is no tithing at all, any more than immersing only half a person's body is baptism. We do not know how bishops can justify themselves in giving temple recommends to such persons. We do not know how a stake president can call a bishop, a clerk, executive secretary, elders quorum president, or high councilor who is not worthy of a temple recommend, which includes paying a full tithe. We do not know how a bishop can call a Relief Society president, Young Women's president, Primary president, or other members of the ward council who are not paying tithing. If there are not enough full tithepayers in a stake or ward to cover these and other key positions, perhaps the unit is not mature enough to be a stake or ward and should be taken back to being a branch and district until the people understand and live the doctrines of the kingdom better. When members do not conform to the law, how can we be justified in conferring upon them the highest blessings that God ever bestowed upon man since the world began, which they will receive in the temple?

"How can we pray to the Lord that a path will be cleared for a temple to be built in Ghana, Nigeria, and other places in West Africa when the people are not obeying this most basic of commandments?

"Brethren, we want you to think of these things, for the Lord has manifested to us most clearly that things cannot continue this way. It is now time for us to wake up, turn our attention to the Lord, and do our duty.

"Our temporal salvation depends on our paying tithing. The poorest of the poor can pay tithing; the Lord requires it at our hands, to lay this matter plainly before the people, and we are going to do it. The temporal salvation of this Church depends upon obedience to this law.

"To paraphrase a famous statement by John F. Kennedy, past president of the United States, it is time for Africans to 'Ask not what the Church can do for you but ask what you can do to help build the kingdom and save the living and dead of your countries.'

"We hope this training session in 1999 will mark the time in the history of Africa that the year 1899 played in the history of Utah Mormons. If our members here will respond in the same way the early Saints responded, the Lord will be able to bless members of the Church individually and collectively. Perhaps a future generation will see Africa self-reliant in tithing and enable you to help other countries as Africans are being helped now by the generous tithepayers of other nations. Are you ready to begin that long trek? Are you ready to help the Lord open up the windows of heaven?

"In all of my travels for the Church I have never seen a more faithful, teachable people than we have right here in West Africa. It is my testimony to you that our members will be faithful tithe-payers if they are taught the doctrine by the power of the Holy Ghost. I also testify that the law of tithing carries with it a testimony of its truthfulness, just as the Book of Mormon does. When your flock hear the doctrine, they will understand it and they will obey it."

It gives me chills to read again how bold and straightforward this talk was, and yet I know it was what they needed to hear and what we needed to teach. As you can read for yourselves, we didn't sugarcoat it in the least bit. Africans love and respond to straight talk, especially when they know you love them. Tithing faithfulness steadily improved and continues to do so. The Lord opened "the windows of heaven, and is pouring out a blessing that there shall not be room enough to receive it" (see 3 Nephi 24:10). But I'm getting ahead of myself. When this talk was delivered there was no light at the end of the temple tunnel in sight.

This meeting of all the priesthood leaders of West Africa was followed by a three-day mission presidents' seminar. During the seminar President Charles D. Martin of the Ivory Coast Abidjan Mission got a phone call informing him that one of his North

American missionaries had been slain—Elder Jonathan Phillip Barrett of Morgan, Utah. This is every mission president's nightmare. We were all devastated, and it cast a pall over the rest of the proceedings. I don't like to dwell on these type of things but they are a reality, and it reminds us of the risks of working in these countries. I express my love and appreciation to the family of Elder Barrett and the sacrifice they have made for the African people.

Fear or Faith?

Four days later, with these realities very fresh on my mind, I was scheduled to go back to the Congo to create the second stake in Kinshasa. Obviously, the members were excited about this historic event. I was to leave directly from Kinshasa to go on the trip to Gabon. However, the day before I was to leave we started getting warnings not to go to the Congo.

That day I went into the office for a little while and then went home to take Jolene to do enough shopping to tide her over while I was gone. While there I got two phone calls warning me that President Merwyn Waite (the mission president in the Congo) was a little concerned about my getting into the country. (He had been unable to attend the mission presidents' seminar because of the same issues.) I then received a panic email from South Africa that read, "In a telephone conversation with the D. R. Congo mission president this afternoon, he expressed fears over the rough handling of white men, especially Americans, at the point of entry into Congo."

The official security report stated the following: "State Department sources indicate that the targeting of U.S. citizens and English-speaking individuals of other nationalities associated with missionary groups is driven by an increasing number of immigration-related conflicts at the Kinshasa airport. Authorities have become increasingly suspicious of English-speaking persons using the missionary label. The reason for this is some recent arrests of mercenaries posing or masquerading as missionaries."

On hearing those reports, I decided not to go to the Congo. But as I drove back to the office I did not feel good about that decision. I met with President Mason, and we decided the worst thing that could happen was that the authorities would send me back to Ghana. (In hindsight, I don't think that was the worst thing that could have happened.) My papers were all in order, and I had never been to either Uganda or Rwanda, the two countries they were suspicious of.

The longer you live in Africa the more you realize that you have to get a confirmation from the Spirit in addition to reading security reports. If you went strictly by security reports, you would stay in your house for the full three years. I used to joke with Angie, my Ghanaian secretary, not to give me a security report for two weeks prior to an upcoming trip because I didn't want to know. In reality, we would look at them, talk to the locals, seek spiritual confirmation, and then move forward with faith.

I hurried home and packed. I then felt at peace about the decision to go. In contrast, I didn't feel good at all when I decided not to go. I knew the people would be very disappointed.

I traveled on Ethiopian Air, which brought back memories of 1985. To get there I had to travel all the way to Addis Ababa. The plane was an hour late leaving, so I got off at 10:00 P.M. and arrived in Addis at 4:00 A.M. Ghana time. After I had waited a couple of hours, some of the local airline employees came into the lounge and got me to take me downtown for breakfast. They had secured a transit visa for me. This was an unexpected treat. They took me on a little tour of the city, which I hadn't seen for many years. I saw the Hilton where I had stayed in 1985 with Elder Ballard (where we watched the rain come down after our sacrament meeting), Independence Square (which was built with much criticism during the famine by the communist regime), and a few other things I recognized. It was a real trip down memory lane. The big difference was the lack of the presence of the Russian military, who no longer had control of the country.

After the five-hour layover I was on my way to Kinshasa. It was a five-hour flight and I was a little apprehensive about what I would find at the airport, but I was still at peace.

When I arrived, I could see five friendly faces of people I knew on the other side of customs, so I waved to make sure Immigration could see I would be missed if they hauled me away. Rather than state that I was a missionary, I said I was a pastor. They were preparing to wave me through when I recognized an airport employee I had met on my previous trip. He thought I was having trouble and so he came to my "rescue" and told the nice officer I was a missionary. With that they took my passport and walked it back to the supervisor, who looked at it and scowled at me for about five minutes.

I'm sure if my passport had contained visas from Uganda or Rwanda I would have been detained and possibly kept out. Except for that little glitch everything went smoothly, and my protectors rushed to my aid as I emerged and took me to their car through the usual crowds of beggars. It was a great relief to be with them (Da Tar and others). I always feel better moving around when I am flanked by Africans.

Early the next morning Elder David Eka and I began interviews with priesthood leaders, called a stake president, Kola Tusey, and his counselors, and held our priesthood and combined leadership meetings. I don't remember ever being more tired, but I was grateful I had arrived safely and happy for the Saints that on the next day there would be two stakes in Kinshasa. I turned on the television and collapsed in bed. I then received a shock. Right there in Kinshasa, Congo, on a Saturday night at about 8:00 P.M. the Utah Jazz versus Houston Rockets game emerged on television, being telecast in French. All of a sudden I didn't feel quite so far from home.

President and Sister Kola Tusey of the Kinshasa Masina Stake.

On Sunday I met with the wives of the counselors I had been unable to interview the previous day, then we held the general session of the conference. Our meeting was in the Parliament Palace again, just like the previous time. It was the best facility I had ever met in since going to Africa. It was full with twenty-five hundred people from the two stakes, which represented about 75 percent attendance. Many walked for two hours, and others spent a lot of money they didn't have on transportation. I was so grateful I had followed the prompting of the Spirit and not given in to my own fears of the unknown. The meeting was so wonderful I wrote of it, "It was a Pentecostal experience."

Baptisms in Gabon

After this stake reorganization, I left with Da Tar for our much-anticipated trip to Gabon. We passed through Cameroon and stayed

Priesthood leaders, including twenty-one stake presidents.

overnight in Douala. We had a small branch there, which was very isolated because we could no longer service it from Kinshasa—the mission president was spread too thin and travel was dangerous. To make things worse, once you got out of the country you might not be able to get back in.

We hired a taxi to take us around the city; our tour included a visit to the home of the presiding elder of the little Douala Branch. He was traveling, but we met his wife and daughter. They live in a very modest home in a humble neighborhood and hold their meetings in their home with about twenty-five in attendance. As we went into their living room we could see sacrament trays, hymn books, manuals, and Church pictures hanging on the walls.

It was a thrill to see how that little group of Saints could keep functioning with a few supplies and even less supervision. The Holy Ghost doesn't seem to need a formal organization prior to communicating with individual hearts.

It was good to get to know Da Tar very personally on this trip. If I found myself lost in a jungle somewhere in Africa, he is the one I would cry out for. He has been through so much. He is from Liberia and in his young married life he lived with his wife in Monrovia. He had a good job working with the U.S. Embassy, which threw a lot of suspicion on him from both sides during their vicious civil war. He was also the district president of the Monrovia District. One time the military picked him up and took him, along with many others, down to the beach and lined them up to kill them. They would just shoot them and let the strong undertow in that area take them out to sea. As he was standing in line an officer drove up in his jeep. He stopped and pulled Da Tar out of the line and said, "You don't belong here." He was taken away and dropped off where he could walk home. To his knowledge, everyone else was killed. I knew I could always rely on Da Tar to get me out of tight places.

At five o'clock the next morning we left for Libreville, Gabon. Libreville, like Douala, is more modern than the other big cities of West Africa I have visited. We hired a taxi to take us around the city. We also visited with a couple of attorneys to explore what we would need to do to become registered in the country. We also wanted their opinion on whether we would be acting within the law to baptize and ordain some people in Mouila, which is where the little handful of members were living. We were assured that we would indeed be acting within the law, and they were surprised we asked. Nevertheless, we are always careful because the work could be held back for years if we ever get careless about honoring and obeying the laws of the land, even if those laws seem extremely primitive to us.

By 9:00 A.M. we were on our way to Mouila, Gabon, where two or three isolated families had been waiting for years to have some of their children baptized and to receive the priesthood. My first impression as we flew into the city was how small it was. It contains

Da Tar giving precious curriculum materials to Ava Bessey in Mouila, Gabon.

about twenty-five thousand people, and doing much work there would not be consistent with the principle that we should build within centers of strength. I was somewhat saddened at that, but I was overwhelmed with a desire to see these members. I think deep down I was trying to practice the principle Elder Ballard taught me in Ethiopia when we went through so much trouble to see one member.

We were greeted with enthusiasm by Ava Bessey, the brother who had been pleading for the Melchizedek Priesthood for so many years. By the look on his face, our visit was second only to the ushering in of the Millennium. He had a great big smile on his face and was very excited to tell us about the people who wanted to be baptized.

He took us to the hotel, which stands in the bush alongside a big river called the Ngounie. This was probably the most isolated spot I had ever been to in Africa.

We gave him the manuals and pamphlets we brought with us.

He picked them up one by one like they were pure gold. He informed us that the rest of his family wanted to be baptized. We were soon joined by Brother William Botulu, the only Melchizedek Priesthood holder in the city. He and his wife are members who had joined the Church in Egypt about ten years earlier.

We were informed that three adult men would join us soon; they wanted to be baptized, and their wives would join soon after. There were also about ten eight- to sixteen-year-olds who wanted to be baptized. We explained we would not be able to baptize anyone until we were assured of their worthiness and their understanding of the Church. We were also told there was a meeting at 5:00 P.M. where friends and dignitaries were going to come to hear about the Church. This was all more than we had asked for or approved.

With this deadline, we began teaching and asking questions to see the extent of the understanding of all these people. My room was full, as was Da Tar's. The first thing we found out was that some of them were not legally married. We informed them we would teach them but couldn't baptize them until their marriages were formalized. They were disappointed, but accepted the decision.

We taught for four hours straight and found their understanding to be quite good. We quit at about 4:45 P.M. to prepare to go to the meeting and didn't have time to privately interview any of them for worthiness. It became obvious that if there were going to be any baptisms they would have to wait until after church on Sunday.

At 5:00 P.M. they took us to the civic center, a very nice little building with air conditioning and a sound system. There was a crowd of about sixty waiting patiently for us, and only three of them were members. They had a choir made up of the youth who wanted to be baptized. I addressed them about the Church in very general terms. Brother Botulu invited the whole crowd to return for the service on the next day and to attend the baptisms.

By the time we were finished it was 8:00 P.M., and we hadn't eaten since the previous night. We went into a "restaurant," where they gave us a menu and then proceeded to let us know they only had two things, goat meat or beef. Neither choice sounded very appealing, but since I was hungry enough to eat a cow I ordered the beef.

When we came out at about 9:30 P.M., Brother Botulu pulled up in a taxi and told us he had another family of ten that wanted to be baptized the next day. I asked where they had been all day and he said they hadn't known about the meeting. They thought they could just show up and be baptized. So I set that interview up for nine o'clock the next morning.

It was exciting to see that thirty people wanted to be baptized. I felt like the first missionaries must have felt back in 1978. I also gained a greater respect for the challenges they met in having to teach the most basic things. Dampening my excitement somewhat, however, was a lingering worry about how these new converts would survive without training and supervision.

On Sunday morning the Ngadzoukou family came in for their interviews to see if they could be baptized. Two of them were under eight, and it turned out that of the remaining eight only four wanted to be baptized, the father and three children. The wife wanted to wait and see. The father teaches science at the local high school and is quite well known in the community. Thankfully, they had been taught well by Brother Botulu so I didn't have to delay their baptism.

We held a Sunday School that was attended by fifty or sixty visitors. Just as we were about to start, a television crew came in and started the cameras. Rather than create ill will, I allowed the cameras to roll. I had William Botulu sustained as the group leader or presiding elder and gave a talk about the Savior. After the service, I did a couple more interviews for baptism and then we headed for the "font."

I got in the front of a pickup truck, and fifteen people climbed

Members on their way to a baptism in Gabon.

in the back. We were joined by three other vehicles equally full. The next thing I knew we were at the airport driving down the runway. I asked, "Can we do this?" Brother Bessey said, "Yes, I'm in the military and I got permission." At the end of the runway was a little swimming and washing hole in a tributary beside the Ngounie River. As we arrived, ladies were doing their washing and a bunch of boys were swimming. I was impressed at how respectful they were when they found out we were coming to do some baptisms. They cleared the river and watched. There were probably a total of sixty people present, including our own party.

We ended up baptizing seven people. We also ordained Cedrick Bessey a priest. (He was nineteen years old.)

The setting was beautiful. The backdrop was the jungle, and the water was just waist deep. It was a thrilling sight to see those black faces in all-white clothing and the hands of those priesthood brethren raised to the square. We had brought four sets of baptismal

Boys swimming in a tributary just before the Saints used this site for their baptismal service in Gabon.

clothing from Kinshasa. The people were thrilled that we were going to leave the clothing with them. As the first new convert came up out of the water the crowd began to applaud. After getting them shushed, we went on. I glanced up at the people lining the bridge just in time to see a monkey climbing on it. That really made it feel like Africa.

Just before the last person was baptized there was a rustle in the crowd, and several people headed for their cars. They had been alerted that a plane was coming in and they would have to move their truck and cars. I don't suppose I will ever see a more unique baptism the rest of my life. For a brief moment as I stood at a river in oppressive heat, watching a monkey climb around a bridge, not understanding French, watching Africans baptize Africans, I wondered to myself, "Am I really here? Yes, I am here. *Why* am I here?"

After the baptism we got back in the truck and headed for the civic center to do the confirming. All this time the television crew had continued with us. After the confirmations I was interviewed.

The Botulus and the Besseys

We returned to our hotel late that evening wondering if it had all been a dream. While pondering in my motel room, I jotted down these thoughts about the weekend: "Building from centers of strength is an inspired strategy. If we had not exercised restraint, we could have baptized thirty or forty people and started a branch of 100 to 150 within three months, but they are so isolated we need to be careful because we can't adequately service them. Small branch problems would kill the little branch without adequate supervision and teaching. Mouila, Gabon, is not in a center of strength, to say the least. We will need to wait until a mission is formed in Cameroon and Gabon. Nevertheless, there are seven more people who have now received the Holy Ghost to guide and protect them."

As I thought about the events of the day, I increased in my respect for the missionary pioneers of the 1970s and 1980s. I was able to see firsthand how easy it would be to get members and yet how much teaching had to be done in the most basic of doctrine and procedures. These pioneers also had to deal with the interpersonal relationships of the members of a small branch. Even on that baptism day in Mouila we had to put out a fire that erupted with three of the families. Some were questioning why their friends couldn't be baptized when others could. They argued that their friends had been attending church longer than the ones who were baptized. They settled down when I reminded them that these friends could be baptized as soon as their marriages were formalized.

Later in the evening we had a wrap-up meeting with the Botulus and Besseys at the hotel. We had earlier called Brother Botulu to be the presiding elder. We gave him authorization to have the sacrament, promised to send him some copies of the Book of Mormon, authorized him to baptize the three men and their families when they legalized their marriages, authorized him to baptize the eighteen- and nineteen-year-olds living at home when they received their parents' permission, and told him he could ordain Brother Bessey an elder on August 1. He was cautioned not to let the branch grow any larger than what we had authorized.

One last experience of the day was reported by Brother Bessey. That afternoon as we were leaving the civic center, a policeman came by waving his arms and wondering why we were gathered there. For some reason he was concerned that we were organizing anti-government activities. We talked our way through it, but later that day Brother Bessey looked the officer up and gave him the pamphlet *For the Strength of Youth*. Later that night the policeman approached him and asked where he could get more of those pamphlets. The policeman had gone home and read it and gathered his family around him and read it to them. He then told them, "This is what you should be doing."

The next morning we went to breakfast at the motel "restaurant." I asked for a ham omelet, but the waitress said, "We don't have any ham." So I said all right, just give me the omelet with no ham. She shuffled away (we were the only ones there) and came back with rolls, butter, and orange juice. We asked about the omelet and she said, "No eggs." We asked what else they had and she said, "Just this." She then shuffled back to the kitchen, and we never saw her again.

In the middle of the night I woke with a start and realized with everything going on I had neglected to set Brother Botulu apart as the presiding elder. I was in a panic as to how I would get that done, since the plane would leave at 11:00 A.M. However, at 9:00 A.M. he and his wife "dropped by" to tell us good-bye, so I was able to set him apart before we left.

This is just one of many little miracles we have seen. Communication in West Africa is such a problem that the Lord seems to fill in the airwaves with the Spirit when there is a real need. At home, where we aren't as dependent on him (or at least we don't think we are), these things either don't happen or we don't recognize them when they do. Here, the people need the intervention and have the faith to follow the Spirit's promptings, and they give credit to the right source when those promptings do come. As a result, they come more often.

We left for the airport, which consists of a couple of carport-type structures that protect the luggage and the people if it rains. Other than that you just stand on the runway and wait for the plane. While we were waiting, two policemen approached us. They said, "Pastor, will you come and pray for a young woman who is afraid to get on the plane?" As it turned out they were taking a mentally disturbed young woman to an institution in Libreville, and she was out of control. So we went over and stood by the police truck and prayed for her. Subsequently she settled down. I couldn't help but compare that to home, where it might actually be against the law for the police to ask you to pray. It also demonstrates the natural faith of the people and their reliance on God.

As we waited, I witnessed something that absolutely broke me up with laughter. A lady came walking toward the luggage cart. All she had in her hand was a dead animal that looked like a cross between a rat and a beaver. She was carrying it by the tail and nonchalantly laid it on the baggage cart. I couldn't believe my eyes. Soon a man came over with a bag, placed the dead animal in it, tagged it, and gave her the claim check.

Our experiences in Gabon illustrate two of the key principles of this book: *The Savior's love for his children is universal, and the doctrines of the kingdom have a universal appeal.* That experience also demonstrated to me how long-suffering members can be once they have been touched by the Spirit and know the Church is true. This dedication of the African people has been repeated countless times over several decades and will continue into the future. In my opinion, the patience and faith of the African people will result in a membership in the millions in the not-too-distant future.

This particular experience also demonstrates the theme of this chapter, which is the blessing of becoming "dissolved in the work." In Gabon, every waking hour was spent teaching because there was so much for the members in that pristine environment to learn.

Shortly after my return from this trip, the Masons left for home. The challenge of obtaining approval for the temple now fell upon my shoulders.

7

THE TEMPLE APPROVAL
ROLLER COASTER

In June 1999 we continued to get rumors and promises that the approval of the temple by the planning commission was imminent. Here are some journal entries that are representative of the types of things we heard. Each of the following paragraphs was pulled from a different day in June:

"Carl Champagnie, an employee of the temple department, came in all excited this morning and said we should get the word from the planning commission on the temple Thursday. Of course, I have heard that before, but it does feel like it is getting close. This means we could be breaking ground in July or August."

"We got good news that our work in public relations to get the temple approved is going well and that we could get a letter as early as this week. The only glitch is they would like to see us tone down the temple some and make it shorter and the office building higher. We'll deal with that later. We aren't getting too excited until we see it, but it would be great if we do get the letter."

"Elder Opare called me at home at 6:00 A.M. [Africans get up very early] to tell me the latest news about the temple. It appears they are going to be preparing a letter tomorrow approving everything but the temple. They don't want to start a precedent of allowing churches to be built on Independence Avenue. They actually said if we toned it down (hid it behind the office building), it might be acceptable. The good news is they are making decisions. Apparently they are getting pressure to move on it from every sector of government."

On June 29 we got the best news about the temple since President Hinckley had announced it a year and a half earlier. My journal entry reads: "We had a letter handed to us that said the temple had been approved contingent on a couple of minor concessions on our part. We are holding back getting too excited until we are sure what it means."

A day later: "We had a meeting with our architect and a member of the planning commission. It looks like the letter is for real and we can start as soon as we are ready. The pressure is on our own people now to get bids. We still may be three months away, but at least everything is in our control. This is very exciting. We also got news that we will be piloting a family history project that will allow work to be done from oral histories. This will allow the most humble of the Africans to take their ancestors to the temple by just knowing names and relationships. This will be an exciting couple of years the way things are coming together."

And then only two days later: "When I got home, Carl Champagnie came to the house all discouraged because he had just left the planning committee and had been given another letter that was to supersede the letter we got last week. This letter stated the temple was to be excluded from the plan. He was so discouraged. The committee's shabby treatment of our case is matched only by their lack of professionalism. We keep trying to rule out discrimination against the Church, but we can't see any other reason for this.

"We have all been a little down due to the new temple problems. I see no alternative than to keep fighting. That piece of ground just seems so right. If we abandon it, we assume we will have a very difficult time finding another acceptable piece, and even if we located one we have no guarantee it would be approved if indeed our problems are political."

A few days later: "We had a meeting with our attorneys and architects this afternoon on the continuing saga of getting the temple approved. The latest version is that the mayor was not in the meeting when they sent out the letter last week and he was upset they didn't consult him and sent out the second letter. We decided to have the attorney and architect meet with the mayor and try to resolve the question as to why we are having these problems. Once we know the real reason we are being refused we can prepare an appeal. If that doesn't work, we will be going to a higher level."

The news went downhill from there. Two further journal entries illustrate that:

"The news we are getting on the temple isn't good. They have told us the majority of the committee voted against the project for zoning reasons. If the zoning law is sound we won't have much to appeal."

Finally, on July 13, just four weeks before the Masons were to go home: "The temple situation is looking very bleak right now. No news at this point is bad news. We are preparing an appeal. . . . If we have to abandon the site, it could delay the temple for years."

For a year we continued to have our excitement thrashed to pieces time after time. I felt nearly as bad for Elder Mason as I did for the African Saints. He would return home four weeks later, and this would have been the best send-off he could possibly have received for his great service. This sympathy was replaced by empathy during the next two years, as these problems became my own. Of course, in the face of such disappointments, you can't really do anything but keep going and teaching the people.

Challenges at Home and on the Road

Getting the temple approved was far from the only problem. In late July Jolene and I were traveling to Brazzaville, Congo, for a district conference and then a mission tour. Brazzaville was a city that had been racked with intermittent war since 1997. In fact, our mission president was evacuated from there a year or so earlier right in the middle of a civil war.

The night we left, our youngest daughter (Jo'ell) was going into the hospital to be induced to have her second child. She was having some problems with her pregnancy, so we were very concerned about her and felt helpless because we wouldn't be able to reach her and her husband for several days, if not longer. I remember kneeling at our bed just before we left and pleading with the Lord to be with our daughter since we could not. I felt especially sorry for Jolene. It seems that a mother has a right to be with her daughter at a time like this. Yet all we could do was put the matter in the Lord's hands and be about his business.

Our flight to Kinshasa (the first leg of our journey) was on time and all went well, although airport immigration officials took a long time approving us. We were the first ones in line and the last ones through. When we were picked up at the airport, we asked if there had been any word by email about our grandson's birth. The answer was no. Later that night President and Sister Waite called to let us know they had just received a message saying the birth went fairly fast, but there was some concern for the baby so the doctor had sent him to intensive care. It sounded like it was fairly routine, but we anxiously awaited further word.

We were so tired all we could think of was a nice hot bath and bed—but since this was Africa there was no hot water. We were also hungry, but I couldn't communicate with the nice person over the phone in French so I went downstairs and drew a picture of a sandwich and French fries and handed it to the waiter. That worked just fine.

The next morning the Waites picked us up and took us down to the "beach" to catch a boat to cross the Congo River to Brazzaville.

The scene at the dock was something straight out of the movies. There was a mass of humanity (generously sprinkled with thieves) on the outside, with many begging for food. Fortunately, we had our African escorts with us. They had arranged for people to carry our bags and paid them so we didn't end up with twenty people all wanting money for helping.

We parked the car, paid someone to watch it, and made our way to the gate, which was guarded by police. All kinds of people were trying to "crash the gate"—there was a lot of pushing and shoving going on and people screaming at each other. It was utter chaos. Once we got through the gate things got a little more organized, but I wouldn't say they got more efficient. You rent the boat in one place, show your passport in another, go to a third place to get your name on a list of passengers for government control, and go to a fourth to have your bags searched.

The ferries had a stream of people carrying sacks of flour and other commodities and animals to be shipped across the river. As we walked down the ramp to the boat, we had to be careful where we stepped because there were big holes in every other plank. Getting into the boat was interesting as well, because one just stepped off the dock onto the front of a speedboat. I pictured myself losing balance and falling into the water, much to the delight of the Africans.

In some ways I thought it would have been worthwhile to have taken the ferry just for the experience. We desperately wanted to take a picture, because the scene cannot adequately be explained. But it was against the law to do so, and I'm sure we would have lost our cameras (or worse) and so it wasn't worth the risk. After all the time-consuming preliminaries, it took only about ten minutes to cross the river, even though it is huge and carries several times more water than the Mississippi.

When we reached the other side, we found a delegation of about ten people waiting for us, consisting of the district presidency and auxiliary leaders. The sisters presented Jolene and Sister Waite with bouquets of flowers.

On the way to the hotel we could see that building after building had been destroyed. Two large hotels had been completely gutted, and no effort had been made to rebuild them. One was a Hilton and the other a Sofitel; both were ten to fifteen stories high. Every building we saw was pocked with bullet holes, and devastation was everywhere. The hotel they took us to was called the Meridian, which is part of a chain. The owners had just finished rebuilding it. But we saw that the mirrors in the foyer had a spray of bullet holes in them. After checking into the hotel we left for the chapel. It had also recently been renovated, since it too had been heavily damaged by the war. I felt the devastation to the buildings seemed worse than in Liberia, but Brazzaville at least had some electricity.

Our members had been living in the bush to escape the war and were just working their way back to their empty homes. As I contemplated this visit, I was troubled, wondering what I could possibly say to members who had been through what they had experienced. When I finally arrived at the leadership session, I was somewhat perplexed to feel compelled to speak about tithing. I didn't want to. Here I was looking at people who were as impoverished as any of our members in the world, and I was impressed to speak very boldly about tithing. I was surprised with the strong feeling I had that that was the most important thing they could do as they began rebuilding their lives.

As I stood to speak in the combined stake and ward council leadership training meeting, I realized that at that very moment, 4:00 P.M. Congo time, the Days of '47 Parade was starting in Salt Lake. I thought of the stark contrast between the events of that day in Salt Lake and those in West Africa. I described the scene to them and concluded by telling them the whole day would be a celebration of the Mormon pioneers and all of their sacrifice. I said I would love to be there in Salt Lake City, "but at this moment, I would much rather be *here*, doing what I can to help the African pioneers who are struggling, than at home celebrating the accomplishments of my ancestors." It was a special feeling of the moment, and they responded with much love.

That evening at the hotel Jo'ell's husband, Rusty, reached us on the telephone. The connection was very poor, but we found out the baby was just fine. However, Jo'ell had serious complications, so serious that we could have lost her. As Rusty was explaining the situation, I was grateful to feel that the Lord would intervene, to a large extent because we had sacrificed being with her to help the people in the jungles of the Congo. We had been feeling helpless to be so far away, but we remembered our prayer when we left her welfare in the hands of the Lord, and we were comforted.

In Their World but Out of Their World

The general session of the conference was held in the hotel's largest room. The first thing we found was that they didn't have any chairs because they were all stolen during the war. We had visions of eight hundred people showing up an hour early and standing through the entire meeting for lack of chairs. Thankfully, we were able to "hire" some, and they arrived just before we began. We could still seat only about four hundred people, and we had seven hundred in attendance. It was humbling to hear of the sacrifice they all went through to reach the meeting; I could only pray that I might say something to make their sacrifice worth their while. At the same time, of course, I knew that only the Spirit could repay them for such a great sacrifice and that my real job was simply to try not to do anything to detract from the work of the Spirit.

As I sat waiting for my turn to speak, I found myself trying to think what President Hinckley would say to them if he knew of their situation. Several things came to my mind, which I passed along as if

I was speaking in the first person. I hope President Hinckley wouldn't mind my assuming that investiture of authority. Without question, it was the most effective part of my talk.

When we retired for the evening, before dozing off, I remember wondering if we had made a difference. What can you do to help people in such dire need? From a physical standpoint, I was at least able to assure the people that they would have food and clothing. (Yet as you say those things in one breath, you have to teach self-reliance in the next.) From a spiritual standpoint I felt I had brought them comfort by speaking of President Hinckley.

The next day we repeated the Congo River experience in reverse. It felt unreal to observe the life going on all around us. I felt somewhat like I was in a protective bubble or was just seeing these things on a movie screen. It didn't seem fair in some ways that we were living in their world but were still out of their world. However, as long as the Lord would allow it, I was willing to let their cup pass me by. I spent a lot of time wondering if I was as grateful as I should have been for all I had been given.

In Kinshasa, we had a zone conference for the forty missionaries serving in the Kinshasa area. There are another twelve in Lubumbashi, whom I would see a month later. I was very impressed with their skills as well as their spirit. None of them had attended a missionary training center, but their skills, as demonstrated in role playing, were as good as any I'd ever seen.

We met a sister missionary who received her call during the war in January and walked more than two hundred miles, including crossing the Congo River in a canoe, to get to Kinshasa to honor her mission call from a prophet. The journey took her about three months. These fifty-two missionaries were baptizing about seventy-five people a month, and retention of new members was high.

That evening Jolene and I went to the hotel restaurant for dinner and bumped into two Church employees who were visiting from

South Africa. We learned they had gone for a walk in the afternoon and hadn't gone one block before a car pulled up beside them. The men in the car said they were government officials and instructed the Church employees to get in the car. They unwisely did so. The men in the car drove them some distance away, then robbed them at gunpoint of $1,200. They were very shaken, but the Lord was merciful and they were unharmed.

Detained by Armed Soldiers

All of our official duties were over the next day, so before the flight home we decided to go on a little drive along the Congo River. We specifically wanted to see a place where the elevation decreases resulted in some gigantic rapids. As we started to take some pictures the people in a nearby village began to scream and yell at us, so we drove to a place where there were no people and took some more.

When we turned around to go back, two soldiers pulled up in a car, got out, and walked over to us. They said we would need to go with them for questioning. They got into our car and we went back to about where we took the first batch of pictures. When we arrived, the soldiers were joined by several others, some of whom had rifles. Our driver got out of the car and tried to reason with them. They responded by taking our passports and President Waite's digital camera. We learned that we were in a secure area because the river separates the two Congo countries, and when there is an attack from rebels they would cross at that point.

After about a half hour we could see our driver was getting very nervous. He asked us to call Da Tar (my jungle fighter who took me to Gabon); Da Tar talked to the soldiers on the phone and then told them he was coming. We also called the embassy to let them know what had happened. The embassy spent ten minutes telling me how stupid we were to take pictures. I pled guilty to all their accusations and concluded, "Now could you help me deal with the fact that I've got soldiers standing next to me with rifles pointed at me?" With that their tone changed, and we received some instructions, including telling the soldiers the embassy was aware we were there.

At this point we started attracting a lot of attention from the roadway, and the soldiers instructed us to go down the road behind some buildings. I said, "We're not going anywhere." In a half hour Da Tar arrived, and the negotiations began anew. He and the driver would periodically give us a status report. By now we knew the soldiers mostly wanted money. When Da Tar refused to give it to them, they said we would have to go with them to their superior. Da Tar said we were perfectly willing to do that.

Again they rode with us as we drove our car to an army office out in the middle of nowhere. When we arrived, the soldiers took their officer off to the side and told him the story. As soon as they came back, Da Tar said, "Sir, I can tell you right now your soldiers are lying to you. If they were honest they would have talked to you in front of me." To this the soldiers all laughed.

We were watching the conversation from the car with much interest. When they all laughed, Jolene said, "Well, it must be going well." I wasn't convinced because they had laughed two hours earlier as well, and I suspected the laughter was at our expense. Right after that they all became animated again and started shouting at each other. Then, all of a sudden, we saw the camera come off the shoulder of one of the soldiers, and the passports were handed back to our heroes. The superior officer came over to the car door, and I stepped out. He extended his hand and apologized for our inconvenience. I told him if we had done something wrong it was us who owed him an apology. He smiled at that.

We found later that Da Tar had explained we were missionaries and meant no harm. The officer asked if the soldiers had asked for any money, to which we responded they had. He said they would be disciplined. We pleaded with him not to do anything, because we were obviously in the wrong. We also learned that since the people in the village had seen us take the pictures, they had to detain us or lose the respect of the people.

We decided visiting one site was enough and thankfully drove back toward town. This experience demonstrates how fast an innocent action can be transformed into a huge problem. It could have become very ugly or even fatal. They could have done anything they wanted to us, and nobody would have known the difference.

When we got back to the mission home, Da Tar brought his wife and children over to meet us. We tried to explain to them what a hero their father was. He wouldn't accept the praise. He has faced so many challenges in his life that he now just takes such things in stride. He says, "I have been saved from death so many times, I just know I cannot be killed until Heavenly Father says I have lived long enough." That is the way he lives his life.

Our flight was not until three o'clock the following morning. We had heard the drive to the airport was not safe at that hour, but we had no other options. After our experience with the soldiers we were feeling a little jittery. But we arrived without incident. Da Tar went back home after he got us situated at the airport, but another employee stayed with us all night to make sure we got on the plane safely. How can I sufficiently express gratitude for those Saints who risked their own lives and would gladly give up their lives for us? You can't pay a person enough for what they do, and they wouldn't do it for any amount of money. As I pondered my feelings of gratitude, the answer came to my heart: "You can thank them by getting them a temple." That didn't bring too much comfort, since I had tried and failed miserably for over a year.

Taking the Temple to the Top

When we got back to Accra we learned the temple approval was dead. Just a day or two before the Masons returned home, we decided to make one last attempt. We had nothing to lose. We had a member who had access to the president of the country, Jerry Rawlings. We gave him a blessing and sent him on an errand to ask President Rawlings if he would intercede. We had hesitated doing this earlier because we felt it would be better to work within the system. But at this point our application on the temple had been rejected. We finally decided it was time to play our trump card.

August 10 was the Masons' last day. They had been out of the United States for five years—four years in Johannesburg and one in West Africa. They deserved to be home with their family. I went to the airport and dropped them off.

Our home is directly under the flight path, and the planes rattle the house and set off the car alarms as they take off. As I heard their plane I walked out the back door and watched it fly over the house at about 8:45 P.M. I missed them immediately and felt the weight of responsibility descend upon my small shoulders.

A few days later, however, Elder H. Bruce Stucki and his wife, Cheryl, arrived. I will be forever grateful. He had been serving as a mission president in England for two years and was called to be a General Authority in April 1999. Two years later he would replace me as the Area President and serve for another year, which means he and his wife would have been away from home for five years. They also are my heroes. Elder Stucki was a very successful businessman and had been his own boss for years. I was tremendously impressed with his humility and ability. I have never had a better counselor. Without him and Elder Opare, the Area Authority Seventy who remained as our second counselor, I would not have been able to throw myself into the temple issue as fully as I did the next few months. So many people have made and are making a difference in Africa. At the top of the list are the African Saints themselves.

The lobbyist we sent to speak with the president of Ghana

returned a couple of days later with a report. He spent over two hours with the president, including time standing on the temple site itself. I was thrilled as I envisioned the president of the country standing on the temple site with one of our members. At least we could now know our voice had been heard at the highest level. The only troublesome remark that seemed to come up in the conversation was "Do you realize this is right on our ceremonial road?" It appeared that there was some question as to whether the temple was something they wanted to put in such a prominent place.

On August 31 I recorded in my journal: "We understand President Rawlings, Vice President Mills, and the mayor of Accra are meeting to discuss the temple. I don't know how we could get at a higher level than that. In my opinion we have now done all we can do. Anything more would just make the officials angry and hurt us in the long run. I'm ready to leave it in the hands of the Lord. We are getting to the point of groveling, and I feel we need to display some amount of dignity."

That statement shows I was wearing thin that particular day. I groveled continuously for another two years. However, another feeling began to emerge that gradually took precedence over the mechanics and politics of getting the temple approved. That was getting the members worthy to enter it. On September 1, I wrote:

"I've been brooding a lot about the temple. It honestly feels like there is nothing more we can do but place it in the hands of the Lord. I feel like we have done everything we can do temporally. I'm not absolutely sure the members have done everything they can do spiritually to prepare. If they had, I think we would have approval."

African Pioneers

During this week I wrote a talk that summarized my feelings as I began my second year of service in the area and my first as the president. The first part of the talk summarized our experiences two weeks earlier in Brazzaville, Congo. I shared feelings I had had on the twenty-fourth of July in Brazzaville, thinking about the pioneers in Utah and the pioneers in Africa. I continued:

"After seeing the devastation I had just witnessed and seeing these members come out of the bush at great sacrifice to attend meetings, I counted myself blessed to be there. At that moment, and many others, I knew I would rather be right there doing what I could to help these pioneers than home celebrating the accomplishments of my pioneer ancestors.

"We are making history right here, right now. These members are pioneers. We have just concluded our first year of an historic opening of the Africa West Area. Who would have thought twenty years ago we would have twenty stakes in West Africa? Who would have thought we would have a temple? Sooner or later that baby is going to be born. We are having a difficult labor, but there will be a delivery and the mother and baby are going to be fine.

"I used to look upon my ancestors with a certain amount of envy to have lived in such an exciting time of the Restoration. In a way this assignment is an answer to that wishful thinking. We find ourselves right in the middle of the most exciting time on this continent. Imagine a temple in Ghana, Nigeria, and other countries. They have been delayed but they won't be stopped. Imagine twenty stakes, forty stakes, and many more. Imagine a million members in West Africa in your lifetime. Here we are on an adventure that is worthy of several chapters of canonized scripture.

"President Benson has spoken of history as follows:

"'[Historical] events are foreknown to God. His superintending influence is behind righteous men's actions. And though mortal eyes and minds cannot fathom the end from the beginning, God does.

"'Great moments in history are made by colliding influences: the personalities in the drama, an issue or crisis, and a timing which synchronizes these influences into an event' (*Teachings of Ezra Taft Benson*, 700).

"It is my testimony that we are in the middle of one of those great moments in history. Occasionally we need to step back and look at the big picture and enjoy the struggle by seeing it for what it is. Of all people, we should be very happy in our work, in spite of a few disappointments.

"Studying past history has limitations to what it will do to make a difference in our own lives. Truman Madsen has said, 'Religiously we are condemned if we cling vicariously to the highest experiences of the past in the absence of our own' ("Guest Editor's Prologue," *BYU Studies*, 9 [no. 3]: 239).

"Our reflection on history should give each of us an incentive to live our lives in such a way that those who follow us can gain additional inspiration from the way we respond to the challenges of our lifetime. It is now our turn to walk across the stage of this last dispensation.

"Goethe, one of Germany's distinguished poets and philosophers, wrote: 'Whatsoever you have inherited from your fathers, you must earn it in order to possess it' (as quoted in Joseph B. Wirthlin, *Finding Peace in Our Lives*, 137).

"On this subject President Benson said: 'Can we keep and preserve what they wrought? Shall we pass on to our children the heritage they left us, or shall we lightly fritter it away? Have we their faith, their bravery, their courage; could we endure their hardships and suffering, make their sacrifices, bear up under their trials, their sorrows, their tragedies, believe the simple things they knew were true, have the simple faith that worked miracles for them, follow, and not falter or fall by the wayside, where our leaders advance, face the slander and the scorn of an unpopular belief? Can we do the thousands of little and big things that made them the heroic builders of a great Church, a great commonwealth?' ("Our Priceless Heritage," *Ensign*, Nov. 1976, 35).

"President Hinckley put it this way: 'Each of us has a small field to cultivate. While so doing, we must never lose sight of the greater picture, the large composite of the divine destiny of this work. It was given us by God our Eternal Father, and each of us has a part to play in the weaving of its magnificent tapestry. Our individual contribution may be small, but it is not unimportant' ("An Ensign to the Nations," *Ensign*, Nov. 1989, 54).

"It is my prayer that all members in Africa will understand how blessed we are to be on earth at this pivotal time in the history of Africa. You are in the position to see this stone cut out of the mountain cover this whole continent. It can't be stopped."

Challenges and Blessings in Lubumbashi

In September I attended a stake conference in Lubumbashi, Congo, the furthermost stake in the Africa West Area. In fact, it is much closer to Johannesburg than to Accra. It is the most isolated stake in the area; it is also the closest stake to the bloody war that has been going on for years in Eastern Congo. With travel the way it is, it takes an investment of thirty-six hours to get from Accra, Ghana, to Lubumbashi, Congo.

I flew from Accra to Kinshasa and stayed overnight. Then I returned to the airport to catch a domestic flight from Kinshasa to Lubumbashi. Since I was flying between two cities in the same county, I assumed I wouldn't need to go through the long routine of checking in. I was wrong. The airport was absolute bedlam. As we were passing through the first checkpoint, which is located at the outside door to the airport, a man came up unsolicited to help us with our bags. Suddenly I heard a big thud and turned around to see the poor guy lying on the ground writhing in pain. The security guard at the door had clubbed him between the shoulder blades with a long club. Security is very strict on who they let in to the airport because the people are so desperate; otherwise, utter chaos would reign there. We went through about five checkpoints. They looked at our passports several times, even though we were on a domestic flight. They searched our bags and even weighed our carry-on luggage.

I came to learn that the reason for the tight security is that Lubumbashi is where President Laurent Kabila is from, and there is always a threat of war breaking out in that area. (Just a few months later, Kabila was assassinated in his own palace, and we evacuated our mission president and two senior missionaries.)

The plane stopped in Kananga and Mbuji on the way. As we landed in these places, I was sobered by the military presence. Big tanks and large, cannon-type heavy artillery lined the runway. There were bunkers every thirty feet or so, with soldiers in them with machine guns. It hardly seemed real. But thousands have died in the civil strife in the Congo, and it is very real. The major fighting was a couple of hundred kilometers distant from any place we went, but it was a little unsettling nonetheless. Things are so volatile you can never feel for certain that you are safe.

When we landed in Lubumbashi, the stake presidency were there to greet us, dressed in their suits and smiling broadly. None of them owned a car, but they had "hired" a car and driver. The driver wasn't a member of the Church. They put me in the front. As soon as we got in, the driver put a tape into the tape deck and looked over at me for my approval. It was a tape put out by the Church of children singing Primary songs—in English. I looked at the stake president, and he was beaming.

After checking into the hotel, we held a zone conference with the twelve missionaries who served in the area. They were about 1,500 miles away from their mission president. These sweet, child-like missionaries soaked up every word. The last fifteen minutes was in complete darkness because the electricity stopped working. All I could see was eyes and teeth. They would have stayed as long as I was willing to keep them. After the meeting they still wanted photos, photos, and more photos. So we went outside to join the swarms of mosquitos.

The missionaries picked us up the next morning to take us to priesthood leadership training. Their car was a real clunker. They had to leave it running because they couldn't get a starter motor for it. They had to push it whenever they wanted to start it.

The training meetings were excellent. I'm astounded at how much you can communicate, even when you have to use a translator. I was able to use a returned missionary to translate for me, and he was thrilled to do so. He translated my English into Swahili because all the members understand it, but they don't all understand French. He was very good and got very excited as he proceeded. He made everything I said sound like I was a Pentecostal preacher.

One of the big problems of the Lubumbashi Stake was contention. There was contention within the Church and between the missionaries and leaders. I spent quite a bit of time talking to them about that, teaching some hard doctrine that rubbed against their culture, but they were absolutely accepting it. When I said, "Well, I guess you've had enough of that," they answered, "No, no, teach us more. We need to know these things."

On Sunday we held the general session in a huge movie theater. I had had no idea they had theaters so big. There were about 1,500 people there, which represented 68 percent of the stake. The Lubumbashi Stake is located more than 1,500 miles away from any other stake. As I recorded, "My overall impression is that the stake has many big problems and needs training very badly. On the other hand, they have 68 percent attendance at sacrament meetings; forty-two missionaries are serving from the stake; they have all kinds of faith and love of the gospel; they are teachable and humble. The success they are having gives you a greater appreciation of the purpose and power of the Holy Ghost.

"They have their problems, but it is miraculous how well they are able to do, considering their isolation and also the fact that most of their members have joined within the last five years."

Tithing for the Temple

As I returned to Accra from that conference I had a very meaningful experience in regard to the payment of tithing. It occurred on the airplane between Lubumbashi and Kinshasa. I had been studying the Doctrine and Covenants, and as I read some of the verses, it was as if the word Ghana or Nigeria was superimposed over Kirtland. It was a special spiritual feeling, and I knew I would need to continue to ponder it, develop it into words, and teach it. We are always counseled to liken the scriptures unto ourselves, but this was the most powerful example of this counsel I had ever experienced.

Over the next few weeks I tried to put these feelings into words and made it my major message for our area training with all stake, mission, and district presidents on October 23. Following are some excerpts:

"In the last weeks of his life, the Prophet Joseph Smith affirmed: 'We need the temple more than anything else' (Journal History of the Church, May 4, 1844).

"We are sure you are wondering what is happening with the Accra Ghana Temple. There is not a lot of new information we can pass along to you. We continue to work within the system to obtain zoning approval. To date, however, we have been unsuccessful and are in the middle of the appeals process. We have also done all we can to persuade various leaders of the city and national government that the temple would be a great asset to the neighborhood, community, and country. We are doing everything we can to get this temple under way. However, as one might expect, opposition is everywhere.

"We shouldn't be too surprised at this opposition. As George Q. Cannon said, 'Every foundation stone that is laid for a temple, and every temple completed . . . lessens the power of Satan on the earth, and increases the power of God and Godliness, moves the heavens in mighty power in our behalf, invokes and calls down upon us the blessings of eternal Gods and those who reside in their presence' (as quoted in Boyd K. Packer, *The Holy Temple*, 179).

"This is why Satan will continue to do everything in his power to prevent a temple from being built here. Currently we have less than 1 percent of our members who have been endowed with the power that comes from the endowment. Satan knows that as soon as the temple is built there will be thousands who will receive that power and he is in a rage about it.

"We are currently in a situation on the approval of the Accra Temple site that can only be reversed by the hearts of men being softened. I know of only one source to call on to accomplish this miracle. Last April the Area Presidency issued a plea to the membership throughout West Africa to help by becoming worthy to attend the temple. It is my conviction that the Lord will intervene when the people have prepared themselves.

"Many have asked that we conduct a special fast and petition the Lord's intervention. As a general rule the Brethren discourage special fasts; however, we would be pleased to have the members include a petition to the Lord on this issue during the regular fast Sunday. In fact, we would suggest you consider making it a part of our members' personal and congregational prayers in Church meetings this coming fast Sunday, November 7.

"It is my conviction that the Lord will not assist us in this matter until we are worthy to go to visit him in his house. He is standing with arms outstretched, waiting for us to be worthy to receive all he has.

"In December of 1832 the Lord commanded the Saints to build a temple in Kirtland. As we read in the Doctrine and Covenants:

"'Organize yourselves; prepare every needful thing; and establish a house, even a house of prayer, a house of fasting, a house of faith, a house of learning, a house of glory, a house of order, a house of God' (D&C 88:119).

"Six months later the temple had not been built. The Lord very firmly but lovingly chastised them for neglecting this important commandment.

"'Verily, thus saith the Lord unto you whom I love, and whom I love I also chasten that their sins may be forgiven, for with the chastisement I prepare a way for their deliverance in all things out of temptation, and I have loved you—

"'Wherefore, ye must needs be chastened and stand rebuked before my face;

"'For ye have sinned against me a very grievous sin, in that ye have not considered the great commandment in all things, that I have given unto you concerning the building of mine house; . . .

"'Yea, verily I say unto you, I gave unto you a commandment that you should build a house, in the which house I design to endow those whom I have chosen with power from on high; . . .

"'Verily I say unto you, it is my will that you should build a house. *If you keep my commandments you shall have power to build it.*

"'If you keep not my commandments, the love of the Father shall not continue with you, therefore you shall walk in darkness' (D&C 95:1–3, 8, 11–12; emphasis added).

"'Verily I say unto you, that it is my will that a house should be built unto me in the land of Zion, like unto the pattern which I have given you.

"'Yea, let it be built speedily, *by the tithing of my people.*

"'Behold, this is the tithing and the sacrifice which I, the Lord, require at their hands, that there may be a house built unto me for the salvation of Zion' (D&C 97:10–12; emphasis added).

"Our current leaders are stressing the payment of a full tithe. Just three weeks ago President James E. Faust stressed this point with all General Authorities when he said, "We should be challenging members to get ready to go to the temple. We cannot lower our standards of worthiness. Local bishops cannot compromise standards. The humble Saints throughout the world will be blessed spiritually and temporally as they live the gospel, including the law of the tithe."

I was so thankful when I heard President Faust's talk that I had had the strength of my convictions to teach tithing to the Saints in war-torn Brazzaville.

"Brethren, six months ago we pleaded with you to teach our people the need to sacrifice so the Lord would intervene and speed up the time when a temple will be built. Specifically, we suggested that the percent of full tithepayers should be doubled.

"It is very difficult for the Area Presidency to lay this problem with the temple at the feet of the Lord and ask for his divine intervention when only a relatively small percentage of our members are worthy to enter his house if the doors to the temple were open tomorrow. In some ways I feel like we are laying a blemished sacrifice on the altar.

"I catch myself thinking about your ancestors constantly. They have been waiting for years, even hundreds and thousands of years, for these blessings. I see them looking down at us and saying, 'Please prepare yourselves so the temple can be built and you can perform those ordinances for us. Our spiritual progress has been held up long enough, and now the Lord is prepared to give us all he has, and the only thing holding us back now is your lack of worthiness. Please don't make us wait any longer.'

"I can envision you going to the temple and performing their work for them. You will feel their presence. There is no place on earth where the veil is as thin as it is in the Lord's house. I can envision your children being baptized on behalf of an ancestor. I can see the font surrounded by the beautiful spirits of those who have passed through the veil. I can hear joyous singing, praising God and praising you for making this possible. Is any price too high? Is there anything you wouldn't give?

"President Wilford Woodruff said: 'We have a great work before us in the redemption of our dead. The course that we are pursuing is being watched with interest by all heaven. There are millions of people in the spirit world who are being preached to by Joseph Smith, and the Apostles and Elders, his associates, who have passed away. The eyes of these millions of people are watching over these Latter-day Saints. Have we any time to waste in neglecting our dead? I tell you no' (*Journal of Discourses*, 22:235).

"If the temple was opened tomorrow and you were worthy to go in, would you be able to take any of your ancestors' names through the temple? We cannot neglect this important aspect of preparation. As a minimum, are you writing down your oral histories and those still in the memories of people in your village? As your members return to their villages this Christmas season, is this one of the top priorities of their visit?

"I suggest we are long past the luxury of being able to talk the talk without walking the walk.

"'But be ye doers of the word, and not hearers only, deceiving your own selves' (James 1:22).

"'He that saith he abideth in him ought himself also so to walk, even as he walked' (1 John 2:6).

"If we are going to receive all God has, we must be willing to live the gospel in its fulness."

During the special fast in November I committed to the Lord

that I would do anything he placed in my mind to move the approval of the temple along. This was the beginning of an exhausting and consuming flurry of temple activity that would last for the next four months. I also believe the fasting of the members on November 7 had a significant effect. As I wrote to one of the Twelve:

"I feel we got over the hump on the temple issue with the November 7 fast. We had a beautiful reaction to the request for fasting and prayer from our members. Nigerians are praying for a temple in Ghana. Different tribes in Nigeria are praying together for a temple in Nigeria. Members in Lubumbashi are praying for the temple in Ghana, even though Johannesburg is closer to them. I believe we will soon have enough of a critical mass of worthy members for the Lord to intervene."

Things Begin to Fall into Place

One week later Georges Bonnet arrived in Accra from Salt Lake City. He had been working in the Church physical facilities department for several years, but previously he had been the director for temporal affairs in South Africa. I had traveled to West Africa with him in 1990 and 1992. He was sent on a special assignment to use his experience to assess the current situation on the temple. He was especially valuable because of his experiences with the government years earlier, when the Church's activities were frozen in 1989. His perceptions were very helpful.

Georges is another example of one of the heroes in the history of the Church in Africa, one of those who worked as employees of the Church, living lives of righteousness and receiving revelation in their areas of stewardships.

I was convinced that Georges' arrival was not a coincidence but was the Lord's response to our effort to fast and to be obedient. I recorded in my journal: "The Spirit seems to be hovering over the community. It just feels like the pieces to the puzzle are starting to come together. All I know is at a time when we have every right to be discouraged I am very optimistic."

On November 26, about three weeks after the fast, I was able to have a private meeting with the mayor of Accra. He talked about the zoning process and asked how long I had been in his country. That gave me a chance to explain how the Church had picked Ghana above all other African countries in which to locate our headquarters. He seemed pleased. I also had a chance to tell him we would be very flexible and were willing to discuss changes in our architectural plan. I indicated that we knew some had thought we were inflexible and even arrogant and apologized if we appeared to have been either. He said he hadn't thought of us that way and counseled us not to listen to all the rumors we hear.

The next day we went to a concert by the choir at the Lartebiokorshie Stake. The deputy chairman of the National Commission on Culture, Ebo Hawkson, was there with members of his family. He had recently visited Salt Lake City and was asked to say a few words. He told us how impressed he was with the Church. He mentioned that several years earlier the ministry of culture received some false information about the Church that resulted in our being expelled from the country. He then said, "I now stand in front of you as a goodwill ambassador." The members burst into applause.

After the concert I approached him with a request for a meeting. I felt this was another example of some of the good things that were happening in our pursuit of the temple approval.

On December 8, I was reminded we weren't alone out there. Elder Jeffrey R. Holland, my first contact among the members of the Twelve, called with the following message: "The Ghana temple is still being singled out on the prayer roll in the temple, and when President Hinckley read it, he said there were some positive developments going on." It was good to see that President Hinckley and the other prophets, seers, and revelators are brooding and praying over this temple. Too often we feel very lonely here in the jungle.

It would not be appropriate to go into all the details of the people we saw and the private discussions we had with various leaders of the community. There was not a level of the government we didn't penetrate. Many citizens both within and without the Church were working behind the scenes at their various levels of influence. Many laid their reputations and credibility on the line because they believed we were not being treated fairly. Many people in high places felt the Church was doing the country much good and that a temple would greatly benefit the city and the country. In an effort to protect these friends, I won't go into detail. It suffices to say that the Lord's hand could be seen in the effort, and many hearts were being touched. Thankfully, good counselors enabled me to work on this "divine obsession" full time whenever I was in town.

While getting the temple approved was the primary focus of my time since becoming the Area President, another very historical event occurred during this time period. For over a year we had been working on getting the right piece of land for a missionary training center. On December 7, 1999, we succeeded. On that day, I went with Elder Stucki, Elder Opare, and others to Lartebiokorshie to examine an old chapel that was going to be refurbished. The thought was that we might use it as a missionary training center. It looked worse than we had remembered. There were some large cracks in the walls, which suggested there might be some problems with the foundation. We noted that there was no place for the missionaries to have recreation. Worst of all, there was no room for future growth.

Later, we drove out to Tema, which is about fourteen miles from our office, and looked at a future stake center site. As we were leaving that site, I asked if we could drive past the chapel in Tema so I would be able to find it Sunday to attend church. It is a very nice chapel just off the motorway. Next to the chapel was a plot of land where bananas were growing. "Who owns that land?" I asked. "We do," came the answer. It was a full acre. It was peaceful all around, with good but distant neighbors. I looked at Elder Stucki and Elder Opare and could see they were thinking what I was thinking. We immediately started asking why we couldn't build the MTC on that location. There were no reasons.

We submitted our recommendation to the missionary department; a few months later plans were begun and we never looked back. While standing on the site we all received an overwhelming witness that this was the right location. I suspected this must be the way the First Presidency feel about a temple site when they stand on it. We just knew it was right.

On December 31 we celebrated New Year's Eve with the terrific couples laboring with us. We rang in the New Year with some bells, pots, and pans and were all on our way home by 12:30 A.M. Jolene and I stayed up a while longer watching more New Year's celebrations from around the world. Then Jolene went to bed, but I actually stayed up until 5:00 A.M. to see the ball drop on Times Square in New York City. After all, a new millennium rolls around only every thousand years! Throughout my life I had wondered where I would spend New Year's Eve to usher in the new millennium. I have fantasized about numerous possibilities, but never in my wildest fantasy did I think I would spend it in Accra, Ghana, on the continent of Africa.

I was looking forward to the year 2000 for one big reason, and that was to see a temple started in West Africa. It seemed fitting that this great event would usher in the next millennium.

8

FREE FALL

The day dawn is breaking, the world is awaking,
The clouds of night's darkness are fleeing away.
The worldwide commotion, from ocean to ocean,
Now heralds the time of the beautiful day.

In many a temple the Saints will assemble
And labor as saviors of dear ones away.
Then happy reunion and sweetest communion
We'll have with our friends in the beautiful day.

> *Beautiful day of peace and rest,*
> *Bright be thy dawn from east to west.*
> *Hail to thine earliest welcome ray,*
> *Beautiful, bright, millennial day (Hymns, 52).*

As this new millennium burst upon us in Accra, Ghana, I caught myself humming this song. I don't hum very often, but I had never felt more positive about our course in regard to the future temple.

But the song in my heart was short-lived. On January 4, a rumor reached us that the temple had been rejected outright. I called my sources, who confirmed the rumor. I felt helpless. I couldn't stop thinking about the temple but didn't know what to do.

Finally I held a strategy meeting with all of our contacts. It felt like the war room at the Pentagon. I got as many different opinions as participants. Some said, "Be patient and take your time"; others said, "We need to do something fast." After hearing all of the conflicting advice, I knew I was the one who had to make the final decision.

The suggestion to be patient was the most intriguing. It had now been two years since President Hinckley announced the temple. At the thought of continuing in patience, I told the strategy committee about my favorite African cartoon. The cartoon depicts two vultures sitting in a dead tree high on a cliff overlooking an African plain. On the plain is an endless number of African wildlife foraging for food. Unfortunately for the vultures, all the animals look very healthy. The vultures are getting hungrier by the minute, with no immediate prospects of a dying animal. One vulture then turns to the other and says, "Patience? Heck, I'm going to kill something." Those were my sentiments on that particular occasion.

The Darkest Hour

A few days later, we heard some additional bad news. The president and first lady of Ghana had decided against supporting the temple. I think that was some of the worst news I had heard since I'd arrived in Africa. That message sent us into a free fall.

For two years we had worked within the system, assuming our problem came from various members of the planning commission or that there was some mysterious zoning law. We knew the commission contained members who were antagonistic toward the Church. As I got more involved personally, it seemed that the problem was with the mayor, then with the vice president. We started working with the president and first lady in hopes that they would use their influence to help our cause.

Now we had learned they themselves had strong reservations.

Without their support we had no other place to turn. This blow seemed final, and the problem looked insurmountable. I felt at the time like a Moses who, if given a chance to sit with the Pharaoh, could reach an understanding, and he would "let my people go."

This was the darkest hour of our three years for me. My testimony of the Master's plan was not shaken to the least degree, but questions about whether I was meeting my responsibilities within that plan received a jolting test. What could I have done differently? Had I let these people down? Had Lucifer been working overtime on me, trying to get to me and others through an Achilles' heel? At my lower moments, I felt I had an Achilles' heel, foot, calf, thigh, and so forth up all the way up to my head. It was a dark feeling that was hard to shake.

At times like that you just have to keep going. And, on reflection, I realized that the terrible news we'd received about President Rawlings' attitude toward the temple was actually good news. Now, for the first time, we could get to work on the real problem. For the first time in two years we finally knew what the real problem was. All of our efforts for that two years had been directed to a source that could not make the final decision. Therefore, we started to get the wheels in motion to gain an audience with the president and first lady of Ghana.

On January 20 my free fall was ended. Elder David E. Sorensen called to inform me of a decision reached by the Brethren in a special meeting with President Hinckley: "Let the temple matter lay fallow for a while."

I immediately felt good about this direction from the Brethren; and I felt a large burden lift from my shoulders. I was comforted to know that attention had been given to this issue at all levels of Church government, even the highest.

We would basically go forward with the long-term plan we had already been following but without the pressure of feeling we had to push for approval immediately. I was relieved to know that our success didn't hinge on one visit with the president of the country. I was willing to go to the Pharaoh, but I had been instructed to spend more time in the wilderness. Still, I felt bad for the members who had waited so long for the blessings of the temple.

Thus came to an end the latest episode of false labor. At first I felt a little bit like an elder without a cause, but then I realized that my focus should be on teaching and training the members.

Meanwhile, I soon found the labor wouldn't stop just because we stopped pushing. We had so many balls in the air and so many people in high places working behind the scenes that I couldn't rein them all in or even remember where they all were. Hardly a day went by when I didn't receive a phone call about some development. A certain momentum or inertia had been created that was beyond my control. One of the biggest irons in the fire at the time was a potential visit to Salt Lake City by the first lady of Ghana.

I continued to get reports from people of influence who conducted private conversations at the highest level on our behalf. I personally was letting the issue lay fallow, but the Lord wasn't.

Long Distance Bad News

During the second week of February we were scheduled to go to Sierra Leone. I looked forward to getting back to testifying to the people, but at the same time I was all too aware of their dire, sad circumstances.

At Lungi Airport in Sierra Leone we experienced a merry-go-round of checks, taxes, and other hassles. But other than that, travel was much better than I thought it would be for a country buried in civil war. From there we flew into Hastings Airport. At the airport was a city of tents that was housing the six thousand United Nations peacekeepers.

We were sobered during the hour-long taxi drive from the airport to Freetown. There were checkpoints about every mile, but none of them stopped us. The buildings were pockmarked from bullets, and many were burned. The people looked weary, but it was amazing to me how life just goes on. In the midst of the horrible killing and maiming they had endured, we saw them carrying their produce and other goods to market, hauling water, and repairing buildings. We could even see a little hope. Children were playing and laughing. I've found that children are very resilient—if you can just get them some food.

Our driver and his family had initially fled to Guinea. When they made their way back, they found their home damaged and completely empty. The rebels had taken everything. A friend lent him a car so he could get back on his feet; he gave the friend a percentage of his earnings for its use.

His youngest child was a daughter of three years. We were taken aback by his very sobering and serious offer to take his little girl. He and his wife were struggling to take care of their four children, and he knew she would have a much better life with us.

Our hotel, the Cape Sierra, had once been a quality hotel, but it was now showing the wear and tear of war. It is located on a point of land that overlooks a beautiful coastline. When we got to our room we wanted to collapse but there was no electricity and, therefore, no air conditioning, fans, or lights. We were later informed that they would turn on the generator in a couple of hours.

We had rested for only a few minutes when the phone rang. It was Elder Stucki with a message from our son Darin. My mother had experienced a heart attack and was in the hospital. She was doing reasonably well, so we decided to continue with our schedule.

We then went to dinner in the hotel. We were the only ones there, and the menu consisted of two choices: spaghetti or chicken. When we got back to our rooms the generator was on so we had lights but no air conditioning. We checked at the desk and found the generator wasn't strong enough for air conditioning—but the power from the city would turn on about 8:00 P.M. Eight o'clock came and went, as did 9:00 and 10:00 and 11:00. Finally we gave up and went to sleep in the heat. We didn't dare open the windows because of the mosquitoes and threat of malaria. About 4:00 A.M. the air conditioning came on, but we didn't really care by then.

We got up the next morning to no water. Jolene had bathed the night before (for all the good it did her, since we slept in humid hot air all night). Since there was no water for bathing, I moistened my hair with our drinking water and combed it and was ready for the day. Jolene used her butane hair curler and we were ready for a tour of the city. We visited most of the chapels in the area. I was impressed that they had received very little damage from the war and was touched at how clean they were. The people didn't know we were coming, and it was obvious they took pride in their church buildings. They are all leased, and they were in much need of repair, but landlords didn't have the desire or money to do it. All of them had a little modest landscaping; one had sayings written with the arrangement of small plants. One such pattern spelled out "Happy Zion."

We then went to the service-center office. It was comforting to go into a little room in the middle of that war-torn city and see the curriculum materials of the Church. Also in the yard were two forty-foot containers of hospital supplies and another with emergency supplies. These shipments had come from Salt Lake City during the devastation; they were soon sent to devastated areas of Sierra Leone.

When we got back to the hotel they offered to give us another room, since we had no water. We had barely made the transfer when Darin phoned. He caught us in the only five minutes we were in the hotel in ten hours. He had the bad news that my mother's condition was much worse than we thought. She was having difficulty with her kidneys. I can't explain how helpless I felt to be in Sierra Leone, of all places, when my mother was seriously ill in Utah. I was utterly trapped—the only way to leave the country was to fly, and no planes were scheduled to depart for several days.

I thought my free fall had been stopped a month earlier, but I found myself falling again. I guess I must have just glanced off a cliff the first time.

I decided to try to call the hospital to talk to the nurse. Jolene and I went to the desk, picked up a phone card, and went to the public telephone since you can't call out on the phones in the hotel rooms. Much to my surprise, I got through on the first attempt, and my mother's nurse answered the phone. I started to introduce myself and she said, "I know who you are. Your mother has told me all about you. She is so proud of you." I asked if my mother was well enough to talk, and the nurse put her right on. The connection was clear; she sounded better than she usually does when I talk to her at home. I was able to tell her how much I loved her. I also said, "If Dad happens to show up at your bedside, you have my permission to join him even though I'm not home." (My father is deceased.) She said, "Okay, honey," as if I'd just given her permission to go on a little vacation. I then said my preference was that she would be there when we went to Salt Lake City for general conference in April. She said, "Oh, I'll probably be here." But she sounded tired.

"Just Bring Them Hope"

There was nothing more we could do, so we went back to work the next morning. We met with the district presidencies beginning at 8:00 A.M. It was interesting to see the problems they were facing. I learned that they had been out of funds for two months but were nervous about asking for any more money from Church headquarters. I got that straightened out in a hurry.

One of the district presidents had an office filled with curriculum materials that hadn't been distributed. We had worked hard to make

Young girl in Sierra Leone,
a victim of the atrocities of war.

sure the service centers got the supplies to the districts, and now much of it was still sitting there. He said he was "rationing it." He also said, "If we give it to the sisters, they will lose it." I also fixed that in a hurry.

We then went over to a large convention center to have our priesthood leadership and combined stake and ward council leadership training meeting. There was no air conditioning in those meetings, so the heat really took a lot out of us. As I stood in front of these brethren with my prepared materials on the Aaronic Priesthood Achievement Program; *Teaching, No Greater Call;* and other standard priesthood instruction, the feeling came over me, "Just bring them hope and encouragement." So I spent most of the time letting them know the Lord and the Church will go forward with them into the future.

During the conference we were introduced to a beautiful little three-year-old girl whose arm had been cut off by the rebels. Her mother and father had been killed, and she had escaped with an uncle. That was a stark reminder of the ugliness that was going on just weeks earlier and was still alive in some places of the country.

Of course, the situation at home was in the back of my mind all this time. Darin called shortly after we returned to the hotel and reported that my mother wasn't doing well and that my sisters were having a difficult time.

We held a different general session for each of the districts on Sunday. I felt I should continue the theme of encouragement and hope. I let them know we would be sending more resources so no member of the Church would go to bed hungry. I also let them know we would begin building more chapels as soon as possible and that it appeared that before too long they could become a stake. I then went on to say that after one stake comes two, then four, then eight—and who is to say there might not someday be a temple sitting on one of these sites where there are only ruins now? I was touched to see that talking about a temple brought a larger response from the congregation than the announcement that we would send food.

As the conference proceeded, I was inspired and gratified to see hope and joy replace defeat and despair in the faces of the congregation. Attendance at the general session was an incredible 70 percent.

The next morning I decided to call my sister, Collene, in Utah, even though it was the middle of the night where she was. I was glad I did. I could tell that our mother was doing worse and that Collene was carrying a lot on her shoulders. She told me that the doctors didn't expect Mom to ever leave the hospital. I prayed that she was not in a lot of pain.

Before catching our plane we paid a visit to a refugee camp filled with people from the city and villages who had no place to go. In the middle of the camp were a group of children and teenagers who had been kidnaped by the rebels, drugged, and forced to commit murder and other atrocities. Their portion of the refugee camp was run by one of our members. I resolved to see if these children could receive some assistance from LDS Charities.

We went straight from there to the helicopter pad, which took us to Luni Airport, where we began to go through all the red tape of leaving the country. We boarded the plane and the pilot started to taxi, but then he stopped and announced that the control tower was requiring us to wait for a VIP passenger.

After we waited an hour in this humid, stuffy, and intimidating situation on an airstrip surrounded by military, the VIP finally arrived on a helicopter with an armed entourage. It turned out to be Foday Sankoh, the leader of the rebel movement. He was the man responsible for all the atrocities being inflicted by the rebel troops of boy soldiers. He sat right across the aisle from me, looking just like anybody else.

Permission to Go Home

On February 15 we were back in Accra when I wrote: "As we drove to the devotional this morning both Jolene and I were very melancholy as the reality that I would soon lose Mom started to set in. It feels like my past is dying with her. She was the link to the good old days of childhood, teenage, and young married life. She was 'grandma' to the children and my remaining link to Dad. Therefore, the loss is magnified. I won't be able to go into my childhood home, lie down on the couch, and become the little boy again that Mom or Dad will always take care of. However, when you think of her circumstance, you can't have any feelings but relief for her. She will soon be with Dad, Grandma and Grandpa Wilde, and all the others. She will be able to walk and run, feel no pain, have more energy than she has ever had, and start serving other people again like she always used to."

Once we were warned that the time was very short for Mom, we received permission to go home. I tried to make sure that all the bases would be covered while I was gone, but the time soon came to let my mother be the top priority and to let the other things go. We boarded the plane on Sunday, February 20. I didn't know when I left whether I was going home for a funeral or to be at her side during her last hours.

Twenty-four hours later we arrived in Salt Lake City and drove straight to the hospital in Provo. It was the same hospital where Kyle and Rikki (our oldest children) were born, where my father had a bleeding ulcer, where my mother had knee and hip replacements, and finally where my dad died about five years earlier.

From everything we had heard, my mother had just a few days to live. With those gloomy feelings we walked in and were surprised to see my mom sitting up in bed smiling at me. She was quite coherent, but it was difficult for her to say more than a few words at a time.

She passed away six days later. What a blessing it was to be able to communicate up until the last day. Then I was able to release her by the power of the holy priesthood, and she died peacefully. The events of that week were spiritual and sacred. I can summarize them by saying I was able to say all I wanted to say, and she was able to understand. It was also a joy to hear her speak of communicating with those on the other side waiting to receive her. This experience brought vividly to my soul the reality of the closeness of the spirit world. It gave me another personal witness that we are not alone in our labors. I wondered how many times I had been helped from the other side while laboring in Africa. Now Mom would be able to come over and see what we were doing and, for all I know, join Dad in helping the African people on the other side of the veil.

After her passing on February 27 we went through all the normal arrangements, including the funeral and burial. Then it was time to start going through the house she had lived in for fifty-five years. All these things were sad but spiritual. It was soon time for me to return to Africa. Jolene stayed home, since we would be returning in two weeks for conference. With the hope of getting Ghana's first lady to visit Salt Lake City, I headed back to Accra alone.

Back to Africa in Time for Crises

It didn't take long to see why I felt I needed to return for those two weeks—Nigeria was in a new crisis. For some time the country had been racked with holy war between the Muslim and Christian factions. The Muslims were trying to make Muslim law (Sharia) the law of the land, and the Christians were fighting that with their lives. Now several hundred Christians had been killed in the north, which precipitated a similar slaughter by Christians against Muslims in the Aba area. All this was happening in the shadow of the temple site.

While we were in Utah, the Stuckis had gone on a mission tour in Aba, Nigeria, where they experienced this civil war firsthand. They drove past burning bodies and vehicles and even around road blocks. Thankfully, they were with some street-smart local missionaries who helped lead them out of trouble. They were protected, and I was grateful to learn that none of our members or missionaries had been injured thus far.

The next day we received the disappointing news that the first lady would not be going to Salt Lake City after all. As I wrote that day: "We came back and licked our wounds. This was a huge setback for me emotionally. [That is one of the biggest understatements of my journal.] We keep getting closer and closer. One day we'll make it. I continue to be impressed that our local members won't give up."

On Saturday, March 18, I found another reason I was prompted to return to Africa instead of staying home. I decided I'd better go into the office and send an email home to let my family know exactly when I would arrive in Salt Lake City. When I entered our offices on the fifth floor of the building, I was immediately confronted by heavy smoke. Even though the office was closed on Saturdays, I thought I had seen the car of our executive secretary, Elder Larson, outside, so I crouched down and crawled on the floor to their office to make sure they weren't in there. I also checked the other offices. The windows to the financial office were black, so I couldn't see in there. Ashy smoke was coming out from underneath the door. I felt the door and windows, and they were very warm. I hurried downstairs and informed security, who ran upstairs to investigate and then called the police and firemen. I thought we were in deep trouble at that point, because I'd heard that typically a building would burn down by the time firemen arrived.

In the meantime, security guards and others were trying to knock down the door of the finance office to get to the fire. I didn't have a key to that office. I didn't think beating down the door was the best idea. I was afraid the additional oxygen would really feed the fire, if not cause an explosion. (At least that is what they say in the movies.) However, by now it was me against ten big Africans, so their opinion had the most weight.

I was impressed at their wanting to help without worrying about their own safety. When they broke the door down, the smoke was so black, they couldn't see anything. So they just turned their heads and sprayed until the fire extinguisher was empty and then went back for another container. I suspected that they used all ten canisters without hitting the fire once.

They had opened all the windows, which really started to feed the fire. I was surprised to hear sirens in the background. By then, with the windows open, the smoke was clearing a little bit. I went to the door and saw the fire on top of one of the desks. It looked like a computer was on fire, and it was spreading very rapidly.

When the firemen arrived, they had to run up five flights of stairs since the power was off. They took a look and then went back for their hose. (No, I don't know why they didn't bring it the first time.) While they were gone, we found two more fire extinguishers to give them when they got back. Within ten minutes they announced the fire was under control. In the meantime, they had broken a window and started throwing stuff out. This included ten big envelopes full of membership records that had recently arrived

One of the rooms in the Africa West Area office after a fire.

from the Congo. At this same time Elder Bob Linnell, our area welfare director pulled into the parking lot and saw the envelopes flying out of the window five floors up. When he saw what they were, he ran around the parking lot picking them up and then carried them back upstairs. It took an hour to clean the ash off everything in my office. It was black as coal. Four hours had gone by since I'd discovered the fire. And all I had planned on doing was to send an email!

The financial office was a disaster, but it could have been so much worse if I hadn't gone in. It could have burned not only our floor but the entire building.

A Surprise Assignment

On my birthday, March 21, I was back on the airplane for the pilgrimage to general conference—and the hope of getting a little rest. Wrong! The day after I arrived back in Utah, I was visiting with family when the phone rang. The caller was Michael Watson (executive secretary for the First Presidency) informing me that I would be speaking in conference on Saturday afternoon. I had four days to turn my written remarks in. Typically I would have had a month.

I struggled to collect my thoughts and prepare an address. With all the events of the past six weeks—from seeing our temple hopes thrashed, the Sierra Leone carnage, watching my mother pass away, returning to Africa, being sick with a bad cold all the time I was there, seeing the first lady's visit fall through, and seeing the office nearly burn down—I didn't know how I could do it. But I knew I had to, and I knew the Lord always gives extra help when it is needed.

As Jolene and I drove back to the hotel, I told her I didn't have a clue what I would speak about. As you would imagine, I had a very sleepless night.

In the next few days, I had commitments with the family, including a birthday party they planned for me and a day's work at my mother's house with my sisters to help decide what to keep and what to throw away. As a result I had Sunday and Tuesday to actually write the talk. By Friday night I still hadn't decided on a topic. At three o'clock on Saturday morning I awoke pondering that reality. As I was lying there the answer came to me very forcefully, almost in a humorous way. I thought, "Glenn, you're so dense. What has been on your mind the last two years?" My thoughts responded, "The temple." The answer was so obvious I had to chuckle at myself. After that I had a great feeling of relief, even though I still wasn't able to turn to the writing.

On the following Tuesday I handed in my talk. On Wednesday we had a meeting with the temple department to bring them up to date on the Ghana temple. Now that it appeared the Ghana temple was going to be a long-term project, I wondered about the possibility of moving forward on the Nigerian temple. Every time I had raised that question, the objection was always that the country lacked stability. On this occasion they asked me about the current status of Nigeria. I answered, "We just had riots in the north over the passing of Sharia law, and several hundred Christians were killed. In retaliation, several hundred Muslims were killed in the south, including many right in Aba where the temple site is located. In the delta region, where the oil fields are located, many hundreds of people have been killed. Whole villages have been burned from explosions caused by sabotage of oil lines. Oil executives are being kidnapped and held for ransom. In Lagos there have been serious riots in the streets. Vigilante groups are springing up all over the country—and they are recognized, condoned, and even encouraged by the police and military. In summary, things are better than they have been in thirty years."

Then I added, on a serious note, "Brethren, if we wait for Nigeria to be stable before we build a temple, we might as well forget it. I feel we have to move forward and support the people. I understand your apprehension. However, if I remember right, there was a lot of instability in Nauvoo when we built that temple."

"A Temple for West Africa"

With this background I feel it is appropriate to include the talk I gave on April 1, 2000, in the Saturday afternoon session. This was also the historic day of the first conference to be held in the new Conference Center.

"Several years ago I attended a BYU football game with some of our young children. We lost the game. I really hate it when that happens. We listened to the coaches' show on the ride back to our home in Bountiful. When it was over, my children had no alternative but to listen to my own postgame show. Just as I had completed my final analysis of what went wrong in the game, my seven-year-old daughter asked, 'Dad, when you see the temple, do you get a good feeling

228

inside?' I wondered, 'Where in the world did that come from?' As I was trying to figure out what that comment had to do with the football game, I glanced over at her and could see she was looking out the window at the Salt Lake Temple. For some reason the game no longer mattered.

"My whole life has been enriched by experiences of the temple. Our parents would take us to Temple Square in Salt Lake City on a regular basis. They would point to the temple and tell us that they were married there and because of that we would always be together as a family. What comfort that brought to a little boy whose biggest fear was that his parents might die. Now what comfort it brings to a grown man whose parents have passed on to the other side.

"When I was ten years old, in the shadows of the Salt Lake Temple I first read the Joseph Smith story and received a powerful testimony of the truthfulness of the Restoration.

"I remember with thanksgiving going to the temple with my parents and receiving my endowment prior to departing for my mission.

"My wife and I were married in the Salt Lake Temple about three years later. In subsequent years I have had the honor of performing the temple marriages of each of our six children.

"We know many members of the Church have not had the luxury I have had of growing up around temples. Because of this knowledge we were all thrilled with the announcement made by President Hinckley in October 1997 when he said, 'We are determined . . . to take the temples to the people and afford them every opportunity for the very precious blessings that come of temple worship' ("Some Thoughts on Temples, Retention of Converts, and Missionary Service," Ensign, Nov. 1997, 50).

"Since that time we have rejoiced and marveled as we have heard announcements of numerous temples and subsequently read of their open houses and dedications. We are witnessing a modern-day miracle and fulfillment of prophecy. What a wonderful time to be alive!

"Our excitement over the building of temples is not shared by all. The adversary in particular is having a major temper tantrum as he sees his power threatened.

"Over the last two years I have witnessed his wrath firsthand in West Africa. He has been very active, trying to prevent the building of a temple in that part of the world. Two years ago President Hinckley announced that there would be a temple in West Africa located in Accra, Ghana. Since then the adversary has been relentless in trying to prevent that from happening. Why is Lucifer so concerned?

"We have 85,000 members in West Africa, and the Church is growing very rapidly. Sacrament meeting attendance is over 50 percent, but currently only 400 members have been endowed because of the prohibitive expense of traveling thousands of miles to Johannesburg or London. We have over 700 full-time African missionaries serving in the mission field, and very few of them have been endowed.

"The African people have waited for centuries to receive the fulness of the gospel and have been through much pain and suffering. Now, at last, they can receive every blessing available to God's children. Worthy members can receive the temple endowment and be able to have their families sealed together for time and for all eternity.

"Elder John A. Widtsoe explained, 'They will attain more readily to their place in the presence of the Lord; they will increase more rapidly in every divine power; they will approach more nearly to the likeness of God; they will more completely realize their divine destiny' (*Evidences and Reconciliations*, 300).

"That is why Lucifer is so concerned. In addition, he is aware of the large number of Africans who have accepted the gospel on the other side of the veil and are anxiously awaiting their proxy baptism and temple endowment, as well as being sealed to their families. When a temple is dedicated, the dam in the spirit world will break and there will be a flood of humanity who have lived on the African continent flow into the temple of the Lord as their descendants do their work for them. We should not be surprised that Lucifer is using every means at his disposal to keep a temple from these people.

"Through centuries of suffering, the people in general have not become bitter. They are humble, teachable, and God-fearing. They know the scriptures, and they recognize the Shepherd's voice.

"I have faith in their faith. I know the Savior loves the African people. Therefore, to paraphrase verse 33 of the 121st section of the Doctrine and Covenants, 'As well might man stretch forth his puny arm to stop the [Congo] river in its decreed course, or to turn it up stream, as to hinder the Almighty from [building a temple for the African Latter-day Saints].'

"As the Savior has said, 'I will not suffer that [the enemy] shall destroy my work; yea, I will show unto them that my wisdom is greater than the cunning of the devil' (D&C 10:43).

"It has been inspiring to see the Lord's hand in bringing the forces together that will lead to an inevitable victory. There will be a temple in West Africa.

"Last week we were driving from Provo to Bountiful again. As we left Provo, we could see the temple up on the hill. Before it was out of sight, the Mount Timpanogos Utah Temple came into view, and then the Jordan River Utah Temple appeared, followed by the Salt Lake Temple. And immediately thereafter we could see the Bountiful Utah Temple standing like a jewel above that city.

"I thought back to my daughter's question, 'Dad, when you see the temple, do you get a good feeling inside?' I realized the overwhelming answer is, 'Yes, when I see a temple I have a wonderful feeling inside.' However, my heart aches for our African brothers and sisters who have never seen a temple in their whole life.

"It is my hope and prayer that we will never take temple blessings for granted. I also have a prayer in my heart for West Africa and any other place in the world where outside influences are preventing the Saints from enjoying the blessings of a temple.

"I testify to the divinity of this work. Jesus is the Christ. He stands at the head of this Church, and He is orchestrating the building of His kingdom here on earth. We are witnessing miracles, and therefore I can testify that they have not ceased. In the name of Jesus Christ, amen" ("A Temple for West Africa," *Ensign*, May 2000, 25–26).

"We Announce . . . a House of the Lord"

With the relief that comes at the "Amen" after giving a conference talk, I settled in to enjoy the remaining sessions. I was touched by Elder David B. Haight's extemporaneous comments on his perspective on Ghana: "As Brother Pace was speaking here a few moments ago about the challenges that we have in Ghana, I know that that will be taken care of. I stood under a tree on the campus of the university there and dedicated Ghana for the preaching of the gospel. Brother Banyan Dadson, who was vice president of the university and a member of the Church, stood there on that day and explained to the people how the natives in Ghana had settled that part of West Africa, and what a blessing it had been for those tribes of people. I know that that problem will be resolved; that will only be a chapter in the on-rolling of this work" ("Faith, Devotion, and Gratitude," *Ensign*, May 2000, 35).

I knew his last sentence was true, but the thought came into my mind, "When you are the one living every word of that chapter, it feels more like several volumes."

The showstopper for me came Sunday afternoon at the end of

President Hinckley's remarks: "Now, additionally, we announce at this conference that we hope to build a house of the Lord in Aba, Nigeria. Brother Pace, we may be delayed in Ghana, but we hope there will be no delay in Nigeria" ("A Time of New Beginnings," *Ensign*, May 2000, 88).

I just about fell out of my chair. I looked down in the audience to where I had previously spotted some familiar black faces. At the "amen" I bolted off the stand and began a sacred, tearful celebration with a few African friends. We would have remained all night had we not been expelled from the premises by ushers and security guards. I couldn't wait to get back to Africa to hear the reaction of the Nigerian Saints.

The next day I was invited to a meeting with President Hinckley, where we discussed both temples. It was a fitting climax to two years of work. When I walked in he was beaming from ear to ear. It was as if he was saying, "I really put one over on you, didn't I!"

He apologized for not conferring with me on the Nigeria Temple before announcing it, but, he explained, the decision was only made Sunday morning. I told him I was so thrilled about the temple being announced, I hadn't even thought about that. This thoughtful little visit with him at an extremely busy time for him will remain one of the highlights of my ministry.

On April 6, I attended the broadcast of the Palmyra Temple dedication in the Church Office Building. Of course, I was thinking about what it would be like to attend the first temple dedication in West Africa. I had accepted the fact that I would not be present at such a dedication, but I was thrilled to think of the possibility of attending the groundbreaking of at least one of them.

9

GOLDEN CALVES

B ack in Africa, I was still on an emotional and spiritual high as we held our area training for all the mission, stake, and district presidents of West Africa. And yet I knew there was still much for the members to do in the way of personal preparation.

As I met with these brethren, I said, "Because the Church is so young here there is a tendency to think of the Church as if in our infancy. I have described you to others as being very childlike. That is meant as a compliment, because the Savior told us we must all become as teachable and humble as children in order to return to him. As we read in Mark, 'Verily I say unto you, Whosoever shall not receive the kingdom of God as a little child, he shall not enter therein' (Mark 10:15).

"However, there is another scripture that reads, 'When I was a child, I spake as a child, I understood as a child, I thought as a child: but when I became a man, I put away childish things' (1 Corinthians 13:11).

"It is time for the Church in Africa to grow out of its infancy and to put away childish things. We are going to have to grow up fast, and we don't have time to be rebellious teenagers. If we don't mature quickly we will not be able to accommodate the growth ahead, and the branches will outgrow the roots. The future of the Church is in this room and those you train in your local areas.

"As Lehi said to his sons, 'And now that my soul might have joy in you, and that my heart might leave this world with gladness because of you, that I might not be brought down with grief and sorrow to the grave, arise from the dust, my sons, and be men' (2 Nephi 1:21).

"The fact that President Hinckley has announced the Nigerian Temple just three weeks after the killings that took place right near the temple site tells me we have all experienced divine intervention through the Lord's living prophet. There was every reason in the world to postpone this temple until we could see what would happen with Sharia law, problems in the delta region, and many other civil disturbances.

"We have much work to do to prepare our members to enter the temple. Are we satisfied with the number of members in our stakes who could enter the temple if its doors opened tomorrow? I'm not. I think we should have at least twice as many worthy recommend holders next year as we have today.

"I trust we are all excited about what has happened and recognize the hand of the Lord in the affairs of our members in Africa. Will that excitement be enough to thrust you into a new day? Are you rejuvenated enough to meet the challenge? If this isn't enough to move you onward and upward, what is it going to take?

"Now, what about Ghana? I can testify that since the special fast on November 7, 1999, there has been movement. I am a witness to seeing the hand of the Lord moving things around. He is touching certain people. The pieces of the puzzle are coming together in a beautiful manner. Hearts are being softened. I believe if we remain patient with the Lord's timetable but become more impatient with getting our own lives in order, we could well see two temples being built in West Africa at about the same time. We have done well, but we must do even better. We thank you and the members of the Church throughout West Africa for the increased worthiness that brought about the Lord's intervention in Nigeria and is bringing about an inevitable victory in Accra."

Major Setbacks

During the next few months we had some major setbacks that began to burst my bubble of elation about the approval of the Nigerian Temple. We discovered some major instances of embezzlement by Church employees in three different countries. I have not mentioned any of their names in this book. I say this to make certain that what I write now will not cast any suspicion on any of the people I have praised herein. Nevertheless, the employees in question had traveled with us, eaten with us, prayed with us, and protected us. It caused me serious heartache then and much sorrow today that the same people who would have laid down their life for us and did risk their lives for us would also steal from the Church. I have never felt so betrayed. A journal entry at the time recorded my heartbreak:

"I met with an employee today who was involved in a transaction where he took money under the table to purchase land. It makes you shudder to consider how common this is in this culture. He had shown us around various places in his country and would have done anything to protect us. It really breaks your heart to be so betrayed and think they would risk their standing in the kingdom. I'm trying hard not to become so cynical that I don't trust anyone. There are so many problems in Africa. On days like today you wonder if the Church can survive it. I suspect there will be a real sifting before it is over."

Corruption is a major problem in these countries. You see it in the government from top to bottom, and it has a tendency to carry over into the lives of members of the Church. It is one of the biggest problems we face. Complete honesty is a virtue that has not been internalized by large segments of the population, in spite of its being as old as the Ten Commandments. Concern about conflict of interest is totally foreign to many. Their culture of "dashing" (bribing or tipping) is acceptable and not thought to be akin to bribery. Money under the table is often viewed as a finder's fee.

Contention was another major problem that began to increase about this time. In Africa when you go to a conference and have the annual sustaining of general and local leaders of the Church, you live in fear and trembling that the leaders won't be sustained. It was not uncommon at all to have several raise their hands in opposition to a stake presidency. Part of the problem was that they didn't understand the difference between a sustaining vote and a popular vote. When I interviewed those who would not sustain the leaders, I would find the most common objections arose from tribal loyalties.

Tribalism manifests itself in many other areas. Loyalties to a tribe are usually much stronger than loyalties to a nation and often much stronger than loyalties to the Church. This results in numerous serious problems in the missions, stakes, and wards.

These problems, all normally serious enough, seemed to be magnified at this particular time. The adversary was hastening his work even as the Lord was.

Modern-Day Golden Calves

I had been studying the Old Testament the previous year and came to realize that many things we were experiencing were similar to some Old Testament problems. In fact, I believe I came to a better understanding of the African people by reading the Old Testament. I began to develop some teachings based on that insight. My objective was to help prepare the people for the temple, and to do so I felt I needed to speak very boldly. That talk became my main theme for the next several months. After repeating my observations about how the people of Africa were childlike in a positive way, and my counsel that we not persist in childishness, I continued:

"It is time for the Church in Nigeria to grow out of its infancy and put away childish things. A temple has been announced in your backyard. The temple will not bless the lives of the Saints in Nigeria unless the members are spiritually mature enough to enter it. It does no good to go through the temple if the temple doesn't go through you. Now is the time to prepare. . . .

"Other countries in the world refer to Nigeria as a Third World country. It is my vision that the Church in Nigeria does not have to be a Third World church. If we don't want to stay a Third World church, we need to stop acting like one. Some of the things we observe are much like the spiritual immaturity of the children of Israel at the time of Moses. It took them forty years in the wilderness before they were able to inherit the promised land. Even then, the Lord told Moses that the Israelites' success was more due to the wickedness of the people already possessing the land than it was to the righteousness of the children of Israel.

"As written in Exodus Moses went up to Mount Sinai where he received the Ten Commandments. 'And he gave unto Moses, when he had made an end of communing with him upon mount Sinai, two tables of testimony, tables of stone, written with the finger of God' (Exodus 31:18).

"We are all familiar with the story of the Ten Commandments. However, something else happened during those forty days. Almost immediately after giving the Ten Commandments and other terms of the covenant (Exodus 20–23), God gave some other instructions. What did he say?

"'And let them make me a sanctuary; that I may dwell among them' (Exodus 25:8).

"The Lord gave directions for fashioning a tabernacle (Exodus 24–27), the most sacred structure of Moses' Israel. Moses not only came away from the mountain with the Ten Commandments, but he also came down out of the mountain with plans for a temple.

"Moses was gone for forty days and forty nights. While he was gone what happened?

"'And when the people saw that Moses delayed to come down out of the mount, the people gathered themselves together unto Aaron, and said unto him: Up, make us gods, which shall go before us; for as for this Moses, the man that brought us up out of the land of Egypt, we wot not what is become of him" (Exodus 32:1).

"Meanwhile back on the mountain the Lord warned Moses of what was going on in camp. 'And the Lord said unto Moses, Go, get thee down; for thy people, which thou broughtest out of the land of Egypt, have corrupted themselves' (Exodus 32:7).

"So Moses took the tablets and the temple plans back down the mountain. 'And it came to pass, as soon as he came nigh unto the camp, that he saw the calf, and the dancing: and Moses' anger waxed hot, and he cast the tables out of his hands, and brake them beneath the mount' (Exodus 32:19).

"So Moses went up to the mount, received the Ten Commandments, and received permission and instructions on how to build the temple (tabernacle). And while he was speaking with the Lord and receiving this instruction that would enable the children of Israel to become purified and sanctified, what were the people doing? They were constructing and worshiping a golden calf.

"Last April this Area Presidency went to the mountain of the Lord's house and met with our current prophet. He revealed to us there would soon be a temple in Aba, Nigeria. As we came back from Church headquarters last April so excited about the temple in Aba, what did we find in the Africa West Area? Golden calves!

"Anything that keeps a member from being temple worthy is a golden calf. There are some golden calves in this stake, and I'm going to speak very plainly about some of them.

"What percentage of adults in this stake do you think will be endowed when we open the temple in Aba? It will be far too low because those paying a full tithing is very low. Golden calves! I continue to believe we would have a temple in Ghana right now if we had prepared ourselves better by paying our tithes and offerings.

"The other day I heard a report coming from one of your stakes that many members excuse themselves from paying their tithing because "the Church is rich" and the people need the money more than the Church. Golden calves!

"How are our members doing in legalizing their marriages? Golden calves! They cannot obtain a temple recommend unless they are paying a full tithing, and they cannot obtain a temple recommend if they have not legalized their marriage.

"One of the temple worthiness questions is, 'Are you honest in your dealings with your fellowmen?' We sometimes pass over that one very fast because most people think they are honest with their fellowmen. Honesty and integrity need to be taught and lived. We are living in a culture where corruption has become such a fact of life that it is accepted by many as part of being a clever businessman. This filters down into the individual lives of our members. Golden calves!

"Theft is much too common in the Church. Far too many members have had to be excommunicated for embezzling Church funds. Others have been caught doing so and no action has been taken by priesthood leadership. Golden calves! When disciplinary action is not taken on an embezzlement of Church funds, two problems result. First, it suggests stake and district presidents don't realize the gravity of dishonesty. Second, it sends a signal to members of the Church that dishonesty is condoned. We receive many letters from members asking why no action has been taken on certain cases.

"'Honesty implies freedom from lying, stealing, cheating, and bearing false witness' (quoted by Marion G. Romney, "'We Believe in Being Honest,'" *Ensign*, Nov. 1976, 36).

"Lying and bearing false witness in Nigeria is far too common. Golden calves!

"I would like to bring to your attention that overstating sacrament meeting attendance is a form of embezzlement. The budget allowance is based on attendance, and if we overstate it, we are stealing Church funds. Golden calves!

"I would now like to speak about tribalism. Many place tribal loyalties above loyalties to the kingdom of God. This isn't a golden calf, this is a gigantic golden bull. There is no room for tribalism in the Church when it is in conflict with divine priesthood government or the doctrines restored to the earth by living prophets. Callings come to an inspired leader. That leader must be 'tribe blind' or he won't be able to function in his calling. We understand this attitude spills over into our missionaries. If we aren't careful, there is an underground network in a mission that builds up around tribal lines. When this happens we are no different from a Gadianton society. There is no room in The Church of Jesus Christ of Latter-day Saints for tribalism. It is a golden bull that can destroy a branch, ward, stake, mission, or area, if we don't get it under control.

"When we joined this church we all became members of the same tribe—the Tribe or House of Israel. Any person who will not sustain and support a priesthood leader because he is from a different tribe is on his way to apostasy; his actions could result in a disciplinary council and excommunication from the Church. Anyone who will not support a local leader because he is not from the same tribe does not support the Area Presidency or the First Presidency of the Church. The only legitimate reason for not supporting a leader is if it is known that leader is unworthy of a temple recommend.

"Bearing false witness against the character of a priesthood leader or anyone else in an attempt to place them in an unfavorable light is an action that is unworthy of a good member of the Church and doing so can bring his own membership into question. Dishonesty, including bearing false witness, and tribalism are golden calves of a great magnitude.

"We hear reports that many members feel it is more important that their son or daughter marry a member of the same tribe than that they marry a member of our church. Golden calves! Brethren, we know this is a very complex issue. We know villages, relatives, and friends may ostracize your family over an issue like this. But somewhere, somehow, sometime, someone has got to stand up and be counted and do what the Spirit tells him is right.

"It is time to accept the full gospel and assimilate it into our lives. We need to internalize what we have been taught. Joseph Smith had some similar problems in the early years of the Church with people wanting to come into the Church and bring their golden calves with them. There was a particular group of people called the 'Shakers.' In the Doctrine and Covenants we read: 'Behold, I say unto you, that they desire to know the truth in part, but not all, for they are not right before me and must needs repent' (D&C 49:2).

"We have some problems with people in Nigeria coming into the Church and wanting to bring their golden calves with them. They are guilty of wanting to live the gospel but not all of it. They want to bring traditional rituals. They continue to treat their wives like they are chattel and their daughters like they are not as loved and respected as their sons.

"I repeat that anything that prevents us from being temple worthy is a golden calf, and it needs to be melted down."

Nothing Short of Miraculous

I know this talk has an "edge" to it and may appear to be hard or even insensitive to the reader. I had been with these people for more than two years at this point, and we had suffered through much together. As concerned as I was over the things expressed above, I would always come out of these meetings with increased love for the people. I'd conclude by saying something like, "Now before you start picking up stones, I want to conclude by telling you how much I love you and that I only want to make it possible for you to receive all the blessings the Lord has to offer you. Have I spoken too harshly?"

They would be unified in their response: "No, no, we need to know these things; teach us more." By then you would want to take it back and just tickle their ears, but the Lord would forbid it.

I attended a Sunday School class once in West Africa and asked the class where they thought they were in the Book of Mormon cycle. They said they were in the suffering stage but hadn't reached the humility and repentance part of the cycle yet; therefore, the Lord had not been able to bless them with prosperity. They were harder on themselves than I ever was.

This book would have been too slanted if I didn't bring up the negatives, and you would think me very naive. I prefer to dwell on the positive, but I can't be blind to the challenges. Nevertheless, I spent a lot of time pondering how we could ever keep up with the teaching and training that needed to be done. After a long day in Nigeria on one occasion I reflected: "They are so new in the Church and growing so fast. We get to each stake once a year, and the stake presidents come to Accra twice a year. How do you keep the doctrine pure, let alone make sure they understand the complex administration of the Church?"

As I prepared for our annual report to a committee of the Twelve, I contemplated the year since our last report and realized we had some major challenges such as described earlier and penned the following: "I vacillate between being overwhelmed by how far we have to go and seeing the miracles of how far we have come. . . .

When you list all the challenges it is overwhelming, but when you concentrate on the progress made it is encouraging and miraculous."

At the end of our report we said: "It may be that Joseph would have been happy to trade the problems he had with the Church membership and leadership in his first fifteen years with those we are experiencing in our infancy in West Africa. It is nothing short of miraculous that we have experienced a 50 percent growth in the last three years and are still maintaining an activity rate of over 50 percent.

"Hence, the word *miraculous* is not being overly dramatic. The results also demonstrate the believing heart of the African people. We have a challenging but fulfilling assignment."

Red Flags

Those challenges continued. On November 9, I wrote: "I really do feel bad about the struggle we are having in Africa right now with the righteousness of the people. I just found out two missionaries in the Congo have been caught in some immoral conduct, which doesn't help the Church in that little district. It just seems like everything is going wrong right now. I know I'm going to face some tough moments in my upcoming trip to Nigeria because of contention in the stake. You'd think we are getting close to building a temple or something."

I did run into a buzz saw at a stake conference in Nigeria that month. When I arrived, a delegation of returned missionaries was requesting a meeting with me. They wondered if it would be all right to set up an organization of returned missionaries for activation, support, and worship. To those without experience in Africa, this may sound like a wonderful idea—but I saw red flags everywhere. It is an example of how careful we need to be during this tender age in the development of the Church in Africa. The proposal sounded very innocent, but before long the organization, which falls outside of priesthood lines, could lead to the group to being critical of local leaders. In some cases we have seen such things lead to outright apostasy.

Many of the priesthood leaders at this time were less experienced in doctrine and Church administration than the returned missionaries. Due to this circumstance, the missionaries can get prideful and start to give inappropriate "counsel" to the priesthood leaders. On the other hand, some priesthood leaders feel threatened by returned missionaries and don't issue meaningful calls to them. They feel this will "keep them in check." As I considered these things I found myself wondering: "How do you make certain the kingdom stays in order when we are growing so fast? Are we growing too fast?"

I felt the priesthood leadership session of the stake conference went very well, in spite of my being very direct on the "Golden Calf" issue, which included things we must root out or melt down in the African Church culture. When I was finished I asked, "Can you go back and teach this to your wards and quorums?" They responded, "Please, will you do it tomorrow?" I said, "In other words, you want them to get upset with me and not you?" Nevertheless, I told them I would teach those same things in the general session.

In the general session they all seemed to take the tough medicine I was doling out, which I tried to mix with heavy doses of testimony, humor, and love. We left walking on air, thinking our mission had been accomplished. But just before we got into the car we were met by a delegation of about twelve very angry men. The spokesman shook his finger in my face and screamed, "We want to see you!" to which the stake president said, "There is no need." I asked what was going on and they yelled, "You didn't let us sustain the prophet!" Translated, that meant, "You didn't give us a chance to 'vote' against the stake president." I explained we do that only once a year, in the first stake conference of the year.

This didn't satisfy them, so they stomped off saying they were going to write the leaders in Salt Lake City. I've never seen a member of the Church so angry. Nigerians are very demonstrative and can get a little agitated. All twelve of these members belonged to a different tribe from the president of the stake. My fantasy about "fixing everything" with my golden calves speech quickly flew out the window. This left a little sour note on what I thought was one of the most powerful general sessions we'd had.

I would like to interject a testimonial about the inspiration and wisdom of having Area Authority Seventies. Over and over again we would call upon our local Seventies to deal with some of these tough issues. I was able to assign Elder Eka, a Nigerian, to get to the bottom of this situation in Nigeria.

Later in the year, in another area, the stake president was accused of serious transgressions. I knew we either had an apostasy and false-witness situation on the part of the accuser or a transgression problem on the part of the accused. Either way it was a lose-lose situation. I was grateful I could assign an Area Authority Seventy to deal with it, sorting through the cultural nuances.

I could have stayed in Africa the rest of my life and not come to a real understanding of what it is like to be an African. Area Authority Seventies are indispensable to the rolling out of the kingdom. They are making all the difference in the world. I would have failed miserably in my ministry without them.

"We've Got a Temple"

At the end of several months of doom, gloom, and golden calves we received a burst of light. We had enjoyed a much-welcomed visit from our son and daughter-in-law, and had just returned from taking them to the airport. We were feeling somewhat melancholy about having them leave us as we went back to the house. Then the doorbell rang. It was the Bonnets. They came in and sat down and then

Georges, in a very somber way, said, "We've got a temple." I thought he was talking about Aba, Nigeria, because the bids were due on the road and bridge that day. He said, "No, I mean we've got the Ghana temple." I waited for the punch line, which was not forthcoming. Finally, I said, "Are you serious?" I soon learned that he was.

Unfortunately, I cannot describe the details of how this came about. Many people are to be thanked but would prefer to remain anonymous. They know who they are. My journal entry for the next day (December 6, 2000) perhaps explains all that needs to be said:

"I've tried to analyze what has happened in the last two years, but I am at a loss to explain it. I think everything that has been done with different influential people has slowly had an impact on the powers that be. All it took was one last little push, which occurred yesterday. After all the analyzing is done, I know the Lord has just taken things into his own hands and slowly and gently softened the appropriate hearts in response to the prayers of the Saints. I feel the Lord has done this because of the critical mass of Saints who have prepared to enter the temple.

"My feelings are hard to describe. I'm feeling very subdued. Jolene said, 'You didn't act very excited.' I'm feeling shocked because the last thing I would have guessed is that something would happen before the elections. I'm also not allowing myself to celebrate until we receive formal approvals and know we are moving forward. The whole thing is somewhat bizarre with the way everything just fell into place overnight. It is miraculous and sacred to the point I have positive, grateful feelings, but 'celebrating' doesn't seem appropriate. This is the crowning moment of my ministry here, but silent jubilation seems in order right now. There will be time for 'Hosanna' later.

"We are a little saddened that we won't be here to see these temples completed but overjoyed that we will see them started. I can go home a happy man."

My journal entry continued: "I'm having a hard time focusing on anything else for very long as I keep thinking of the next steps on the temple, such as how shall we let the members know before the rumors have things really distorted.

"As the day ended, I had that old memory of thinking we had the temple approved many times over the last two and one half years, only to have it fall apart. We didn't receive any more information throughout the day, but I can't imagine getting it done the day before elections."

The temple continued to be constantly on my mind, but thirty months of disappointments had taught me how to cope by keeping my emotions under check. On December 11, I recorded: "Thus far there is no word on the temple of a formal nature. I'm glad I withheld my exuberance until we know we've got it. Otherwise I'd be so anxious I'd be hard to live with. I guess I've been able to do that as a result of riding the roller coaster for so long—I've become accustomed to it. I don't want to become numb or unfeeling, but I don't think my system can take too much more in the agony and ecstasy departments.

"The elections are over in Ghana. Vice President Mills (V.P. to President Rawlings) and John Agyekum Kufour are going to have a run-off election, since neither of them received over 50 percent of the votes. I don't know who is best for us in regard to the temple."

The Strengths of the African People

By Christmas we still hadn't received official word on the temple. I knew I had to continue our other work, and during the Christmas break I crafted a strategic plan for Africa based on our thirty months of experience. I won't get into the details. I listed many of the "golden calf" problems and what we ought to do to combat them.

But I also noted many of the positive things we could see in Africa. In order to provide balance to this chapter, I would like to quote the last part of the document.

"In contrast to these golden calves there are an even greater number of things on the positive side of the ledger. The African people are inherently religious. They know their scriptures. They have a deep but simple faith in God. They recognize the Spirit when taught by the missionaries. They come to a quick and firm testimony of the Book of Mormon. They love to come to church, as indicated by the attendance figures. They love all phases of the Church. They love the songs of the Restoration and quickly learn them. They are teachable and humble. They are bright and learn quickly. They can laugh at themselves and at their old traditions when they are in conflict with gospel traditions. They are acquainted with dreams, visions, and manifestations. They believe God is a God of miracles and that the heavens are not closed. They readily accept the principle that revelation has not ceased and that Jesus Christ stands at the head of this church and reveals his will through apostles and prophets.

"Their family beliefs are such that our teachings as summarized in the *Proclamation to the World on the Family* are accepted readily. Even long-standing beliefs on the inferiority of women are falling quickly under the light of the gospel. The African culture has strong ties to the extended family. They 'take care of their own' much better than the American culture, who leave that task to the Church or government. They love and respect their ancestors, which will lead to an enthusiastic search for those they can take to the temple.

"African men are interested in religion, which has resulted in more men joining the Church than women. The Melchizedek Priesthood base is very high, which gives us the raw material for building a very adequate priesthood base. A generation of returned missionaries is maturing who will be able to lead the people to greater heights.

"The children of Israel had been slaves for four hundred years when Moses was called to free them. It took them forty years in the wilderness before they were ready to enter the promised land. The African people have been slaves in one way or another for thousands of years. We can't expect that all will be well after twenty years in the wilderness. We will have apostasy, embezzlement, transgression, and many other problems. There may even come a great sifting of those who have joined the Church for the wrong reasons. But through it all the Lord seems to be brooding over Africa and desires to give them all that he has. Two temples will soon grace the land, and we will see a change in our members and a change in the countries themselves. Our members will be blessed spiritually and temporally."

These were our feelings as we began our last year in the country. I knew in my heart that there would be a lid on our progress until the temples were built, and those temples were still less than a reality in both Nigeria and Ghana. It was my personal dream and goal to see the ground broken for both temples before I returned home in August of 2001.

10

EUPHORIA

We entered the New Year with new leadership in Ghana. President Jerry Rawling's party lost convincingly. John Agyekum Kufour became the first new president of Ghana in twenty years. This event left much to be pondered. After laboring thirty months with the Rawlings regime significant progress had been made. Now he and his people would be leaving office.

We remained cautiously optimistic about the approval of the Ghana temple. We still had received no official word.

During the next few weeks we received many calls from our members. The word on the streets of Accra was that the "Mormon Temple has been approved." This was encouraging, but until we had that written approval, I was still unwilling to claim victory.

The news on the Nigeria temple was not as encouraging. Thankfully, we had no outside force holding us up, but obtaining an acceptable bid from a reputable contractor was proving to be very difficult.

For the next few days, I spent nearly 100 percent of my waking hours in making phone calls and discussing strategies about the Ghana Temple. I thought of nothing else until I was jarred loose by a phone call on January 16. Elder Stucki called and informed me that Kabila, the president of the Democratic Republic of Congo, had been assassinated in his palace. This brought immediate, intense concerns for the safety of the missionaries and the members of the Church in the area. I felt it would be nice to go through one week in Africa without a serious disaster.

Early the next day I met with Elder Stucki about the safety of the missionaries. We had some leanings toward closing the country down to missionary work until things became more stable. I always felt we needed to continue our work within a country as best we could, but sometimes a country reaches such a state of disarray that we just can't function properly. The mission president couldn't even visit Lubumbashi. When they left the compound they never knew whether their vehicle was going to be commandeered. As a minimum we would need to evacuate the mission president and the missionary couples. The missionaries themselves were African, and half of them were Congolese. They could blend into the community and wouldn't need to be evacuated.

With all these irons in the fire, it was time to go on the road again. Thankfully, Georges Bonnet was returning from Salt Lake City and could resume his command at "temple control." If that were not the case, I would have to cancel my mission tour.

"The Committee Was Satisfied"

We toured the Port Harcourt Nigeria Mission. At the completion of the tour as we arrived in Lagos, Ephraim Etete handed me an envelope he had received from Georges Bonnet. The envelope was handwritten and sealed with scotch tape and said on the outside, "February 7th, Elder Pace, from Georges, Personal." I waited until we had checked into the hotel. I read it and then casually handed it to Jolene, who had collapsed on the bed. It said: "Dear Elder Pace, I called Mr. Osei (of the Accra planning commission) last evening. The committee chaired by the mayor met on Tuesday—Project is

Elder Pace and Elder Ballard on the Ghanaian temple site in November 2000, fifteen years after they first visited Ethiopia.

approved. Tried to call you on Tuesday night, reached the mission home—and that was that—Sorry, could not find you. Will retrieve the letter from the AMA [Accra Metropolitan Assembly] Thursday or Friday. Will give you all the details when you are back. I hope you are well! With love and respect. Georges."

I recorded in my journal that same day: "You would think we would go ballistic. Jolene did let out her patented screech, but over-all we felt exquisite joy and celestial peace. We have been on cloud nine ever since."

The official letter was waiting for us when we arrived home. It said in part:

"In reviewing its decision at its meeting held on the 6th of February, 2001, the AMPC took into consideration the further interactions with your consultant, and head of Temple [temporal] affairs in the West Africa Area and the re-presentation of the project sketches and summary explanation of the proposed facilities, in addressing the issues and concerns raised in our earlier refusal.

"The Committee was satisfied with the explanation that the Temple as proposed in the Latter Day Saints, is not a place of mass worship but for religious instruction and ordinances. The proposed facilities as re-presented largely reflected a predominant mixed commercial land use and would therefore not infringe on the zoning regulation.

"The Committee has therefore, granted approval in principle to your application."

I have reflected on this point in history many times. For thirty months I had felt like I was running into a brick wall. I would get up, clean up my wounds, and run again. I would run at the wall faster, slower, and from further back. I tried jumping over it and dig-ging and crawling under it. The wall didn't fall. It didn't even budge. I just kept getting more bruised and bloodied. Then, when it was time, the Lord just gently blew it over. In hindsight, I believe the wall came down because so many African members got serious about living the gospel. If I had any impact on increasing the righteousness of the Saints, I would be elated.

The rolling out of the kingdom in accordance with the Master's plan cannot be stopped.

Announcing the Good News

As fate would have it, Elders Jeffrey R. Holland and Earl C. Tingey arrived on February 14 for a few days. We had already scheduled a special meeting of the Saints on February 15 in Accra so the members could hear them speak. We decided we would make the announcement about the temple to the members at that time. It seemed very fitting, since Elder Holland was in attendance in February 1998 when President Hinckley made the original announcement. Three full years had now gone by.

I was so excited for that meeting it was hard to get through our strategy sessions with the visiting Brethren. I broke away long enough to draft a letter to be read to the congregation on Thursday night.

When we arrived at the member fireside, we were greeted by Stake Presidents Sono-Koree and Ahadjie. Sister Holland was wearing an African dress the women had given her, and Sister Sono-Koree insisted on putting the head tie on her. Sister Holland was a good sport and wore it to the meeting, and the members loved it.

I conducted the meeting, and after the prayer I announced that the choir would sing "Plea for Africa." I told them I wanted them to sing it better than they had ever sung it before, because we wanted them to sing their ancestors from the other side of the veil right into the meeting with us. I told them that after the song I had a very special announcement to make. I expected everyone would know what was going to happen, but I thought it would be worth their anticipation.

During the song I handed the announcement to President Sono-Koree and watched his expression. He exploded into a broad smile and gave a double take, looking at me and then the paper and back again, with his eyes filling with tears. After the song I said, "God bless Africa and all her sons and daughters. And now the Lord is going to do just that. I would like Presidents Sono-Koree and Ahadjie to stand by my side for this announcement." I then asked President Sono-Koree as the senior stake president to read the announcement. The letter read as follows:

February 15, 2001

To: Stake, District and Mission Presidents in the Africa West Area

Dear Brethren,

   Accra, Ghana Temple (To be read in sacrament meeting)
   It is with great pleasure and gratitude we inform you that on February 8, 2001, we received approval in principle from the Town and Country Planning Department of the Accra Metropolitan Assembly to build our temple on

Independence Avenue in Accra, Ghana. We expect to begin construction within the next few months.

We express appreciation to all who have helped in this approval process and to members of the Church in the Africa West Area and throughout the world who have fasted and prayed for the approval that is now ours. We thank all members who have been living temple-worthy lives and pray that many more will make the changes necessary to allow them to enter the Lord's House.

Above all, we express our love and adoration for the Lord who has lovingly and gently intervened on our behalf. We have been witnesses to a miracle.

> Sincerely your brethren,
> Glenn L. Pace
> H. Bruce Stucki
> Emmanuel O. Opare
> Africa West Area Presidency

As soon as it became obvious by the announcement that the temple had been approved, the audience erupted. They stood up, applauded, and screamed. When President Sono-Koree concluded the letter, reading the words that expressed appreciation to the Lord for bringing about such a miracle, they erupted again. You would have thought we had just made a winning touchdown with one second to go. I told them we would excuse their applause and yelling in the chapel just this one time, and that brought laughter from all. As I put it in my journal, "We were all euphoric."

My feelings at this time can best be expressed in the hymn, "How Beautiful Thy Temples, Lord":

> *How beautiful thy temples, Lord!*
> *Each one a sacred shrine,*
> *Where faithful Saints, with one accord,*
> *Engage in work divine.*

How beautiful some aid to give
To dear ones we call dead,
But who indeed as spirits live;
They've only gone ahead.

How beautiful thy message, Lord,
The gospel, pure and true,
In these our days to earth restored
And taught to men anew.

How beautiful its faith and hope;
All mankind it would save,
Including in its aim and scope
The souls beyond the grave.

How beautiful thy promise, Lord,
That we may grow in truth,
And live, exalted by thy word,
In endless, glorious youth.

With loved ones sealed in holiness
By sacred temple rites,
Worlds without end we may progress
From heights to greater heights (Hymns, *288*).

On March 15 we had another joyous evening when we broke ground for the first missionary training center on the continent of Africa. I thought of how for more than two decades the West African mission presidents had to conduct their own mini-MTCs. Thus, every missionary we sent out was unendowed and only partially trained. I also reflected on the day more than a year earlier when Elder Stucki, Elder Opare, and I stood on that ground and felt very strongly that we should build our MTC there. It was satisfying to realize that dream was about to be fulfilled. My emotions were running deep. Next to being able to announce the temple approval, it was the highlight of our ministry.

With these major events behind us, we left for Salt Lake for conference. We were so grateful for the events of the previous two months that we could have flown back under our own power. On April 3 we attended "the meeting" of all General Authorities, where new assignments were given for the upcoming year. We were quite certain we would be coming back home. It became official at that meeting, and thus began three months of "last time" events in Africa.

More Straight Talk

At the end of April we had our area training with all the mission, stake, and district leaders in West Africa. This gave me a chance to express my love and appreciation to them for the last time, as well as give them my last shot at where we needed to go next:

"The instruction we received at general conference revolved around the family. I would like to spend a little time giving you my impressions of what we heard and what we need to do to follow the prophets on this issue in the Africa West Area.

"Moses 1:39 reads, 'For behold, this is my work and my glory—to bring to pass the immortality and eternal life of man.'

"The Lord has repeatedly revealed the importance of families in assisting him in his purpose 'to bring to pass the immortality and eternal life of man.' This is demonstrated in the experiences of Adam and Eve and their children; Noah and his family who were saved from the flood; Abraham, Isaac, and Jacob (a family); the twelve tribes of Israel (a family); and in many examples in the Book of Mormon, including the first verse: "I, Nephi, having been born of goodly parents, therefore I was taught somewhat in all the learning of my father' (1 Nephi 1:1).

"It was Lehi and his family who traveled to the Promised Land, along with Ishmael and his family. In latter days, it was families who crossed the plains and settled in the Salt Lake valley. Today the

Church is organized into wards and stakes, and they are extremely important and have a vital function to perform. However, we must always keep paramount in our minds that the Church has been established to serve the family.

"You will recall that last October I talked to you about golden calves. I have a few more golden calves to add to your list, which need to be melted down before the family can assume its primary role in bringing each family member back to the presence of the Lord.

"1. We need a better understanding of the role of womanhood and motherhood. Womanhood must be understood, appreciated, and honored.

"2. We need to work together to convert and baptize more women. Currently in the Africa West Area there are 43,000 adult men in the Church and 28,000 women. What this means is that one out of three men will not be able to receive the full blessings available in the temple because he will be married to a wife to whom he cannot be sealed.

"3. Marrying within the Church must become a higher priority than marrying within the tribe.

"4. We must find some way for our young men and young women to marry at an earlier age. Too many are getting dangerously beyond childbearing age before marrying and, therefore, the commandment to multiply and replenish the earth becomes impossible to live and the opportunity to raise a righteous generation passes them by. It may be that the financial responsibilities inherent in dowries need to be looked at in light of the Church culture.

"5. The practice of husbands and wives living in different villages or countries for long periods of time can diminish the opportunity for husband and wife to become as one and deprives children of being raised by a mother and father in the same home. In addition, it provides Satan with an opportunity to tempt the parties to break their covenants, thus destroying the marriage.

"6. The custom and practice of sending youth to boarding schools at a very young age deprives our youth of the love and teaching available from father and mother in the home. It also deprives them of some tender, loving sibling relationships.

"I'm sure you can think of many other examples of cultural traditions that could be working against our family focus.

"These traditions can strike at the heart of what we are being counseled to do in relation to family relationships. These traditions run deep, and hearts will need to be touched through teaching the doctrine. Frankly, I don't know how to overcome these traditions, but I believe the Lord will inspire you, the local leadership, to solve them. I have a testimony that as you study the doctrine contained in the *Proclamation on the Family* you will be inspired to find ways to put the doctrine into practice.

"Stake and ward councils would be a wonderful forum to discuss the doctrine behind these issues and to develop ways to lead the people into compliance with the doctrine so they can receive the attendant blessings.

"We have a wonderful window of opportunity as we are preparing our people to enter our temples and be joined together as families for time and for all eternity. The ultimate blessings received in the temple don't come just by participating in the ordinances. These blessings are available after we earn them through our righteousness. Eternal family relationships must be developed through association one with another in righteous lives and acts of love and service one to another.

"There is much that is right in this culture, and we have success stories unique to Africa. President Faust used Ghana as an example in a recent talk to General Authorities. He spoke of what happened during the time the government froze the activities of the Church.

He talked of 'how blessed the people were by continuing to worship as families even though they couldn't worship in churches. They will be further blessed when the blessings of a temple are available. Nothing will strengthen the members like preparing for a temple.'"

Another "last time" experience occurred on May 1, as we said good-bye to the great mission presidents we had grown to love. I cannot say enough for the dedication of those who have served as mission presidents and couples in the Africa West Area. They have dealt with unbelievable challenges, endured physical discomfort, and no small amount of danger. I pay a special tribute to the wives, who labor as partners to their companions, set an example of womanhood, live away from children and grandchildren, teach the doctrines, nurse the sick, and, in short, play a crucial role in the building of the kingdom throughout the world. It is my firm testimony that the couples who serve in Africa demonstrate one of the underlying principles of this book: *Each of us has a role to play in the Master's plan and each of us can make a difference.* I have never met a set of missionaries who come home feeling more fulfilled than the couples who have served in Africa. God bless them for their sacrifices.

After spending our final time with these good mission presidents, "I walked around alone for a little while and watched the stream of natives walking down the beach at sunset after their May Day celebration. I had that tug at my heart that I'd be leaving it all soon. The sky was red but my mood was blue."

The BYU Singers

In May the BYU Singers came to the country. They were a joy to behold—fifty bright-eyed, enthusiastic students ready to take on the world. One of my favorite nights was a concert at the Cape Coast Castle, which was one of the castles used in the slave trade. To have these wholesome, refreshing students perform there was a real treat. As I listened to the music and simultaneously thought of

Africa West Area presidency and Area Authority Seventies in 2001. From left: *Elders Chukwurah, Stucki, Pace, Opare, and Eka.*

the atrocities that had occurred in that slave castle—and then fast-forwarded to the realization that a temple was about to be built to free them all—it gave me a chill. I recorded the following:

"It was a very special night. The breeze from the ocean kept it cool, you could hear the waves crashing against the castle, and a full moon made an appearance halfway through the concert as it rose over the ocean. The Singers were great."

At one point the choir gave a special concert for a very high-ranking chief and his superior, the main chief for their tribe. He said to me, "As they sang I felt as if the heavens opened and angels were around us." I explained that "it was because of the lives the choir lead, as well as the music they sang." The report I got was that the main chief felt the same way and didn't want them to quit.

The choir had a very successful two weeks, which was concluded with a concert on the temple site on May 26. Before they began to sing, I said to the audience: "We thought it only fitting that this concluding concert should be on this sacred ground. The stage upon which the choir is standing has been placed where the holy temple will stand.

"When Moses approached the burning bush he was commanded to remove his shoes because he was on holy ground. After the temple is built and dedicated we will be asked to remove our shoes before entering. Today, we will not ask you to remove your shoes, but out of respect for the sacred, holy ground upon which we stand we are asking that the audience not applaud. This will also show respect for the Traditional Council of Chiefs in Accra who have asked that drums and clapping be discontinued in outside settings during this period of time.

"I would suggest at the end of each number when we would ordinarily show our appreciation with applause that we instead just wave our appreciation to the singers.

"We have arranged this concert on the temple site for two reasons. The first is to reward the singers for coming to Ghana by letting them stand on the temple site to sing. The second is to bring the members here together to unitedly pray for the speedy issuance of the final building permits that will allow us to begin construction. Monday, the day after tomorrow, we will submit our detailed plans to the planning commission as the last step prior to beginning construction. Therefore, as you listen to the singers please ponder and have a prayer in your heart that there will be no delays."

When we arrived that night, we could see that all six hundred of the chairs were quickly filling up. I had had some concern that we might have only fifty or sixty people there due to the threatening weather. Earlier in the day, when I had talked to the people setting up the chairs and putting final touches on the stand, the supervisor had looked up at the threatening sky and said, "We are finished, and our only concern is the weather." I responded, "Well, that's my responsibility."

As it turned out the whole sky was cloudy, which provided shelter from the sun, but it didn't rain the whole evening. We even had dragonflies appear in swarms to eat the mosquitoes.

I sat back ready to savor the evening as they sang their first song, but halfway through the second number one of the singers fainted, then another, and another. Evidently many of them had gotten sick in Benin and were dehydrated. We started packing them off the stage. Luckily, we had several doctors there, including some visiting physicians from the HART Foundation who were doing some humanitarian work.

After the embarrassment and inconvenience of the interruptions, things started getting better and better. By the time they finished we had regained the spiritual high we started out on and everyone loved it. The waving instead of clapping turned out to be so unique it will always be remembered. When the choir sang a couple of songs in the native language of the Ghanaians, the people waved so hard they almost fell off their chairs.

It was a magical night, and I was emotional all evening just looking into the faces of our wonderful members and realizing we would be leaving before long. On the other hand, I was so grateful we were leaving behind the gift of a temple approval. I asked the members how many of them had stood on the temple site before, and 95 percent of them had not. That alone was worth having the event.

The Chapel in Jos

At the conclusion of this event, the sudden realization was upon me that I had only one more major assignment—to dedicate a chapel in Jos, Nigeria. It seemed like the first time in the three years I had been in Africa that I had time to take a breath. I didn't really enjoy it. I felt lost.

On June 7 (our thirty-eighth wedding anniversary), we left for our last assignment to Jos, Nigeria.

The background of the chapel in Jos is noteworthy. When I was on my first mission tour of Africa in Enugu in 1998, I received a phone call at the mission home. It was the leaders of the Church in Jos wondering if we were going to build our new chapel on the current site, where we had been meeting in an old building, or look for a new site. The question related to the fact that the current site was right across the street from a mosque. We suggested they take a delegation over to the mosque and speak with the leaders there. They did so, and the reaction of the Muslims was that of shock. They said, "No Christian has ever asked our opinion on anything of this nature. We would welcome you as our neighbors."

Several months after the dedication of the chapel more trouble developed in the country, and the Muslims were storming through the streets destroying Christian chapels. As they approached our building, our neighbors came running out of the mosque and their homes and turned away the mob. They said, "These are our friends. They are good people and have been good neighbors."

When we arrived at Jos on the day of the dedication, I walked into the chapel and received quite a shock. The floors were filthy with red dirt. There had been a deluge of rain, and as people had walked along the dirt road leading up to the chapel their shoes had become very muddy, which mud they carried with them into the building. It looked so bad I suggested we might not be able to dedicate the building at that point.

We had a new convert and investigator meeting scheduled for 9:00 A.M. There were about twenty in attendance, many of whom were well educated and will make an immediate contribution to the kingdom.

When we came out of that meeting, the building was teeming with members who had gone home and returned with mops and brooms to clean things up. There was no way they were going to let me leave without dedicating their church.

The general session and dedication was packed with chairs set up in all of the rooms and the hallways. Many of our Muslim friends were in attendance. Since the building had been spruced up as well as they could make it, we went forward with the dedication. It was a spiritual experience. As we started, a hush came over the audience. It reminded me of how the audience in general conference reacts when the prophet comes in. I was very glad we went forward with it. None of those in attendance except Jolene and I had ever seen a dedication before.

On Monday, June 16, we were ready for our last trip from Lagos to Accra. At the airport, as we waited for the airplane to come, I did my usual laps around the concourses and indulged in some reflecting and pondering. I met a man from Connecticut who was furious because his plane had been canceled the previous night and hadn't arrived yet this evening. He said, "I was supposed to leave a half hour ago." I just smiled (I was proud of myself for not guffawing) and nodded knowingly. I assumed he hadn't had much African experience. I was right—he had been there for only three weeks on business. You learn a lot more in three years. I looked out the window and saw our plane taxi in from the domestic airport. It was a good sight and we left on time.

I received word on June 19 that construction on the temple would not take place until October or November. This put to rest any remaining hope I had about being able to participate in the groundbreaking. I already knew the Aba Nigeria Temple would be delayed longer than that, since we still didn't have a contractor.

John Agyekum Kufour

In June, President Kufour made a surprise visit to a corporation in Accra owned by members of the Church from America. Two years earlier these members called asking my opinion on setting up a data-entry business in West Africa similar to what they had done in other developing countries. I suggested Ghana would be the best place to do it. They moved on it very quickly, and now were in a situation where they employed hundreds of people, many of whom were members of the Church, including top management. President Kufour was very impressed with what he saw. He asked, "How did this all come about?" His escort told him the story about the company contacting me about where to set up operations and that it was because of the Church they were in Ghana. The escort hastened to add that only 20 percent of the employees were members. President Kufour said, "Don't you apologize for one minute about that." All that mattered was that they were 100 percent Ghanaians, which they were. He then made a comment that any church that could do something like that must be taken seriously.

A year later President Kufour was hosted in Salt Lake City by the First Presidency. He visited all the main sights, including the temple and the humanitarian center. Of course, he spent time with the First Presidency. This event went unnoticed by most. It did not go unnoticed by me. Imagine my joy, with all I had experienced, to see this come about. The relationship with the president of Ghana is secure! The temple cannot be stopped! *The rolling out of the kingdom in accordance with the Master's plan cannot be stopped.*

During this same period Georges would talk to me every day about the progress of the final plans for the temple. On June 22 he came in again, expressing how spiritual he had felt ever since the special concert on the temple site and that he could tell things would now come together. As I recorded in my journal, "He just keeps seeing miracles. The Lord has taken this into his own hands."

The Stuckis and the Bonnets left for a trip home in July, which left us with our last few days alone. I missed them immediately, and when they left I really felt the curtain come down. With a certain feeling of melancholy, I wrote, "I'm a lame duck figurehead here for two more weeks. Elder Stucki will become the new Area President.

When he leaves there will be someone else, just as there were others before me. I will soon be forgotten, but I will never forget. For my remaining time, I'll put out fires but won't start any new ones. It is beginning to feel like it is over. I'm sure when the moving van picks up our stuff Monday I will feel like an elder without a cause for the remaining ten days."

God Bless Africa!

We got an invitation from the Lartebiokorshie Stake to come to a final fireside on July 22. The invitation read: "This fireside is so important to us because of the good leadership you have exemplified for the past three years of your stay in Ghana. We wish to hear and learn more from both of you before you finally embark on your journey. We wish you both a *Safe Journey.*"

We accepted the invitation, and on July 22 we gave our last address to the Saints in Ghana. It was held at the Lartebiokorshie chapel I dedicated three years earlier. The chapel and overflow were full, and a strong spirit was there. Jolene spoke about pioneers and families and expressed her love. I basically summarized the few points we had been teaching for three years and expressed our appreciation. It was all received very well; and afterwards everyone wanted to shake our hands and thank us, which is different from the norm. The Africans feel it is presumptuous to approach a "dignitary" to shake their hand. Others think they are trying to befriend "the chief" for special favors.

They bestowed gifts on us—a dress for Jolene and a wood-carved puzzle showing a missionary handing out a Book of Mormon for me, as well as a Ghanaian tie. They loved it when I immediately took off my tie and put on the new Ghanaian one.

I recorded, "This will be my last public address to Africans. I will miss the spiritual and emotional response they give to teaching. It will seem very bland when I get back home."

*Elder and Sister Pace dressed in native clothes given to them by
Ghanaian members as a farewell present in July 2001.*

For perspective I include the final talk I gave in that fireside on
July 22, 2001.

"It has been a joy to labor with you at this critical time in the
history of the Church in West Africa. We have seen the foundation
of the Church laid and have watched the building start to take shape.
We have had many problems, some of them very serious, but the
memories we take home with us will be positive. We have developed
a love and respect for the African people. As I said in my general
conference talk last year:

"'The African people have waited for centuries to receive the fulness of the gospel and have been through much pain and suffering.
Now, at last, they can receive every blessing available to God's
children.

"'Through centuries of suffering, the people in general have not become bitter. They are humble, teachable, and God-fearing. They know the scriptures, and they recognize the Shepherd's voice.

"'I have faith in their faith. I know the Savior loves the African people. Therefore, to paraphrase verse 33 of the 121st section of the Doctrine and Covenants, "As well might man stretch forth his puny arm to stop the (Congo) river in its decreed course, or to turn it up stream, as to hinder the Almighty from (building a temple for the African Latter-day Saints).

"'It has been inspiring to see the Lord's hand in bringing the forces together that will lead to an inevitable victory. There will be a temple in West Africa.'

"That talk was given in April of the year 2000. When Elder Holland was here in February of this year, we were able to make the long-awaited announcement. We assure you things are still moving smoothly. We hope to begin construction of the stake center in August, the office building in September, and the temple in October. Nothing on the outside is holding us up now. We are completing the detailed drawings for all of the buildings, and the Accra Metropolitan Assembly has approved everything we have turned in thus far.

"In the last part of May we had the BYU Singers perform a concert on the temple site. It was a very spiritual day and evening for Sister Pace and me. As we walked on the site about noon that day to inspect the site, we both had a spiritual experience. The day became more than a concert on the temple site. It brought together the culmination of three years of work in getting the temple approved and trying to prepare the members to enter. As we walked around the site all alone we had a witness of the Spirit that it was finally a reality. There will be a temple in West Africa!

"Until that time we were feeling a little bit sad and empty that we had worked so hard and were not even going to be present at the groundbreaking. However, as we looked at the stage that was sitting on the footprint of the temple, and saw the Ghanaian flag waving in

*The Angel Moroni atop the Ghana Temple in the summer of 2003,
when the temple was still under construction. (Photo courtesy Michael K. Kirkpatrick.)*

the breeze, it was as if the stage became the temple and the flag became the Angel Moroni. I felt in my soul more audible than a physical voice:

"'The temple is here at long last. You have done what I asked you to do. You can go home now. *Safe Journey.*' Sister Pace felt the same thing at the same time, and we will always remember that experience. The Lord had accepted our sacrifice and yours. I commented to Sister Pace that I could not feel any happier at the groundbreaking or the dedication of the temple than I felt at that moment.

"We want everyone to know that we will be with you in spirit at the groundbreaking and the dedication. No person will be watching the progress with more interest than us. Georges Bonnet has promised to send us pictures of the temple at various stages of construction. We may not be at the dedication, because General

The Ghana Temple, still under construction, summer 2003. (Photo courtesy Michael K. Kirkpatrick.)

Authorities don't attend dedications outside of their assigned area without the invitation of the First Presidency. Generally only members of the current Area Presidency attend. We want you to know that if we are not here it won't be because of lack of interest but out of obedience.

"On numerous occasions I have compared our three years here to Moses in leading the children of Israel out of Egypt. You are very familiar with the story of Moses and his dealings with the Pharaoh. I've often felt the frustration he must have felt when he could not persuade the Pharaoh to 'let his people go.' In my case it was 'Let the temple be built.' Now we have that permission. I'm sorry for the delay.

"Now we reach my final chapter in the story of Moses. After all this time of wandering with you in the wilderness, I am not going to be able to enter the promised land. However, my joy will be full if you will walk the walk into the promised land and on into the temple.

"In closing, I want to express my love and appreciation to you and all the Saints in Africa for what has been the most spiritual three years of my life. I have been a General Authority for sixteen years now and have seen many things and enjoyed many blessings. I have rubbed shoulders with prophets, seers, and revelators, but these last three years have been the most inspirational of my ministry.

"I would like to thank you for the response you have given to our teachings and the improvements you have made. The progress is miraculous. We have numerous problems and obstacles, but with God all things are possible, and he is showering down his blessings upon us.

"I think I can best express the way I feel as I am about to depart your land by quoting the words of Paul to the Thessalonians. I feel for you what he felt for them.

"'For neither at any time used we flattering words, as ye know . . . ; God is witness. . . . But we were gentle among you, even as a nurse cherisheth her children:

"'So being affectionately desirous of you, we were willing to have imparted unto you, not the gospel of God only, but also our own souls, because ye were dear unto us' (1 Thessalonians 2:5, 7–8).

"God bless the members of the Church and their families as they prepare for the sacred ordinances of the temple. And God bless Africa and all her sons and daughters with a *safe journey* back to their Father in Heaven."

EPILOGUE

On July 28, 2001, I left the area office in Ghana for the last time. "At about 6:00 P.M. I packed all the remaining signs of Elder Pace into my briefcase, turned at the door, looked into the empty office, walked down the hall, into the elevator, out to the parking lot, and drove away for the final time. How very, very strange."

About two months later I was conducting a mission tour in the New York Rochester Mission. I was still in culture shock. I was becoming accustomed once again to all the comforts of life available in America. But I had not yet adjusted to missing the people of Africa.

I went to Palmyra. This was my first visit to the restored log cabin residence of Joseph Smith where he was living at the time of the First Vision and the appearance of Moroni. The couples had given me excellent tours of all the buildings, the Sacred Grove, and the Hill Cumorah. I had to pinch myself to see if this was all real. I finally extricated myself from my tour guides and walked into the Sacred Grove alone.

I had been there on several occasions, but never had I appreciated and savored it more. I could not imagine that passing through the veil could bring any more ecstasy, joy, elation, bliss, or any other positive state of mind than I was feeling at that moment. I wondered if I had ever been happier on this earth.

As I was contemplating and savoring the moment, I glanced through the trees and could see the Smiths' log house and the Palmyra Temple in the background, with the spires and the statue of Moroni rising up through the trees surrounding the temple. This immediately brought to my memory the temples that were yet to be built in Accra, Ghana, and Aba, Nigeria.

From there my thoughts went to the Saints in Africa, and I started to feel melancholy. This was not just because I missed them at that moment, but also because I realized that a very small fraction of the Saints in Africa would ever stand in the Sacred Grove. They are so faithful and the experience I was having would mean so much to them, and yet it would never be theirs. It didn't seem fair.

At that moment I received a revelation in the form of an impression. Into my mind came words I could understand. "Oh, Glenn, haven't I taught you anything yet? Haven't you learned anything from your African experience? Do you remember that day in May when you stood on the site where the temple will be built and looked up at the Ghanaian flag waving in the breeze? Is your joy here in the Sacred Grove today any greater than that which you felt while standing on that sacred ground? You don't have to be in the Sacred Grove to know what happened here. I'm no respecter of persons. I can visit my house in Ghana just as easily as I can visit the Sacred Grove."

I finally got it.

The Savior's love for his children is universal.

BOOKS CITED

Benson, Ezra Taft. *Teachings of Ezra Taft Benson.* Salt Lake City: Bookcraft, 1988.

Bowen, Albert E. *The Church Welfare Plan.* Salt Lake City: Deseret Sunday School Union, 1946.

Brown, Hugh B. *Eternal Quest.* Salt Lake City: Bookcraft, 1956.

Cannon, George Q. *Gospel Truth: Discourses and Writings of George Q. Cannon.* Selected, arranged, and edited by Jerreld L. Newquist. Salt Lake City: Deseret Book, 1987.

Hymns of the Church of Jesus Christ of Latter-day Saints. Salt Lake City: The Church of Jesus Christ of Latter-day Saints, 1985.

Journal of Discourses. 26 vols. London: Latter-day Saints' Book Depot, 1854–86.

Kimball, Spencer W. *The Miracle of Forgiveness.* Salt Lake City: Bookcraft, 1969.

Lee, Harold B. *Stand Ye in Holy Places.* Salt Lake City: Deseret Book, 1974.

Madsen, Truman G. *Eternal Man.* Salt Lake City: Deseret Book, 1966.

McConkie, Bruce R. *Mormon Doctrine.* 2d ed. rev. Salt Lake City: Bookcraft, 1966.

———. *A New Witness for the Articles of Faith.* Salt Lake City: Deseret Book, 1985.

Packer, Boyd K. *The Holy Temple.* Salt Lake City: Bookcraft, 1980.

Smith, Joseph. *Teachings of the Prophet Joseph Smith.* Selected and arranged by Joseph Fielding Smith. Salt Lake City: Deseret Book, 1976.

Smith, Joseph F. *Gospel Doctrine: Selections from the Sermons and Writings of Joseph F. Smith.* 12th ed. Salt Lake City: Deseret Book, 1961.

Smith, Joseph Fielding. *Answers to Gospel Questions.* 5 vols. Salt Lake City: Deseret Book, 1957.

————. *Doctrines of Salvation.* Compiled by Bruce R. McConkie. 3 vols. Salt Lake City: Bookcraft, 1954.

Snow, Lorenzo. *Teachings of Lorenzo Snow.* Edited by Clyde J. Williams. Salt Lake City: Bookcraft, 1996.

Widtsoe, John A. *Evidences and Reconciliations.* Arranged by G. Homer Durham. 3 vols. in 1. Salt Lake City: Bookcraft, 1960.

————. *A Rational Theology.* 7th ed. Salt Lake City: Deseret Book, 1966.

Wirthlin, Joseph B. *Finding Peace in Our Lives.* Salt Lake City: Deseret Book, 1995.

Young, Brigham. *Discourses of Brigham Young.* Selected and arranged by John A. Widtsoe. Salt Lake City: Deseret Book, 1975.

INDEX

Italicized numbers refer to photographs.

Aba, Nigeria: Church meetings in, 56–60, 64–67; as LDS gathering place, 60; stake, creation of, 62, 68

Aba Nigeria Temple: announcement of, 95; preliminary plans for, 154; delays in building of, 157, 268; final negotiations for, 253–56

Abak [Nigeria] District, author attends Church meetings in, 117–20

Accra, Ghana: Church area office established in, 77; living conditions in, 110–15; outdoor market in, *111*; author meets with mayor of, 157–58, 209; BYU Singers perform in, 265–66

Accra Ghana Temple: announcement of, 89–91; delays in building of, 139, 230–32, 268; approval process for, 203–4, 247–48, 257–58; author meets with government officials regarding, 209–10; government rejects proposal for, 213–15; final negotiations for, 253; concert at site of, 265–66; construction of, *273, 274*

Addis Ababa, Ethiopia, 42; author's first visit to, 26–27

Adversity: blessings resulting from, 74–75; suffered by Ghanaian missionaries, 82–84

Africa: Church in, xii; first convert in, xvi–xvii; poverty in, 1, 41–42; living conditions in, 32, *59,* 79–80, 114–15; Church involvement in, 43, 50, 77, 122–23, 126–27, 198–200; Presiding Bishopric assignments in, 50, 84–88; welfare needs in, 52, 80; theft in, 79; challenges of traveling in, 85, 120–21, 132–33, 156; author called to serve in, 95–97; author's departure for, 106–8; day of, 123; emerging from Third World, 126; spiritual experiences in, 163; first missionary training center in, *259.* *See also* African people

Africa, West. *See* West Africa

Africa West Area, xi–xiii; author called as first counselor in, 109; presidency, *115, 264;* Area Authority Seventies in, 116; leaders in, *116;* author called as president of, 164–68; rapid progress of Church in, 198; fire in office of, 224–26, *226*; mission presidents and missionaries of, 263; new president of, 269–70

African people: suffering of, 1, 16, 271–72; eagerness of ancestors of, to receive gospel, 18, 206–7; dignity of, 38–39; author's love for, 49–50, 94, 116–17, 244, 275; resourcefulness of, 50–52; kindness of, 54–55, 117; potential of, 67; spirituality of, 122, 182, 250; enthusiasm of, 150, 266, 270; humility of, 168, 244, 272; teachability of, 168, 272; patience and faith of, 182–83; God's love for, 231; tribal loyalty of, 238, 242–43, 261; goodness of, 250; slavery of, 263–64; traits of, 272

Africare, author meets with, 29

Agency: conditions essential to, 7–8; law of, 7–10; wise use of, 8–9

Ahadjie, President Richard Kwesi, 257

Aid, extension of, to victims of corrupt governments, 44–45

Alston, Douglas, 79

American Red Cross, letter from president of, 46–47

Americans, persecution of, in Congo, 169–70

Ancestors, African, awaiting temple blessings, 155–56, 206–7

Angel Moroni statue, Accra Ghana Temple, *273*

Area Authority Seventies, 247; in West Africa, *264*

Area office, author visits sites for, 77

Area presidency, author called to lead, 164–68

Arungwa, Samuel, *61*, 118; letter from, 61–64

Assistance, heavenly, 17–18

Australia Sydney North Mission, author as president of, 89

Baby, Nigerian, 162–63

Ballard, M. Russell: travels to Ethiopia, 26–43; meets with solitary Church member in Ethiopia, 27–29; as executive director of missionary department, 28; prays for rain in Ethiopia, 29; at refugee camp, *37*; called to Quorum of the Twelve, 43; with Elder Pace at temple site, *255*

Baptism: earliest, in West Africa, xvii; of entire village, 60; isolated investigator requests, 145–46; "partial," 166–67; in Gabon, 176–80; monkey at, 179; for dead, 207

Barrett, Jonathan Phillip, 168–69

Beggars, 114, 160–61

Benin City, Nigeria: living conditions in, 159–61; Church meetings in, 161–63

Benson, Ezra Taft, 62; Nigerian Saints' love for, 65–67; on self-improvement, 153; on foreknowledge of God, 198–99; on pioneers, 199–200

Bessey, Ava, *175*; ordination of, to Melchizedek Priesthood, 175; as member missionary, 181

Bessey, Cedrick, 178

Biafran War, xvi

Birth, diverse circumstances of, 10

Bishop, Lars, 76

Blessings: from adversity, 74–75; priesthood, 99–103, 223; gratitude for, 136–37, 192; of temple building, 141–42; of tithe paying, 166; obedience and, 167

Boateng, Michael, *71*; letter from, 71–75; author visits, 81–82

Bonnet, Georges, 79, 208; and temple

approval process, 247–48, 254–55, 269

Book of Mormon, West Africans likened to people of, 244

Botulu, William: sustained as group leader in Gabon, 177; responsibilities of, 180–81

Bowen, Albert E., on self-reliance, 151

Brazzaville, Congo: district conference in, 187–92; effects of war on, 190

Bribery, 78–79, 238

British Isles, Africa becomes separate Church area from, 77

Brown, Hugh B., on recognizing truth, 7

Bushrod, Liberia, district conference in, 129

BYU Singers: concert tour of, 263–66; performance of, at temple site, 265–66

Calabar, Nigeria, conversion of large group in, 55–56

Callings, Church, 134; feelings of inadequacy in, 24; seeking inspiration in, 42–43, 59–60, 64–65

Cannon, Edwin Q. and Janath, as missionaries to Nigeria, xvi

Cannon, George Q.: on becoming like God, 5; on glory of premortal existence, 5; on temples, 141–42, 204

Cape Coast Castle, BYU Singers' concert at, 263–64

Cather, Willa, on happiness, 139

Catholic Relief Services: Church's contribution to, 25–26; author's meeting with, 29; humanitarian projects of, 31–32; letter from chairman of, 46

Challenges, closeness to God during, 108

Champagnie, Carl, 185–86

Charity: blessings of, to giver, 47, 152; to beggars, 114

Chastity, 82–83

Chiefs, African, special concert for, 264

Children, establishing gospel traditions with, 161–62

Choices: agency and, 8–9; suffering due to, 15

Christensen, Joe J., 102

Chukwurah, Christopher, 85–86, *116*, 149, *264*

Church News: on first West African stake, 68–69; announcing Ghana temple, 89–91; on President Hinckley's welcome by Nigerians, 94–95

Church of Jesus Christ of Latter-day Saints, The: in Africa, xii, xv; unofficial African meetings of, xv–xvi, 91; first visit of president of, to West Africa, xvii; beginnings of humanitarian program of, 21, 47; sends aid to Ethiopia, 22–26, 44–47; contributes to Catholic Relief Services, 25–26; growth of, in West Africa, 55–56, 87–88, 198; conversion of entire village to, 60; restoration of, 64; Ghana government suspends activity of, 67, 71–75, 81–82; imprisonment of employee of, on false charges, 76; mission of, 77–78; Africans as pioneers in, 94; Spirit present at meetings of, 131; opposition to, 140; programs of, in West Africa, 143–44; leaders, interview African wives, 150; international, 151; building program of, 166; and Third World countries, 239; marriage within, 261

Commandments, importance of keeping, 205

Commitment, importance of, 207–8

Conditions, mortal, 10. *See also* African people

Conference, stake, in Congo, 202–3

Congo, Democratic Republic of, 129, 132–35; author's first visit to, 76–78; problems in, 78; Church membership in, 132; poverty in, 135; travel conditions in, 188–90; Saints of, 190–92; author detained by soldiers in, 193–95; war in, 201

Contention, 238

Contributions, from special fast, 45–46

Corruption, in Africa, 237–38

Countries, Third World, 239

Creations, God's, 14

Culture shock, after return from Africa, 277

Cunningham, Miles, 52; visits chapel sites, 54–55

Curriculum materials, African people's respect for, 175–76

Dadson, Ato, 85

Dadson, Banyan, *130*, 130–31, 159–61, 232

Dadson, Sister, *130*

"Dashing." *See* Bribery

Davies, Samuel, on intolerance, 149

Dedication, of General Authorities, 103

Discipline, Church, 241

Dishonesty, 237–38

Diversity, 8–9

Divine nature, 5

Doctrine, teaching correct, 123, 168

Douala Branch, 173

Edmunds, Mary Ellen, 57

Education, 262

Ehanire, John A., 85–86

Eka, David William, 65, *116*, 171, 247, *264*; as president of first Nigerian stake, xvii; as first stake president in West Africa, 68; background of, 116

Eket, Nigeria: health care project in, 55; living conditions in, 57–58

Elisha, heavenly assistance given to, 17–18

Embezzlement, 241

Encouragement, 220

Environment, changing, 153

Eternity, 4

Etete, Ephraim S., 68

Ethiopia: famine in, 21–23, 31–32, 45–46; Church's humanitarian aid to, 21–24, 44–47; author's first trip to, 26–43; isolated Church member in, 27–29; miracles in, 29–31; government of, 30; difficulty of travel in, 30–31, 33–35; Russian control of, 34; author visits feeding camps in, 35–41; refugee camp in, *36, 37*

Ethiopian man, rescue effort of, 40–41, *41*

Ethiopians, gratitude of, 39–40

Existence, premortal, 4–7

Experiences, spiritual, 79–80

Faith, 15, 63; and miracles, 33; of African people, 56, 73–75, 81–82, 272; of Ghanaian missionaries, 82–84; test of, 97–103

Faithfulness, to marriage covenants, 261–62

False witness, bearing, 242–43

Families, in scriptures, 260

Family: importance of, 77–78, 260–63; love for, 107–8; teaching correct principles regarding, 119–20; establishing gospel traditions with, 161–62; proclamation on, 262

"Family, The: A Proclamation to the World," 5, 262

Family history: approval of oral

history project for, 186; importance of, 207

Fasting and prayer: for inspiration, 60; for relief of famine, 22–24, 45–46; for author's health, 101–103; for temple, 204; power of, 207–8

Faust, James E., 85, 96–97; on temples, 166; on tithing and temple readiness, 206; on faithfulness of Ghanaian Saints, 262–63

Fire, in area office, 224–26

First Presidency, requests special fast, 22–23

Fisher, Glenn G., xvi

"For the Strength of Youth," 181

Foreordination, 10–16; to missions, 10–11; of Abraham, 10, 13; to nationality, 11; to use talents, 11; to lineage, 11–13; of Saints of Africa, 124

Gabon, 172; members in, 145, 146, 178, 180; baptisms performed in, 176–80, 179; living conditions in, 182; airport experience in, 182

Gambia, investigator desires baptism in, 145–46

General Authorities: concern of, for Africans during famine, 25–26; African Saints' respect for, 58–59, 75; responsibilities of, 59–60; challenges of, 103

General conference, author speaks at, 227–32

Ghana, 147–49; Church introduced in, xv; Church building program in, 50; students in, 53; author's visit to, 67; Church activities "frozen" in, 67, 81–82; sister missionaries in, 70; faith of persecuted Saints in, 70–75, 81–82, 124–25, 262–63; priests quorum in, 71; member missionary in, 72–73; faithfulness

of missionaries from, 82–84, 125; Saints in, 86, 124–26, 143–45; Church growth in, 87–88; announcement of temple in, 89–91; challenges of building temple in, 109; living conditions in, 110–15; marketplaces in, 111; monetary system in, 112; food in, 112–14; people of, 117, 136–37, 270; dedication of first Church-owned building in, 122; need for Church leadership in, 123–24; adversity in, 125; history of, 136; demolished building in, 164; building a missionary training center in, 210–11; dedicated for preaching of gospel, 232; election results in, 249; new president of, 253, 268–69; author's last address to Saints in, 270–75; author and wife leave, 277

Ghanaian Chronicle, The, anti-Mormon articles in, 147–49

God: as Father of spirits, 4–5; purpose of, 7; open rebellion against, 9; foreknowledge of, 10–11, 198–99; omniscience of, 13–14; as Creator, 14; power of, 14, 140–41, 256; omnipresence of, 14–15; reliance on, 33, 80, 108, 158, 182; love of, for children, 35, 231, 278; commandment to love, 43–44; our role in plan of, 68, 80, 119, 263; triumph of kingdom of, 78, 142; fairness of, 156; contribution to kingdom of, 200; hearts softened by, 248; safe journey to, 275

Godliness, power of, 141

Gods, worshipping false, 240

Goethe, Johann Wolfgang von, on good works, 199

"Golden calves," 240–43, 261

Good and evil, knowledge of, 8

Good deeds, of Catholic priest in Africa, 31

Good works, 11, 199

Gospel: purpose of, 5; universal appeal of, 6–7, 118, 134, 182; Nigerian boy's love of, 64; rolling forth of, 74, 78; joy found in, 83; Africa's need for teachings of, 140; gift of, 153; full acceptance of, 243; our role in, 263

Governments: corrupt, aiding victims of, 44–45; West African, 163

Gratitude, 2; for rain in Ethiopia, 29–30; for service opportunities, 45–46; for blessings, 136–37, 192; of ancestors for temple work, 207; for blessings of temple, 232; for missionaries, 263; for African Saints, 275

Grocery shopping, in Ghana, 112–14

Growth, personal, 235–37

Hadlock, Harry, 27–29

Haight, David B., dedicates Ghana for preaching of gospel, 232

Hales, Robert D., on duties of Presiding Bishopric, 49

Happiness, relationship of work to, 139

Hawkson, Ebo, 209

Health: author's challenges with, 97–102; diagnosis of heart, problems, 98; miraculous results of, tests, 102–3

Health care: instructing Africans in, 57; in West Africa, 158

Heaven: war in, 9; opening windows of, 168

Hinckley, Gordon B.: visits West Africa, xvii; on capacity to do good, 11; on Church's relief efforts in Africa, 43–47; on giving aid to victims of corrupt governments, 44–45; announces plans for building temple in Ghana, 89–91; addresses Ghanaians, 90–91; visits Nigeria, 91–93; welcomed by Nigerian Saints, 94–95; thoughtfulness of, 105; interest of, in temple building, 166; on our contribution to kingdom of God, 200; on temples, 229; announces Aba Nigeria Temple, 233

Histories, oral, 186, 207

History, great moments in, 198–99

Holland, Jeffrey R., 209–10, 256–57; visits Ghana temple site, 90; addresses Nigerian Saints, 93

Holland, Patricia, 257

Holy Ghost: as revelator, 5–6; as teacher, 6–7, 278; power of, 66, 75; following promptings of, 88, 131, 182; reliance on, 108, 117–20, 152; African people blessed by, 122; as comforter, 273

Home, sacredness of, 124

Honesty, 237–38, 241–42

Hope, 220

"How Beautiful Thy Temples, Lord" (hymn), 258–59

Humanitarian aid, 55; organizations providing, 24–26; interfaith efforts in, 46; project, 53; to Sierra Leone, 218

Humanitarian workers, 31–32

Humor, maintaining sense of, 75–76, 130–31

Ibadan, Nigeria, author dedicates chapel in, 130–32

Ijebu-Ode, Nigeria, living conditions in, 159–61

Inspiration, 60, 88, 152; sources of, 18; lesson regarding, 42; in Church callings, 42–43, 95, 134, 170, 227; in speaking assignment, 64–67, 117–20, 131; regarding importance of tithing, 203

Intelligence, eternal nature of, 4

Intolerance, religious, 148–49

Israel: children of, 11–12, 239–40; house of, 242; wandering of, 274–75

Ivory Coast Abidjan Mission, missionary killed in, 168–69

Jesus Christ: characteristics of, 6; purpose of, 7; light of, 14–15; love of, for children, 35, 182, 278; man's nature changed by, 153

Johannesburg, South Africa, Church area office established in, 77

Johnson, Joseph W. B., 91

Jos, Nigeria, meetinghouse dedicated in, 266–68

Kabila, Laurent, assassination of, 201, 253–54

Kennedy, John F., paraphrased saying of, 167–68

Kenya: author's first visit to, 76–78; government restrictions on Church activity in, 77–78

Kimball, Spencer W.: receives revelation on priesthood, xvi, 69, 93; on organization of intelligence into spirit beings, 4

Kinshasa, Congo: author visits, 132–35; creation of second stake in, 169–72; stake conference in, 172; missionary zone conference in, 192; theft in, 192–93

Kirk, Jerry V., 121, 156; at Nigeria temple site, 154; with missionaries in Nigeria, 155

Kirtland, Lord chastises Saints of, 205–6

Knowledge: eternal nature of, 6; of good and evil, 8; of God, 13–14

Koforidua, Ghana, 70; first converts in, 81; author visits, 81–82; Saints in, 86; author attends branch meetings in, 86–87; growth of Church in, 87–88

Kufour, John Agyekum (president of Ghana), 253; impressed by Latter-day Saints, 268–69; tours Salt Lake City, 269

Lagos, Nigeria, poverty in, 67

Langevin, Elder, 133

Language barriers, overcoming, 202

Lartebiokorshie, Ghana: stake center dedicated in, 122; author's final meeting in, 270–75

Latter-day Saints, Ghanaian, 86; premortal valiance of, 18–19; faith of, 81–82

Laws, essential to progress, 7–8

LDS Charities: founding of, 24; water well built by, 53

Leaders, Church: education level of, 65; training of, 135–36, 246, 260; sustaining, 242–43, 246–47

Leadership: seeking inspiration in, 92; of Church in Africa, 67, 26–27

Lee, Harold B.: on foreordained lineage, 11–12; on nearness of spirit world, 18

Lepers, in Nigeria, 160–61

Liberia: civil unrest and violence in, 82–83, 127–29; death of missionary from, 127; war-damaged building in, 128; faithfulness of Saints in, 129

Libreville, Gabon, 174

Lindquist, Jaden, 106, 107

Lindquist, Jo'ell, 107; health challenges of, 188, 191

Lindquist, Rusty, 191

Linnell, Bob, 53; assists during fire, 226

Love: of God, for His children, 35, 231, 278; as commandment, 43–44; of author, for people of Africa, 49–50, 94, 116–17, 244, 275

Lubumbashi, Congo: challenges of traveling in, 200–201; stake conference in, 200–203;

missionary zone conference in, 201–2

Mabey, Rendell N. and Rachel, as missionaries to Nigeria, xvi

Madsen, Truman: on recognizing truth, 6–7; on spirituality, 199

Madu, Declan O., 149–50

Makalle, Ethiopia: author visits, 33–41; feeding camps in, 35–41

Malaria, 114

Man: role of, in universe, 3; created in image of God, 4–5; immortality and eternal life of, 7; goodness of, 31

Marriage: common-law, 176, 241; tribalism and, 243; unity in, 261–62

Martin, Charles D., 168–69

Mason, James O., *115*, 125, 187; visits Ghana temple site, 90; as Africa West Area president, 109, 164, 196

Mason, Marie, 109

Maturity, spiritual, 239

Maxwell, Neal A., 96; visits West Africa, 68–69

McConkie, Bruce R.: on agency, 7–8; on war in heaven, 9; on foreordination, 10–11, 12–13; on omniscience of God, 13–14

McKay, David O., assigns mission president to visit West Africa, xvi

Meetinghouse: site for, 54–55; bringing Spirit into, 124; dedication of, 130–32; in Jos, Nigeria, 266–68

Melchizedek Priesthood, African holders of, 250–51

Men, prevalence of, in Church in Africa, 250–51

Messages, from African Saints to prophet, 66

Miracles: recognizing, 33; small, 121; praying for, 158

Mission presidents, first African, 85

Missionaries: in Nigeria, xvi, 118, 154–55; farm, 51; West African, 53–54; in Ghana, *70*; couples, service of, 76, 125; African, 82–85, 139–40, 250–51; death of, 127, 168–69; spiritual experiences of, 137; and adversity, 157; faithfulness of, in Congo, 201–2; tribalism among, 242; misconduct of some, 245; proposal of returned, to form private group, 245–46; safety of, 254; author's gratitude for, 263

Missionary training center: lack of African, 52–53, 139–40; site selected for Ghanaian, 210–11; groundbreaking for, 259

Missionary work: challenges of, in West Africa, 52–53; success of, in Nigeria, 55–56; of members, 72–73, 83

Monrovia, Liberia: living conditions in, 128; district conference in, 129

Monson, Thomas S., calls author and wife to serve in Africa, 96

Mortality, veil of forgetfulness during, 4–7

Moses, 274–75

Mother and daughter, at refugee camp, *40*

Motherhood, honoring, 261

Mouila, Gabon, 174–75

Muslims: and Christians, conflict between, 224, 236; reaction of, to LDS meetinghouse, 267

Nairobi, Kenya, 77

Nationalities, diversity in, 12–13

Needs, physical, of Congo Saints, 192

Ngadzoukou family, baptism of, 177

Nigeria: Church introduced in, xv; first official Church visit to, xvi; first stake in, xvii, 60, 68; Church building program in, 50; faithful Saints in, 56–58, 61–64, 94,

119–20; conversion of entire village in, 60; and temple building process, 60, 95, 154, 157; poverty in, 67; persecution of Saints in, 76; author visits, 76–78; corruption in, 78–79; challenges of travel in, 78–79, 159–61; President Hinckley visits, 91–95; regional conference in, 92; first stake president in, 116; missionaries in, 118, 154–55; living conditions in, 119, 149, 159–61, 227–28; humorous experience in, 156–57; sisters at training meeting in, *162*; civil war in, 224; isolated stakes in, 244; meetinghouse dedicated in, 266–68

Nigeria Enugu Mission, author's tour of, 117–18

Nigeria Port Harcourt Mission, author's tour of, 153–56

Nsirimo, Nigeria: author's visit to, 58–60; first ward in, 62

Obedience, agency and, 8

Obinna, Anthony, first convert in Africa, xvi–xvii

Ojaide, Nduka, 119; on faith of Nigerian Saints, 94

One, seeking after the, 27–28

Onitchi, Lazarus, 68

Opare, Emmanuel Ohenre, *115, 116*, 123, 185, *264*; as second counselor in Africa West Area presidency, 109; Church callings of, 115–16

Opobo District, Nigeria, xvi

Opposition, to temple building, 204

Organizations, humanitarian, 24–26, 44

Owerri, Nigeria, stake organized in, 149

Pace, Darin, 101, 217–218

Pace, Elizabeth A. Wilde (author's mother), 105–6, 217; health challenges of, 218–19, 221; death of, 222–23

Pace, Glenn L., 61, *115, 264*; background and experience of, 1; education and career of, 23; receives assignment to distribute humanitarian funds, 23–24; as managing director of Welfare Services, 28; and children at Ethiopian camp, *36*; at water well built by LDS Charities, *53*; family of, 103–7; death of mother of, 105–6; called as first counselor in Africa Area presidency, 109; with wife and President and Sister Dadson, *130*; at Nigeria temple site, *154*; with missionaries in Nigeria, *155*; with Elder Ballard at temple site, *255*; in African clothes, *271*

Pace, Jolene, *61*; visits Africa, 84–88; with Ghanaian children, *87*; receives inspiration regarding future assignments, 88, 95–97; fasts and prays for husband, 101; in outdoor market in Ghana, *111*; with African woman, *113*; teaches African Saints, 120; at district conference in Abak, Nigeria, *121*; with husband and President and Sister Dadson, *130*; humorous experience of, 130–31; with missionaries in Nigeria, *155*; speaks at Nigerian stake conference, 162; in African clothes, *271*

Pace, Kenneth LeRoy (author's father), 100; death of, 99; memories of, 104–5

Packer, Boyd K., 99–100

Palmer, J. Duffy, 55–56; calls special district meeting, 58–59

Palmyra New York Temple: dedication of, 233; spiritual experience near, 277–78

Parenthood, importance of, 261

Patience, 214

Paul, love of, for those he served, 275

Peace, inner, 60, 97; in fulfilling Church callings, 133; regarding temple delays, 215–16

Peddlers, 114

Persecution, of Ghanaian Saints, 71–75, 83–84

Pioneers, example of, 199–200

Plan of salvation, 2, 9, 49, 263

"Plea for Africa," 257

"Popcorn Popping on the Apricot Tree" (song), Ghanaian version of, 70–71

Port Harcourt, Nigeria: President Hinckley addresses Saints in, 92–93; author visits stake in, 119; author tours mission in, 153–56, 254

Porter, L. Aldin, 99, 102

Poverty: in Africa, 1; in Lagos, Nigeria, 67; in West Africa, 110, 112–15; in Congo, 135; tithing and, 190

Prayer: for safety, 32–33; of Ethiopian refugees, 39–40; answers to, 64–67, 158, 160

Premortal existence: limited recollection of, 4–7; leaders foreordained in, 10–11

Presiding Bishopric: author's call to serve in, 43, 49; author's release from, 84; author's last visit to Africa while serving in, 84–88

Priesthood: revelation on, xvi, 69, 93; power of, 29, 99–103, 223; honoring, 92; African holders of, 250–51

Primary, author visits Ghanaian, 70–71

Principles: teaching correct, 80; welfare, 150–53

Proclamation on the family, 5, 262

Progress, eternal, 8–9, 16–17

Prophet, characteristics of, 65–66

Protection, God's, 33–35

Purification, through service, 152–53

Races, diversity of, 12–13

Rawlings, Jerry (president of Ghana): meets with President Hinckley, 90; Church member meets with, 196–97; loses election, 253

Recognition, of truths of gospel, 6–7

Refugees, Ethiopian, 38–39

Reilly, Daniel P., 46

Relief efforts, success of, in Ethiopian famine, 38–39

Restaurant, humorous incident in, 181

Restoration, 64

Revelation: on priesthood, xvi, 69, 93; seeking, 160

Righteousness, temple blessings predicated on, 262

Romney, Marion G.: on organization of intelligence into spirit beings, 4; on self-reliance, 151–52; on honesty, 241–42

Sacrament meeting, with member in Ethiopia, 28–29

Sacred Grove, spiritual experience in, 277–78

Sacrifice, 85–86; spiritual experiences and, 79–80

Safe, theft of, 76

"Safe journey," 270; significance of phrase, xii–xiii; to Father in Heaven, 275

Salt Lake Temple, 229

Salvation, temporal, 167

Sanctification, through service, 152–53

Sankoh, Foday, 222

Satan: role of, in war in heaven, 9; ongoing war with, 140–41; lessening power of, 141;

overthrowing of, 142; temple building opposed by, 204, 230–31
Schools, boarding, 262
Schubert, Richard, 47
Self-improvement, 153
Self-reliance: Africans' desire for, 51; principles of, 150–53; of early Saints, 165
Service: of General Authorities, 103; sanctification due to, 152–53; love an outcome of, 275
Seventies, challenges of, 103
Seventy, First Quorum of the, author's call to serve in, 89
Shakers, false beliefs of, 243
Sharia law, 224, 236
Sierra Leone: unstable government of, 140; civil war in, 146–47; death of Church members in, 147; effects of war on, 216–18; living conditions in, 217–21; citizens of, 220; humanitarian aid to, 221; refugee camp in, 221
"Sister," as nickname for humanitarian workers, 38
Sister missionaries in Ghana, 70
Slavery, 2, 263–64; Ghana's role in, 136; lasting effects of, 251
Smith, Joseph, 64; on plan of salvation, 9; on foreordination, 10; author relates experiences of, 65; on importance of temple, 203
Smith, Joseph F.: on man as son of God, 5; on eternal nature of truth, 6; on spirit world, 16–17, 18; on assistance from beyond the veil, 17
Smith, Joseph Fielding, on the nature of intelligence, 4
Snow, Lorenzo, on tithing, 165–66
Soldiers, author detained by, 193–95
Sono-Koree, President Charles, 257
Sorensen, David E., 215
Spirit: immortal, 4; African people blessed by, 122. See also Holy Ghost

Spirit world, 4–7; agency in, 8; gospel taught in, 15–16; activities in, 16–17; nearness of, 18
Spirits, rebellious, 9–10
Spiritual experiences: sacrifice and, 79–80; of missionary couples, 137
"Spiritual helps," letter requesting, 144–45
Spirituality, developing, 199
Spouses, establishing gospel traditions with, 161–62
Stake: creation of first, in West Africa, 62, 68; creation of, in Owerri, Nigeria, 149; conference, in Nigeria, 161
Stakes, isolated, 244
Stucki, Cheryl, 196
Stucki, H. Bruce, 196, 253–54, 264; as Africa West Area president, 269–70
Suffering, 15; of African people, 1; purposes of, 1–2
Sunday School, in Gabon, 177

Tar, Da, 133, 146, 171–77, 175; competence of, 174; aids author in crisis, 193–95
Tema, Ghana, experience at fish market in, 113–14
Temple: first West African, xvii; purposes of, 16; African Saints' desire for, 85; announcement of, in Ghana, 89–91; in Nigeria, 95; Pace family visits, 103–4; delays in building process of, 139, 163, 185–87, 213–15, 268; preparing African people for, 139–40, 154–55, 164, 206, 236–37, 239–45, 256; building a, 141–42, 205–6, 229–30, 272–74; importance of, 141–43, 203–4, 228–29; preliminary plans for, 154; worthiness to receive ordinances of, 167; sealing power of, 229; nations without blessings of, 230;

gratitude for blessings of, 232. *See also* Aba Nigeria Temple; Accra Ghana Temple; Palmyra New York Temple
Temple work: for Africans, 19; ancestors awaiting, 155–56
Testimony, xii; growth of, 2–3; joy resulting from, 83; meeting of Pace family, 105
"The Day Dawn Is Breaking" (hymn), 213
Theft: in Africa, 79; danger of, in Nigeria, 159–61
Thrasher Foundation, 55, 57
Tingey, Earl C., 256
Tithing: temple and, 165, 205–6; blessings of paying, 165–66, 206, 240; partial payment of, 166–67; increased payment of, 168; poverty and, 190; inspiration regarding, 203
Traditions, 262, 161
Travel: in Russian-controlled Ethiopia, 33–35; challenges of, 54–55, 85, 114–15, 120–21, 130–32, 156, 170–71; in Nigeria, 78–79, 159–61; in Congo, 188–90, 193–95
Tree, analogy of bent, 123
Trials, closeness to God during, 108
Tribalism, in Africa, 238, 242–43, 261
Truth: recognition of, 6–7; religious, 148
Tusey, Kola, 171, *172*
Tusey, Sister, *172*

Universe, man's place in, 3
Utah, author returns briefly to, 222–23

VanderHoeven, Ludy, 76
VanderHoeven, Tonja, 76
Veil of forgetfulness, 4–7

Waite, Merwyn, 133, 169, 188

War: in heaven, 9; in Congo, 78, 190; in Sierra Leone, 216–18; effects of, *220*; atrocities of, 220–22, 224
Welfare: farm, author's visit to African, 50; challenges in Africa, 52; author's concerns regarding, 80; principles, 150–53
Welfare Services Department, 151; author's work in, 21
West Africa Area. *See* Africa West Area
West Africa: Church in, xv–xvii; Church representative visits, xvi; first branch president in, xvi–xvii; early convert baptisms in, xvii; President Hinckley visits, xvii, 91–92; first temple in, xvii; welfare project in, *51*; lack of missionary training centers in, 52–53; gas station in, *54*; growth of Church in, 55–56, 60, 144, 198, 235–37, 245; living conditions in, 57–58; first stake in, 62, 68; author's desire for temple in, 85–86; poverty in, 110, 112–15; work of women in, *113*; climate of, 114–15; rest rooms in, 114–15; challenges of travel in, 132–33, 170–71; civil unrest in, 140; significance of first temple in, 143; Church members as pioneers in, 146; isolated Church members in, 143–47; health care in, 158; teachable people of, 168; priesthood leaders in, *173*; communication in, 182; author's love for people of, 244; response of Saints of, to temple announcement, 258
Widtsoe, John A.: on man's place in universe, 3; on blessings of temples, 230
Williams, LaMar, xvi
Woman, role of, 261
Womanhood, respect for, 243, 250, 261

Women: duties of African, 51–52; rights of, 243, 250
Woodruff, Wilford: on powers of Satan and God, 140–41; on family history work, 207
Word of Wisdom, 84
Work, 199; immersion in, 139
Worship, freedom of, 148
Worthiness: personal, 124, 143; to attend temple, 204

Young, Brigham, on premortal existence, 5
Youth, willingness of, to serve in Church, 61

Zaire. *See* Congo, Democratic Republic of
Zion's Camp, Nigerian Saints' experiences compared to, 155–56